C000178565

Is There a Desk with
The Politics of

Is There a Desk with My Name on It?
The Politics of Integration

Edited by

Roger Slee

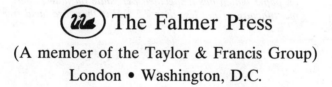

The Falmer Press

(A member of the Taylor & Francis Group)
London • Washington, D.C.

USA   The Falmer Press, Taylor & Francis Inc., 1900 Frost Road, Suite 101,
      Bristol, PA 19007
UK   The Falmer Press, 4 John St, London WC1N 2ET

© Selection and editorial material copyright R. Slee 1993

*All rights reserved. No part of this publication may be reproduced,
stored in a retrieval system, or transmitted, in any form or by any means,
electronic, mechanical, photocopying, recording, or otherwise, without
permission in writing from the Publisher.*

First published 1993

**A catalogue record of this publication is available from the British
Library**

ISBN 0 75070 174 9 cased
ISBN 0 75070 175 7 paper

**Library of Congress Cataloging-in-Publication Data are available on
request**

Jacket design by Caroline Archer

Typeset in 9.5/11pt Times by
Graphicraft Typesetters Ltd, Hong Kong

*Printed in Great Britain by Burgess Science Press, Basingstoke
on paper which has a specified pH value on final paper
manufacture of not less than 7.5 and is therefore 'acid free'.*

Contents

Contents

Acknowledgments

After a long gestation this book emerges thanks to the efforts of a number of people. Special thanks are due to each of the contributors. The value of these chapters is enhanced by their commitment to the rights of all people to participate in an inclusive and enabling education system.

Kim Amos, Eslynn Mauritz and Jocylen Lee took on the additional burden of preparing the manuscript. I am also grateful to Sandra Taylor for her careful reading and useful commentary on parts of this collection, and to Eleanor Ramsay who made the time to play her part in this project. Malcolm Clarkson and Lyn Gorman at The Falmer Press have been very supportive, as was Richard Bates when I first discussed the idea of this book with him.

The enduring commitment and enthusiasm of my colleagues in Melbourne to the expansion and improvement of educational provision is an inspiration. John Lewis, Sandy Cook, Bob Semmens, Tony Knight, Gillian Fulcher, Geoff Emmett and Jim Williamson have each added their piece to the policy jigsaw.

And, of course, thank you Jeanette, Carly and Rowan.

Roger Slee
September 1992

Foreword

Is There a Desk with My Name on It? The Politics of Integration provides historical, theoretical, pedagogical and personal insights of special relevance and significance at this particular moment of educational reform in Australia. At the heart of the material presented in this book lie a great challenge and a difficult question. The question being posed, both rhetorically in the title of the book and implicitly throughout its content, is whether the public school system exists to provide equality of educational opportunity, in terms of access, participation and outcomes, for all students in Australia; and, if this is so, then the challenge facing the educational community is to make this intention a reality, in practice as well as in rhetoric.

Most would readily agree that the purpose and, indeed, *raison d'être* of public schooling is to provide equality of educational opportunity for all students, regardless of their particular circumstances, backgrounds or characteristics. Indeed, many would believe that this is what our schools have been doing for many years. However, as some of the contributions in this book make abundantly clear, and as explored in a range of other research, schools and teachers in them have often held very strong and fixed notions about the 'normal' students they exist to educate, resulting in attitudes and practices which have excluded and disadvantaged students perceived to be different in some way from this norm. This is reflected in the very strong tendency for the education system to make quite separate, different and in many respects lesser educational provision for such students, justified by the belief that their 'different' educational needs are best catered for in specialist settings. This has been the educational experience of various groups of students in Australia who have been defined as different on the basis of factors such as their gender, their socio-economic location, their ethnic or cultural background, as well as students with disability.

This collection makes a significant contribution to clarifying the dangers inherent in responding to educational difference through the provision of a segregated education. In demanding that the educational needs of all students are the proper concern and responsibility of educational systems, and the schools within them, the voices in this collection are demanding that their educational needs be moved from the margins of public educational policies, structures and provision into the mainstream where they belong. This challenges the very nature of this mainstream education and, in particular, challenges it to become inclusive practices which exclude. Policy enacted in systems, schools and classrooms frequently runs counter to the descriptions, official and anecdotal, of what is happening.

Inclusion or Exclusion: Changing Educational Cultures

The central focus for this book is upon inclusion in, or more precisely exclusion from, educational provision. Ultimately, as Barton and Landman (Chapter 3) urge, the issue of integration provides opportunity 'for raising serious questions about the kind of society we desire' and the nature and role of schooling within such a society. As Douglas Biklen suggested while addressing educators in Melbourne in June 1989: 'How schools see integration is crucial: is integration understood as an outsider coming in, or as creating a school culture so that it accepts all comers?'

From the outset it needs to be acknowledged that these questions are intensely political. They are not simply technical problems, addressing contests over the distribution of resources or the deployment of special assistance. Who belongs where is at the heart of the controversies evoked by the politics of integration. Inequality is ineluctably contingent upon the distribution of power and cultures of control. The pursuit of equity in schools requires a multi-leveled approach which confronts questions of organization, governance and administration, curriculum and the construction of worthwhile knowledge, and pedagogy. This book addresses these questions.

Recognizing obstructions to the achievement of equity for various groups in society, schools have been targeted as a strategic site for redressing disadvantage. As I write, Queensland schools are having to respond to the reorganized Education Department's social justice agenda. The implications of inclusive schooling for curriculum, pedagogy and school organization are being acknowledged and responded to in relation to: girls and schooling; race and ethnicity; socio-economic status; disability; and geographical isolation. Responding to disadvantage generated by patriarchy and sexism in schools, strategies were developed to counter sexism at all levels of school operation and organization. Change was not simply a question of mobilizing more support to help girls to cope with sexism in education. Nor was it just a matter of writing new policies at state level. Equity necessitated changing culture to support inclusive school organization, school curriculum and pedagogy. Intervention was required at a number of levels to support departmental policy. This includes confronting the fundamental questions relating to women, employment and career opportunities in the education workforce. Similarly, early initiatives within the Participation and Equity Program and the Disadvantaged Schools Project were amended so that the focus shifted from supplementing perceived deficits (Connell, White and Johnston, 1991; Henry *et al.*, 1988; Kalantzis and Cope, 1992). We must also more carefully theorize disability and the consequent implications for equity and approaches to integration.

The Karmel Report (Commonwealth Schools Commission, 1973) understood equity for disabled students as the provision of additional special resources, special teachers and special educational settings. This perception is echoed in more recent government investigations into special needs provision (see Gold, Bowe and Ball, Chapter 4; Barton and Landman, Chapter 3). *Integration in Victorian*

Education (Ministry of Education-Victoria, 1984) remains unique. By casting integration as a rights issue, and consequently approaching policy development from a systems perspective as opposed to an individual needs basis, the report demonstrated that society had the capacity to enable or disable. A central intention for this collection is a reconsideration of this all-pervasive perception that equity and inclusion are guaranteed through the redistribution of resources. As the contributors to this book collectively demonstrate, the issue is far more complex. Inclusive schooling summons ideological contests about who belongs in regular classrooms and who does not. These contests spill over into notions of what an inclusive curriculum is and how it should be taught.

The delivery of curriculum is not simply an issue for state legislation and guidelines, for it is affected by policy formation and enactment at all levels (Fulcher, 1989). The interpretation and enactment of state policies at regional, school and classroom levels determine the degree to which students are included in or excluded from the classroom. School organization as characterized by the location of physical and human resources, the structure of decision-making and the relationship between the school and its community serves to determine the extent to which schools may be seen as enabling or disabling. The repertoire of teachers' skills and knowledge, together with their preconceptions, also has an impact on the success of policy, as Ainscow demonstrates through the Unesco project (Chapter 13).

All of this is underpinned by community understandings about disability. Anne Deveson has produced a moving account of society's inability to cope with difference in a portrait of her son's premature demise.

> We do not use the word 'mad' anymore. We have banished it, together with words like 'lunatic', 'asylum'; even the word 'insane' is rarely heard. These words evoke oppressions of the past; today the terminology has changed, become more technical and distancing, yet our oppressions remain. (Deveson, 1991: 2)

The deliberate manipulation of language by teachers, psychologists, therapists, educational administrators and special educators alike to regulate the membership of our classrooms exemplifies Deveson's concern. Notions of maladjustment and social emotional disturbance are arbitrarily applied to attract funding or to remove students from their peers when teaching becomes difficult. The accounts of schools' difficulties in dealing with difference and disability in the final section of this collection confirms the resilience of 'old oppressions'. The arenas and agendas for change are chaotic. The challenge becomes that of intervention at a number of levels to support initiatives toward inclusive education. The scope of concerns within the chapters in this collection helps to identify points of entry.

The Organization of the Book

This book is divided into four parts. Simply put, the architecture is devised to progress from an historical understanding of the culture and processes of exclusion in the first part to an analysis of attempts to redress the marginal status afforded to disabled students in educational policy and practice in Australia and elsewhere in Parts 2 and 3, with a reminder in the last part from those at the receiving end that the journey continues.

Many parents experience extreme difficulty as they search for the school with their child's name on a desk. Others are finding that some time into their child's education the lease on the desk has been terminated and that they must seek alternative accommodation for their children. The 'individual gaze' upon students and how they can be specially placed to meet their needs, or the needs of the providers, drives both of these scenarios. What emerges as a particular concern is that too often the greater the attempts to remediate, the greater the disadvantage for the student. Becky Walsh (Chapter 15) lends her experience to demonstrate that attempts to address her special needs would have resulted in narrower further education and career options had she deferred to expert advice. Jenny Corbett also reflects upon the deleterious effects of therapy-based schooling on academic development (Chapter 5).

Exploring what he sees as 'the special education paradox', Skrtic (1991) concludes that special education actually distorts the problem of school failure. Driven by the functionalist imperative of maintaining the present organization and order of regular schooling, special schools serve as a safety valve to contain those who do not conform to preferred individual and social pathologies. Dealing with individuals who do not fit is deemed better than the larger political questions pertaining to the processes and form of mass schooling. Indeed, Len Barton (1988) drew our attention to this paradox when describing special educational needs as a euphemism for school failure. For this reason the major preoccupation of this book is with the regular school and the changes that are prerequisites to more inclusive educational provision.

References

BARTON, L. (1988) *The Politics of Special Educational Needs*, Lewes, Falmer Press.

COMMONWEALTH SCHOOLS COMMISSION (1973) *Schools in Australia* (The Karmel Report), Canberra, Australian Government Printing Service.

CONNELL, R.W., WHITE, V.M. and JOHNSTON, K.M. (Eds) (1991) *Running Twice As Hard: The Disadvantaged Schools Project in Australia,* Geelong, Deakin University Press.

DEVESON, A. (1991) *Tell Me I'm Here*, Ringwood, Penguin.

FULCHER, G. (1989) *Disabling Policies?* Lewes, Falmer Press.

HENRY, M., KNIGHT, J., LINGARD, R. and TAYLOR, S. (1988) *Understanding Schooling*, London, Routledge.

KALANTZIS, M. and COPE, B. (1992) 'The Post-Compulsory Curriculum for Students with Special Needs', in DEER, C. and SEDDON, T. (Eds), *A Curriculum for the Senior Secondary Years,* Hawthorn, Australian Council for Educational Research.

MINISTRY OF EDUCATION-VICTORIA (1984) *Integration in Victorian Education: Report of the Ministerial Review of Educational Services for the Disabled*, Melbourne, Victorian Government Printer.

SKRTIC, T. (1991) 'Students with Special Educational Needs: Artifacts of the Traditional Curriculum', in AINSCOW, M. (Ed.), *Effective Schools For All,* London, David Fulton Publishers.

Part 1

A Segregated History: Legacies for Perceptions and Practices in Our Schools

identifying potential troublemakers. The acceptance of this link was comfortable endorsement for the existing social relationships, and the sanctioning of a subsystem of education as a means of social cleansing was a logical outcome of these beliefs. Special education, through its basic ingredients of categorization and segregation, offered a means of monitoring, if not curing, the problem, while at the same time ensuring the smooth running of the regular schools.

Standardized intelligence tests were increasingly used to identify pupils in regular classes who were considered a problem and to legitimize their exclusion into a subsidiary system of schooling. By this process, regular teachers were able to remove difficult pupils from their classrooms. In drawing on their American experiences, Gartner and Lipsky observe that special education and regular teachers colluded in this exercise, which relieved regular teachers of the responsibility of teaching those pupils functioning at the bottom of their class. Furthermore, this process had consequences for those pupils remaining in the regular classroom:

> Every time a child is called mentally defective and sent off to the special education class . . . the children who are left in the regular classroom receive a message: no one is above suspicion; everyone is being watched by the authorities; nonconformity is dangerous. (Gartner and Lipsky, 1987: 383)

The possibility that these tests might be fallible, or discriminatory, was not keenly interrogated by their Victorian advocates, and the low scores achieved by groups such as juvenile delinquents, Aborigines, the working class and non-Anglo immigrants only served to confirm existing prejudices.[18] These findings were thus a legitimization of the prevailing social order. Cunningham, who established the postgraduate training course prescribed for special school teachers in the 1920s, regarded intelligence tests 'as the most delicate of all the wonderful instruments which modern science has invented for measuring purposes'.[19] It is therefore no surprise that the first Victorian special settings in the then working-class suburbs of Fitzroy, Port Melbourne, Carlton and North Melbourne, or that schools populated by juvenile prisoners or significant numbers of Aboriginal children were modelled as special schools.

The reliance on intelligence testing as the basis for drafting the majority of children placed into special settings occurred at a time when Victoria was undergoing massive industrialization, the workforce was being professionalized, and the effects of liberal immigration policies and rapid urbanization were at a peak. Changes to the Victorian social and economic infrastructure were not isolated from the school system, which represented an important area where a contest for social mobility was played out. Here the spreading use of standardized testing played its part in the maintenance of the existing social order at a time when the established middle class was under threat from an upwardly mobile workforce.[20]

Karier (1976) has argued that it was no coincidence that many large North American corporations supported the burgeoning psychology departments and their research programs because intelligence tests were designed to produce a hierarchy of scores which was in consonance with the notion of a stratified workforce demanded by a rapidly industrializing Western economy.[21] In drawing on information from his own department's extensive research programs, the prominent Stanford University researcher Lewis Terman pointed out what he believed was the relevance of this hierarchy for teachers:

> Preliminary investigations indicate that an IQ below 70 rarely permits anything other than unskilled labour; that the range 70 to 80 is pre-eminently that of semi-skilled labour, for 80 to 100 that of the skilled or ordinary clerical labour, from 100 to 110 or 115 that of semi-professional pursuits; and that above all of these are the grades of intelligence which permit one to enter the professions or the larger fields of business.
>
> Intelligence tests can tell us whether a child's native brightness corresponds more nearly to the median of (1) the professional classes, (2) those in semi-professional pursuits, (3) ordinary skilled workers, (4) semi-skilled workers, or (5) unskilled labourers. This information will be of great value in planning the education of a particular child and also in planning the differentiated curriculum. (Terman, 1923: 27–28)

The belief that intelligence was a fixed and largely heritable characteristic that could be precisely measured and would indicate the most suitable school pathway and work future for individual pupils provided an added catalyst to special education traditions such as categorization, homogeneous grouping, segregation and the teaching of a watered down curriculum with limited academic content and job options. The isolation of some students into segregated classes effectively deprived them of the opportunity for social mobility at a time when there was increasing opportunity for higher paid jobs in the workforce. The Scandinavian Soder has related this concept of exclusion to a modern, internationally connected and fluctuating economy and proposed that the mentally disabled are in fact an organized 'surplus population' that are moved in and out of social participation depending on the availability of positions in social organizations, particularly those which provide employment.[22] This notion might help in understanding why local special education grew so rapidly in the 1930s when the number of special schools doubled. If Soder is correct, then at a time of a seriously depressed economy, as occurred at this time, special education would be expected to expand its influence in response to the subsequent massive unemployment.

Special Education and Integration

In 1982 the newly elected Victorian Labor Government conducted the state's first public review of educational services to children with disabilities. This review occurred at a time when special education was particularly robust. A large central bureaucracy managed more than 300 psychologists, 1700 teachers qualified in special education, seventy-three special schools and more than seventy segregated classes situated in regular schools. Members of the review committee and its working parties were composed of an impressively broad assortment of those interested in disability issues, including politicians, Education Department bureaucrats, teachers, parents, academics and unionists. Previous reviews had

Table 4. Percentage of Students in Special Schools, 1974–92

Year	Students enrolled in all types of government schools	Students enrolled in state special schools	Students enrolled in state special schools (percentages)
1974	618,601	3410	.55
1975	629,745	3522	.56
1976	636,366	4371 (Inc. SDS's)	.69
1977	637,207	5188	.81
1978	633,714	5412	.85
1979	624,400	5461	.88
1980	613,229	5419	.88
1981	602,396	5609	.93
1982	591,358	5711	.97
1983	587,889	5325	.91
1984	578,161	5403	.94
1985	564,984	5364	.95
1986	550,942	5282	.96
1987	542,309	5258	.97
1988	536,794	4993	.93
1989	532,707	4888	.92
1990	530,976	4959	.93
1991	536,754	4967	.93
1992	539,700	4991	.93

Sources: Lewis, 1989; Ministry of Education, *Compendium of Statistics 1989*, 1990.

schools has not shown any significant decrease. This remarkably steady proportion of pupils in the special school system is contrary to the 1984 review's expectations and has in part come about through the traditional special education ability to expand its client base to include extra categories of clients. This has meant that important resources earmarked for integration have not been released for other purposes.

The Future

This overview of reactions to policy development in the area of disability suggests that the future of integration in Victoria schools is problematic. At a systems level, policy strategies thus far deployed have been inadequate to implement the radical change to the provision of educational services to the disabled envisaged by the 1984 review. In seven years the number of pupils in the state school system officially labelled as disabled has doubled — about 5000 segregated into special schools and a further 5000 'integration children' in regular schools. The integration process, which was considered to be largely self-funding from resources deployed from a gradually devitalized special education system, is currently costing the state $43 million a year, while in the period 1984–91 the cost of the special school system grew from about $50 million to $100 million. Traits which characterized Victorian special education over the last eighty years, such as categorization, the expansion of its activities into new areas and the creation of new categories of children and workers, can be seen to have contaminated the integration process. An appreciation of the history of special education is important in understanding how and why these elements have persisted, and in developing alternative integration strategies which are both effective and genuinely liberating.

Notes

1 See Leo Kanner, 'Johann Jakob Guggenbuhl and the Abendberg', in *Bulletin of the History of Medicine*, 33, 6, 1959, pp. 489–502; also Leo Kanner, *A History of the Care and Study of the Mentally Retarded*, Springfield, Charles C. Thomas, 1964.
2 Kanner, *ibid.*, pp. 62–66 reports that in the forty years following the opening of Howe's Massachusettes institution fifteen similar complexes were built in America: one in each of fourteen states and two in New York.
3 Dr Jones's letter dated 2 May 1904 applying for the Victorian position. Held at CRD Brothers Museum, Royal Park, Melbourne.
4 *Victorian Parliamentary Paters*, Vol. 2, 1914, 'Report of the Minister of Public Instruction 1912–13'. See 'Report of Arthur J. Hauser on the Education of Backward and Defective Children', Appendix M, pp. 148–163.
5 *Ibid.*, p. 155.
6 See Maria Montessori, *The Montessori Method*, New York, Schocken, 1912.
7 The term 'lunatic' was commonly used as a general term to describe all types of mental abnormality; and during the nineteenth century there was increasing agreement that a distinction could be made between lunatics born mentally incapable and those who were once mentally capable and subsequently lost their powers of reason. The term 'idiot' increasingly became used to describe the former category and 'imbecile' the latter.
8 See *Victorian Parliamentary Papers*, Vol. 3, 1988, 'Report of the Inspector of Lunatic Asylums on the Hospitals for the Insane, 1887', p. 15.
9 This is recorded in *Victorian Parliamentary Papers*, Vol. 6, 1891, 'Report of the Inspector of Lunatic Asylums for the Year Ended 31 December 1890', p. 53, Table 9.
10 See T.S. Pensebane, *The Rise of the Medical Practitioner in Victoria*, Canberra, Australian National University, 1980.
11 *Victorian Parliamentary Papers*, Vol. 2, 1986, 'Royal Commission on Asylums for the Insane and Inebriate' (the Zox commission), p. cxiii.
12 *The Age*, 6 March 1920.
13 For example, the broadranging and influential British 'Report of the Royal Commission on the Care and Control of the Feeble-minded' was handed down in August 1908.
14 Margaret Archer, in Len Barton and Sally Tomlinson (Eds), *Special Education and Social Interests*, London, Harper and Row, 1984, 'Foreword'.
15 For example, see P. Molitor Bachelard, *The Education of the Retarded Child*, Melbourne, 1934; 'Report of the Remedial Education Committee', Victorian Education Department, August 1965; L. Barby *et al.*, A Step for the Underachiever, BSpEd thesis, Monash University, 1975.
16 For example, see the writings of Goddard and Terman listed under 'References'.
17 Cunningham found a forum for these beliefs as President of the Victorian Eugenics Society, which included Bachelard and Tate as members (Lewis, 1989).
18 See S.D. Porteus, 'Mental Tests with Delinquent and Australian Aboriginal Children', *Psychological Review*, 24, 1, January 1917, pp. 32–42; C.R. McRae, 'The Relation between Intelligence and Social Status', *Education Gazette*, 26, 7, 20 July 1926, pp. 241–242; P. Molitor Bachelard, *op cit.*; J.G. Cannon, 'Victorian

Teachers' Group Test, Grades IV to VIII — Number 1. Description of Test and Age Norms', *Education Gazette*, 26, 3, 18 March 1926.
19 K.S. Cunningham, 'The Theory and Measurement of Intelligence', *Education Gazette*, 23, 6, 1923, p. 201.
20 J. Lewis, The Development of Remedial Education in Victoria 1910–40, MEd thesis, La Trobe University, 1983.
21 Clarence J. Karier, 'Testing for Order and Control in the Corporate Liberal State', in Roger Dale, Geoff Esland and Madeleine MacDonald (Eds), *Schooling and Capitalism*, London, Open University Press, 1976, pp. 128–141. Before the University of Melbourne established its psychology department, the Carnegie Foundation provided the seeding grant for the establishment of the local test developer and importer, the ACER.
22 See Marten Soder, 'The Mentally Retarded: Ideologies of Care and Surplus Population', in Len Barton and Sally Tomlinson (Eds), *Special Education and Social Interest*, London, Harper and Row, 1984, pp. 15–34.

References

BARMBY, L., *et al.* (1975) A Step for the Underachiever, BSpEd thesis, Monash University.
BARTON, L. and TOMLINSON, S. (Eds) (1981) *Special Education: Policy, Practices and Social Issues*, London, Harper and Row.
BERRY, R.J.A. (1928) *Brain and Mind*, New York, Macmillan.
BARRY, R.J.A. (1929) *Report to the Edward Wilson (of 'The Argus') Trust on Mental Deficiency in the State of Victoria*, Melbourne, Wilson and Mackinnon.
BERRY, R.J.A. (1933) *Mental Deficiency — Stoke Park Studies*. London, Macmillan.
BLUM, J. (1978) *Pseudoscience and Mental Ability,* New York, Monthly Review Press.
COOK, S., LEWIS, J. and SWORD, B. (1989) 'The First Five Years of Integration Policy in Victoria', Unpublished research report, Melbourne, Victorian Ministry of Education.
CUNNINGHAM, K.S. (1923) 'The Theory and Measurement of Intelligence', *Education Gazette*, 23, 6.
FLUGEL, J.C. and WEST, DONALD, J. (1964) *A Hundred Years of Psychology 1833–1933,* London, Duckworth.
FULCHER, G. (1989) *Disabling Policies,* Lewes, Falmer Press.
GARTNER, A. and LIPSKY, D.K. (1987) 'Beyond Special Education: Towards a Quality System for All Students', *Harvard Education Review*, 57, 4, November, pp. 367–395.
GODDARD, H.H. (1914) *The Kallikak Family*, New York, Macmillan.
HAUSER, A.J. (1913) 'Report of Arthur J. Hauser on the Education of Backward and Defective Children', Appendix M, pp. 148–163, in *Victorian Parliamentary Papers*, Vol. 2, 1914, 'Report of the Minister of Public Instruction 1912–13'.
JUDGE, C. (1987) *Civilization and Mental Retardation*, Melbourne, Melbourne University Press.
KAMIN, L.J. (1974) *The Science and Politics of IQ*, New York, John Wiley and Sons.
KANNER, L. (1959) 'Johann Jakob Guggenbuhl and the Abendberg', *Bulletin of the History of Medicine*, 33, 6.
KANNER, L. (1964) *A History of the Care and Control of the Mentally Retarded,* Springfield, Charles C. Thomas.
KARIER, C.J. (1976) 'Testing for Order and Control in the Corporate Liberal State', in R. DALE, G. ESLAND and M. MACDONALD (Eds) (1976) *Schooling and Capitalism*, London, Routledge and Kegan Paul.

KEVLES, D.J. (1985) *In the Name of Eugenics*, New York, Alfred A. Knopf.

LEWIS, J. (1984) 'A Socio-historical Analysis of the Origins of Remedial Education in Victoria', *Curriculum Research Bulletin*, 19, 1, March.

LEWIS, J. (1989) 'Removing the Grit: The Development of Special Education in Victoria 1887–1947', PhD thesis, La Trobe University.

McCREERY, J.V. (1892) 'Idiocy and Juvenile Insanity in Victoria', *Intercolonia Medical Congress of Australasia*, 3rd Session, Sydney, pp. 665–668.

MINISTRY OF EDUCATION-VICTORIA (1984) *Integration in Victorian Education: Report of the Ministerial Review of Educational Services for the Disabled*, Melbourne, Victorian Government Printer.

ONIANS, E.C. (1914) *Men of Tomorrow*, Melbourne, Thomas C. Lothian.

PENSABENE, T.S. (1979) *The Rise of the Medical Practitioner in Victoria*, Canberra, Australian National University.

PORTEUS, S.D. (1917) 'Mental Tests with Delinquent and Australian Aboriginal Children', *Psychological Review*, 24, 1, January, pp. 32–42.

PORTEUS, S.D. (1969) *A Psychologist of Sorts*, Palo Alto, Calif., Pacific Books.

PRITCHARD, D.G. (1963) *Education and the Handicapped 1760–1960*, London, Routledge and Kegan Paul.

SCHULTZ, D. (1975) *A History of Modern Psychology*, New York, Academic Press.

SODER, M. (1984) 'The Mentally Retarded', in Will Swann (Ed.) (1984) *The Practice of Special Education*, Oxford, Basil Blackwell.

SWANN, W. (Ed.) (1984) *The Practice of Special Education*, Oxford, Basil Blackwell.

TERMAN, L.M. (1916) *The Measurement of Intelligence*, London, Harrap.

TERMAN, L.M. (1923) *Intelligence Tests and School Re-organization*, New York, World Book Company.

TOMLINSON, S. (1982) *A Sociology of Special Education*, London, Routledge and Kegan Paul.

TWINING, W. (c.1843) *Some Accounts of Cretinism, and the Institution for Its Cure on the Abendberg, near Interlachen, in Switzerland*, London, Parker.

VICTORIAN DEPARTMENT OF EDUCATION (1992) 'Achievements of the Integration Program in Victoria 1984–1991', Ministry of Education, Department of School Education, January.

WEILAND, R. (1982) The Development of Special Education, PhD thesis, University of Queensland.

WYNDHAM, H. (1934) *Ability Grouping*, Melbourne, Melbourne University Press.

Chapter 2

Divide and Rule: A Study of Two Dividing Practices in Queensland Schools

Daphne Meadmore

The drive to test, categorize and select children for differential treatment in educational institutions has a history which is inextricably linked with the provision of state funded education in Western democracies. Mass schooling often paralleled a need made apparent by industrial capitalism for a more docile and morally correct workforce. When education was made available to all children, schools became arenas of competition for life chances. Reasons to exercise control over the outputs of the social machine of schooling found their manifestation in testing procedures which have operated as 'dividing practices' (Foucault, 1982: 208). As 'power-knowledge' technologies, these are manifestations of the exercise of modern power over individual students in the cause of governance (Foucault, 1977). This chapter will focus mainly on two dividing practices used in Queensland schools, but a wider contextual background is also given since initiatives in this state were influenced by trends in other states, as well as from abroad.

The Social Origins of 'Intelligence'

In nineteenth century Britain mass schooling was a result of industrial capitalism and reflected a general fear among the upper and middle classes that industrial prosperity and social stability might be jeopardized by the existence of a large, uneducated and potentially revolutionary working class (Dale and Esland, 1977: 38–39). In the liberal rhetoric of the time, education was promulgated as a source of moral and rational training and also of personal fulfilment, but, primarily, schools functioned as apparatuses of social control (Jones and Williamson, 1979: 61). When all social classes were participating in some form of schooling, the socially competitive nature of mass schooling precipitated the situation where the activity of schools very soon began to be linked with ways that students could be sorted and sifted in the schooling race. Significantly, these procedures were associated with notions of 'intelligence' (Simon, 1983). Thus the idea that one needed to exhibit a particular type of intelligence in order to succeed at school and conversely the notion that those who were deficient in this commodity required different schooling provision have largely been constructs arising out of the whole set of relations of production that industrial capitalism brought forth.

It is not surprising that intelligence had been of little relevance in pre-industrial times. Life in a predominantly rural world where poverty was the condition of ordinary people had meant that physical strength and endurance were qualities which were prized above all others. To illustrate the relative unimportance of 'intelligence' in the pre-industrial French context, Bisseret (1979: 7) traces the meaning of this concept, arguing that it was not well known or understood until the second half of the eighteenth century. However, by the nineteenth century, when social mobility had generally become a possibility, 'intelligence' was conveniently used not only to explain, but also to legitimate the social inequalities which had been made more apparent by industrial capitalism.

The notion of intelligence assumed power in institutional spheres as part of a perceived need for 'normalization'. Normalization procedures constitute an applied form of what Foucault (1977) calls the 'human sciences', e.g. psychiatry, penology and pedagogy. Methods of normalization have been used in hospitals, asylums, prisons, workshops and schools to legitimate internal hierarchies and the treatment of 'inmates'. This could be done through detailed and continuous evaluation which 'established a grid of codeability of personal attributes. They act as norms, enabling the previously aleatory and unpredictable complexities of human conduct to be charted and judged in terms of conformity and deviation, to be coded and compared, ranked and measured' (Rose, 1990: 133). Such information could be recorded and stored so that each individual became a 'case' with a case history. It was as if a human sorting house were needed to assess individuals and determine to what regime they were best suited (Rose, 1990: 133). But most important for this discussion are the ways that schools used normalization procedures as dividing practices by employing strategies of comparison, differentiation, hierarchization, homogenization and exclusion (Foucault, 1977: 183).

Dividing practices are at the heart of school organization as they encompass examinations, testing, profiling and streaming. They also include the use of entry criteria to different types of schooling and the formation of different types of intelligence, ability and scholastic identity (Ball, 1990: 4). Of concern is that these practices largely pivot on the notion of who is intelligent and who is not without giving due recognition to the social and cultural production of intelligence. In addition, dividing practices in schools are closely linked with teachings from the discipline of psychology which developed from psychiatry. Action resulting from psychological testing can mean the separating of those considered to be less intelligent for placement in special educational settings, the selection of 'bright' students for 'gifted and talented' classes and, more generally, streaming and tracking procedures to monitor children in the regular classroom. All this is not to argue that all individuals have the same capacity to engage in the kind of abstract thought embraced by education systems in advanced industrial societies. However, while intelligence is socially and culturally defined and produced, and the organization of education seeks to divide students, there remains unequal access to the sort of bourgeois cultural capital that such notions of intelligence command.

The discourse of intelligence promulgated by psychologists has influenced educators 'to cater for individual differences' in a liberal progressive mode by providing different curricula, different pedagogies and fostering different student-teacher relationships. From these procedures and processes, students learn their individual scholastic identities which relate to perceived levels of intelligence, and these are carried into their adult lives (Ball, 1990: 4). Thus a major outcome of schooling is that life chances are determined in significant ways by the types of scholastic identity produced by schools.

An important means of producing scholastic identity has been through the use of standardized tests for measuring intelligence. In the early 1990s, because all children were participating to some degree in schooling and therefore were ostensibly competing for access to positions of higher status, the testing movement manifested the concern that governance of the outcomes of schooling was necessary. Middle-class people had most to fear from a democratization of schooling since their fairly precarious position depended largely on educational success. In such a competitive social climate the promulgation of the notion that only the intelligent would succeed through schooling led to intelligence as a commodity being regarded as the critical filter to academic success in the public mind.

Scientific validity for psychometric tests was highly desirable, and it was no accident that the earliest proponents of eugenics and psychometrics linked their work with science in the hope of basking in its reflected glory of being the best means of observing and unravelling the mysteries of the natural world. Such was the faith in science at the turn of the century that reified science replaced the church in bourgeois thinking and concomitantly was the ultimate legislator of bourgeois ideology (Rose, Lewontin and Kamin, 1984: 31). It is important to note that even after the scientific basis of intelligence testing had been exposed in the 1970s as being a pseudoscience with an ideological function (Kamin, 1974; Blum, 1978; Gould, 1981; Rose et al., 1984) there remain restorationists who seek to breathe new life into this degenerating research paradigm.

To return to the heady days of scientific acceptance: psychometricians and psychologists espoused the science of individual differences by placing emphasis on the treatment of the individual. It was reckoned that if intelligence as a fixed, heritable commodity could be isolated in certain individuals, then the schooling process could be designed to differentiate individual differences in intellect. On the grounds of this logic, biologistic discourse influenced the way teachers and others thought about the ability of individual children. Prior to the twentieth century there had been a degree of optimism that the ordinary child was capable of intellectual development and that this could be brought about by sound and thorough teaching in school. Mental abilities were believed to develop as the child progressed through education (Simon, 1983: 89). Initially mass schooling tended to embrace such ideas, but eugenicism and psychologism were to change teacher thinking because of their insistence that a child was born all that s/he would become; and that the most teaching could do was to bring to light a given, inborn quota of intelligence. Psychometricians produced classist, racist and sexist tests which were used on whole populations (Kamin, 1974; Blum, 1978; Gould, 1981; Rose et al., 1984). For example, in Britain tests were used to legitimate and control social mobility, while in America the problems of difficult race relations presented a forum for testing (Sutherland, 1984: 283). Race, gender and class intersect in discrimination and social injustice, and those at the bottom of the social ladder were considered by eugenicists and psychometricians to be 'genetically inferior victims of their own immutable defects' (Kamin, 1974: 15).

Closely linked to beliefs about intelligence are those of 'individualism'. It has been argued that industrial capitalism of the twentieth century produced the modern form of individualism (Turner, 1988), and that no other aspect of social thought and culture is as widely acknowledged and as deeply felt as that of individualism (Cagan, 1978: 228). Indeed, industrial capitalism and individualism have fused to create the 'Foucault paradox' (Turner, 1988: 60). This paradox is evident in the manner by which individualism has produced a double-edged impact, occurring when the separation of individuals has invoked subsequent consequences for the individual through bureaucratic processes, such as in methods of surveillance. Irreparably the cost to the individual through such a relationship with the state is expressed in the term 'individuation' (Turner, 1988).

It is a relatively recent phenomenon that individuals have been singled out for individualized treatment. In pre-industrial times individualization of ordinary people was not common practice. Ordinary folk were part of a family, a community, but not 'knowable' in the sense of having an individual identity. It was those closest to the sovereign who were knowable individuals — the wealthy, the holy, the noble. These were the people whose lives were recorded. But as Foucault (1977) demonstrates so clearly, it was the individualizing 'gaze' of the nineteenth century which illuminated the entire social fabric, by shedding its light on those previously obscured, i.e., the mad, the indigent, the delinquent, the criminal, the sick, the poor, the young, all of whom were a problem to the new order. With the provision of mass schooling in Western democracies it also came to shed its light on the 'normal' population, and in this instance it was students in schools who were targeted. Thus the gaze was designed to make knowable the entire population, for it is only through knowing that a society can be tested for its ills and solutions can be found. Interventions by way of the techniques of 'moral statistics' resulted in new forms of social investigation and political calculation (Hunter, 1988: 53). By knowing the individual, one could train, change, classify, normalize, exclude, by the use of time and space (Foucault, 1977).

An example of how the gaze, i.e., surveillance, as a form of modern power can be more intrusive and pervasive than earlier forms of power is found in the workings of the 'psychological complex' (Rose, 1979, 1990). This term embraces more than the discipline of psychology to include the agents, discourses and apparatuses which are inextricably part of its workings. Foucault (1977) likens such surveillance to Bentham's panopticon where the gaze was unidirectional, synoptic and individualizing. Historically the position of those carrying out these functions on modern individuals, that of the psychological complex, has become stronger to the point where the expertise of the 'psy' people elicits the respect, even the awe, of the public at large (Kapferer, 1990: 43), and where the insertion of psychology in modern social practices has helped to constitute the very form of modern individuality (Henriques *et al.*, 1984: 1). Thus while it is through social and cultural practices that human beings are made into subjects, it is through further individuation procedures of classification and division that objectification of subjects occurs. Objectification within the subject or between the subject and others makes the individual a 'case' wherein the acts of classifying, correcting, normalizing and/or excluding are regarded as legitimate means of treatment.

The Initial Australian Response

It is significant to note that for the first three decades of this century eugenics and psychometric testing found few adherents in Australia because the social climate was different (Bacchi, 1980: 200). This was due to a general feeling that a superior social and physical environment gave Australians a better chance in the 'New World' far removed from the entrenched class system and flammable race relations of the 'Old World'.

Changes in attitudes came about with the 1930s Depression when, coupled with a falling birth rate, many middle-class people began to worry that the 'unfit' might outbreed the 'fit' (Bacchi, 1980). The term 'unfit' was used specifically to refer to those with mental or physical defect, but was also more generally used to refer to the poor in society. Because their faith in social reform has been damaged, the middle classes became increasingly fearful that their formerly privileged position would be eroded. They were also alarmed at the prospect of supporting the 'wastrels' of society (Bacchi, 1980: 211). Since mental deficiency was believed to be the root cause of personality disorders which led to immorality, crime and poverty, it seemed appropriate to use mental tests to identify and categorize those children who should be separated from the mainstream for schooling purposes, and perhaps later to decide if such children should be sterilized (Miller, 1986). For these reasons, mental tests were given to Australian children with the objective being to weed out (scientifically of course) those children for whom education was a waste of money. This was in accordance with the idea that social cleansing of this nature was in the national interest of technical and social efficiency (Lewis, 1987; McCallum, 1990).

Increased attendance in secondary school, which partially was precipitated by the lack of jobs due to the depression, was also a reflection of a growing belief that universal secondary education was needed for the purposes of industry and advancement, both nationally and internationally. Furthermore, secondary education was now considered a right rather than a privilege. In response, secondary education broadened its base to provide different types of courses with varying statuses which led to different kinds of jobs. Yet there remained questions about how much education was desirable for the rank and file. For instance, in 1935 K.S. Cunningham, a leading Victorian educator, argued that 'secondary education is primarily, if not solely, the prerogative of the intellectual aristocracy' (Hyams and Bessant, 1972: 135). He was, of course, referring to the ruling class, those who had received a secondary education from its limited private beginnings in Australia in the nineteenth century and who were demonstrating their 'natural' fitness as eminent leaders in society.

Significantly, psychological theory was conveniently used to justify the provision of limited secondary opportunities for the working class (Henry *et al.*, 1988: 195). Stemming from the notion that it would be socially efficient not to waste precious time and money on those who were proven to be of low intelligence and therefore ineducable anyway, influential Australian educators followed a lead initially taken by the medical profession of defining those who had normal intelligence and those who did not. 'Proof' was now available through the use of scientific tests that the privileged classes were superior to the poor, criminals, immigrants and, of course, the Aborigines. On the grounds of such evidence there was an increase in the use of special classes, which, not surprisingly, were set up in working-class areas. However, the stigma attached to attending such special classes, coupled with a curriculum which centred on acquiring skills related to jobs that required 'working with one's hands', seriously closed off future life options for working-class children (Lewis, 1987).

Increasingly educators involved themselves in the discourse of the psycho-logical complex to the point where they regarded standardized tests as a legitimate means of treating the uniqueness of the individual child. Difference could be codified, mathematized and standardized (Rose, 1988: 194), thereby shoring up the 'efficiency' of schooling by the deployment of dividing practices.

'On Our Selection':[1] The Case of Queensland

As a dividing practice for almost 100 years in Queensland education, the State Scholarship Examination needs to be placed in its socio-historical context; but first some time needs to be spent in analyzing the notion of 'the examination' as a focal point of disciplinary power. Foucault (1977) refers to the examination as a 'slender technique' which combines the two aspects of disciplinary power, hierarchical observation and normalizing judgment. This technique possesses a normalizing gaze, a surveillance that makes it possible to qualify, to classify and to punish. Moreover, 'it establishes over individuals a visibility through which one differentiates them and judges them' (1977: 184).

Hoskin (1982: 213–236) traces the history of the examination, especially in the area of 'schooled science', as a technique of modern power. He sees the modern written examination as one of the most significant transformations in the history of educational practice and refers to the examination as a particular and special microtechnology which, in Foucault's words, 'combines the deployment of force and the establishment of truth'. The 'written material makes it possible to generate a "history" of each student and also to classify students *en masse* into categories, and eventually into "populations" with norms' (Hoskin, 1979: 137).

In Queensland the State Scholarship Examination (commonly known as the 'Scholarship') during the years from 1873 to 1962 was a useful means of deciding who had the 'ability' to benefit from a secondary school education and what sort of education was appropriate (Meadmore, 1990). Foucault's (1977: 184) description of the examination as a 'power-knowledge' technology can be accurately applied to the Scholarship because of its disciplinary power simultaneously to give 'rewards' and 'punishments' as a 'ritualized mechanism of discipline'. The educational and social effects on the recipients of these rewards and punishments were enormous. This examination at first effectively ensured that only a social élite would be involved in secondary schooling, but later the scope widened slightly to include an academic élite when state universal secondary provision was made from 1912 onwards (Tyrrell, 1970).

Not only was the Scholarship an efficient gate-keeper to secondary education; it also proved useful as a device for tracking students in 'appropriate' courses. In fact the examination, as a dividing practice, acted surreptitiously as a test of intelligence, and the assumption was that the 'brightest' children should pursue the academic courses, while the less clever should be placed in vocational courses.

There was also a gender component in tracking since non-academic courses for girls and boys were different, e.g. 'domestic science' for girls, 'technical' for boys (Department of Public Instruction, 1928: 11). Academic courses leading to matriculation were more likely to be taken by boys than girls, with middle-class males being disproportionately overrepresented. This reflected a wider societal view that education was to fit girls for home duties (Queensland, *Report of the*

Secretary for Public Instruction, 1914). In fact 'Queensland was a man's [sic] world' and 'girls were not regarded as having the same place in high school education as boys' (Goodman, 1968: 223). Overall decisions made on the basis of Scholarship results were more likely to be gender- and class-based rather than located in sound educational considerations of ability. Thus the State Scholarship was a dividing practice par excellence and was very successful in 'sorting out the sheep from the goats', thereby achieving its mission. However, in the 1950s it became increasingly unpopular, mainly for educational and pedagogical reasons, and remained as something of a dinosaur since the other Australian states had long since abandoned entrance examinations to secondary education. Finally it was abolished in 1962, when the state was financially prepared to open the gate wider and allow more of the goats to benefit from the richer pastures of secondary education. Not surprisingly, attention began to focus increasingly on notions of normalization to legitimate policy and action.

Normalization procedures were applied to 'retarded' children later in Queensland than in the southern states (Wyeth, 1955: 183). However, by 1923 psychological tests were being used to determine entry to 'backward' classes. The special classes were later officially called 'opportunity schools' after unsympathetic teachers threatened to send low achieving children 'to the Dunces' school' (Queensland, *Report of the Secretary for Public Instruction*, 1926). The District Inspector's Report made specific reference to this practice, and in fact a note was included in the *Education Office Gazette* (*EOG*) (1926: 28, 7) warning teachers against referring to opportunity schools in derogatory terms. Nevertheless, the stigma of being singled out for opportunity classes was felt despite official decrees and was reflected in diminished life chances for the students involved.

After the 'abnormal' population had been dealt with, it was time to turn the gaze to the 'normal' students in classrooms, and increasingly dividing practices to select and stratify the entire population were implemented. Mainly this was done by giving 'vocational guidance' as a supplement to Scholarship results. In 1948 the establishment of the Research and Guidance Branch in the state Department of Education formalized the influence which psychologism had come to exert in educational matters. Guidance officers from the branch administered psychological tests to pupils in their final year of primary school. Their role involved carrying out testing programs and helping make decisions about whether individual students should continue to secondary school, about what courses (academic or vocational) individual students should take, and about career and/or job opportunities. However, there was a problem. While guidance officers were traversing the vast expanses of Queensland armed with intelligence tests, and although several thousand students were tested and interviewed with their parents, the task was enormous and many students could not be reached. New strategies had to be adopted since faith in vocational guidance was firmly located in policy as an 'efficient technique' to avoid the 'social wastage of round pegs in square holes' (Haine, 1961: 190). There was to be no turning back. After all, psychologists asserted that the occupation best suited for individual students could be gauged from the test results. For instance, university professors, doctors, highest posts in science required an IQ score of 133+, while a sorter and packer could get by with 85 IQ points (Haine, 1961: 190)!

Associated with demographic problems was the very cost of testing. On the one hand, the tests were generally considered to be both valid and socially useful, but, on the other, the costs of administering them were prohibitive in a society whose education system faced the urgent need to expand rapidly in response to the unprecedented growth in the numbers of children engaging in secondary education. This marked increase in participation in secondary schooling stemmed from four main sources: the transfer of Grade 8 of primary school to secondary school when the Scholarship was abolished after 1962; the concomitant raising of the school leaving age from 14 to 15; the baby boom which had been experienced since the end of the Second World War; and migration.

For these reasons, secondary schooling had to expand rapidly, and it was at this time (1963) that primary teachers instead of guidance officers were used to administer group tests to their own classes in the final year of primary schooling. Teachers were then acting as 'scientists in the classroom' (McCallum, 1985), a role for which most of them would have had no specific training. Educational psychology had achieved a small but firm footage in the curriculum of Queensland teachers' colleges in the 1960s when the textbook written by Haine (1961) especially for teacher training purposes was used in the state's colleges. However, it is obvious that only one subject out of a curriculum of twelve (Queensland. Department of Education, 1966) was no basis for teachers to be considered to be qualified to act as psychologists. However, because psychologism was firmly entrenched in the public mind as a legitimate practice, teachers had accepted its relevance and importance to teaching and learning. Kapferer (1990: 42) states that so widely has psychologism been accepted by practitioners in classrooms that 'no-one escapes the amateur psychologising of teachers.'

It is significant to note that although the democratic gate to secondary education was being opened wider, control was seen to be necessary to oversee the procedure. The testing program in the final year of primary schooling, which was implemented to fill the gap left by the abolition of the Scholarship and to help alleviate the problems of providing vocational guidance on a large scale, became unofficially known as the 'October Tests'. Details of this program were first published in August 1963 (*EOG*, 65, 8, pp. 224–226), and the purpose of the testing program was explained to school principals and to teachers who would be administering the tests. The official purpose of the testing program was:

  to provide information to secondary schools to assist in the placement of
    students in appropriate courses; and
  to indicate to secondary schools those students who could benefit from re-
    medial and developmental reading courses.

The first stated purpose of this program clearly demonstrates that these tests were expected to provide data which schools could use to place students in different tracks, e.g. academic, commercial, home science, industrial. However, in 1964 an alteration was made to the wording of the first purpose for the program when the phrase 'placement of students in appropriate courses' was altered to 'placement of students in appropriate classes' (*EOG*, 66, 7, p. 229). The implication of this change is significant because it formally approved and legitimized the practice of streaming.

This testing program as a dividing practice was thus able to continue the streaming and tracking functions formerly provided by the Scholarship and psychological testing. Ironically, one set of dividing practices was replaced by another despite the deleterious social and educational effects of streaming and standardized testing being well documented for their contribution to the phenomenon of the self-fulfilling prophecy and of labelling practices (Hargreaves, 1967; Rosenthal and Jacobson, 1968; Good and Brophy, 1973; Willis, 1977).

It must be emphasized that in such a highly centralized system policy laid down in the *Education Office Gazette* had to be carried out to the letter. There could be no departures without incurring reprimands or punishments, and on this basis the practice was closely aligned to the policy. Under these conditions, variously described tests of 'scholastic aptitude', 'general ability' and 'attainment' were given to all children in their final year of state schooling. In 1976 there appeared a test entitled 'Test of Learning Ability 6' (TOLA 6), which was designed and produced by the Australian Council for Educational Research (ACER). This particular test stands out for its longevity because, having survived the demise of the other tests in the battery, it alone remained until August 1991, when the *EOG* (93, 16, p. 176) informed teachers that the 'annual Year 7 Testing Program, which involved the administration of the TOLA 6 . . . to Year 7 students in all State and participating non-State schools in October, will be discontinued.' It is interesting that no rationale was given for the discontinuation of a testing program which had been in operation in one form or another for twenty-seven years. It seems that educational and social reasons were not major considerations because further on the same *EOG* states: 'Existing TOLA 6 testing materials (including test booklets, answer sheets, score keys and manuals) in primary schools are the school's property for disposal or use as required. Secondary schools wishing access to the materials should make arrangements with their local primary schools.' While the test may not *officially* be given in the primary school, there is still scope for its use in the secondary school!

As an illustration of problems which group testing presents, there is some value in taking a closer look at TOLA 6. Not only have psychologists long recognized the shortcomings and indeed the dangers of group testing, but also problematic is the fact that the same test was used year after year, with *EOGs* regularly making a plea for it to be securely kept away from prying eyes. Annually a master sheet of results was forwarded to the Education Department to provide an indication of pupil achievement relative to others throughout the state, but, more importantly, individual scores were sent to appropriate secondary schools, possibly arriving before the student. The role played by the test results in the construction of student profiles and ultimately in the production of scholastic identity is clearly articulated thus:

> The standardized results from the TOLA 6 can be used in conjunction with accumulated information of pupil achievement to provide Guidance Officers and high school personnel with comprehensive profiles of pupils transferring from primary to secondary schools. (*Queensland Primary Testing Program: Administration Manual for Year 7 Tests*, 1987: 4)

While the *Administration Manual* (1987: 20) does go on to state that TOLA 6 'is not an infallible indicator of student ability' and that the test results should 'supplement' and 'not be substituted for the other information about individual pupils', the test results provided an efficient and 'scientific' way for acting on ability levels for streaming and tracking purposes. For instance, in informal discussions over the last three years with students studying within the Faculty of Education of the Queensland University of Technology the majority have reported that they clearly remember doing the October Tests, and many have given anecdotal evidence that test results were used to stream and/or track them. It is interesting that so many students remember the testing program and its implications, five or more years down their educational paths, since it was not a widely publicized event at Department level. Parents were not issued with official information about the purpose of the testing program, and it is stated in the manual that advance notice to students to ensure their readiness and attendance was to be 'brief and low key' (*Queensland Primary Testing Program: Administration Manual for Year 7*, 1987: 6).

Apart from educational considerations, there were other concerns. First, because ethical considerations were not covered adequately in the manual, teachers and school administrations treated confidential information differently. Again this exemplifies the problem of using 'amateur psychologists' in professional roles. Second, an insidious characteristic of this particular group test is that it yields an individual score (out of 15) which was easily used as a referent when making educational decisions. Examples have been widely reported of teachers who were encouraged in many schools to keep the scores next to students' names in their mark book. Third, it is alarming that of all the possibilities which were encompassed in this dividing practice, it was not recognized that children who were socially or culturally different could not hope to score well on a test which demanded both an extensive conceptual understanding of the English language and a deep involvement with the dominant culture. Merely being able to 'speak English' was not a viable prerequisite for success in this test, but nowhere did the manual suggest that recently arrived migrant children, Aboriginal children or working-class children might be disadvantaged through this testing technique.

In spite of the dangers apparent in the use of standardized tests, they are commensurate with a national policy of economic determinism where selection is critical and where such processes need to be carried out as cheaply and efficiently as possible. The problem, of course, is not merely with TOLA 6, but with any single group test which is meant to be used in a selection process. In the future it could well be that national testing in Years 7 and 9, as outlined by the Federal Education Minister (Stanaway, 1991), might replace the function of TOLA 6 as Australia moves towards the introduction of a national curriculum.[2]

Conclusion

It can be seen that these examples of dividing practices which were used in Queensland schools to determine and control the outcomes of secondary schooling have had significant social and educational effects. There is an ongoing need for teachers as professionals to question the power of the 'experts' and to take the opportunity to be advocates for their students in ways which are likely to lessen the disadvantage faced by those who are socially, culturally, physically and/ or intellectually different. What is problematic is that teachers, through the influence of psychology in their preparation courses and in its widespread acceptance in society, involve themselves in the rhetoric of psychologism to the point where they welcome standardized tests as a way to treat the uniqueness of the individual child. Individuation processes and the issues of social justice and desirable pedagogy escape their notice in their quest to make each individual a 'case' whereby the need to classify, correct, normalize, exclude is legitimized.

Dividing practices of the sort discussed in this chapter are in fact disciplinary techniques in that they simultaneously give rewards and punishments which ultimately produce scholastic identity in inequitable ways. As such, they are examples of the use of modern power in the cause of governance (Foucault, 1977).

Note

1 'On Our Selection' borrows the title of Rudd's classic Australian literary work. A 'selection' referred to the tract of land that European settlers violently misappropriated from Aboriginal Australians. Ownership of such 'selections' brought prestige, privilege and political power, as qualification for a parliamentary position was on the basis of 'ownership' of land.
2 In June 1992 the state Education Department announced its intention to implement a new testing program called 'Performance Standards' to assess six levels of competence in Years 1–10. It could well develop as yet another normative measure for the governance of difference.

References

AUSTRALIAN COUNCIL FOR EDUCATIONAL RESEARCH (1974) *Test of Learning Ability 6*, Hawthorn, ACER.

BACCHI, C. (1980) 'The Nature-Nurture Debate in Australia, 1900–1914', *Historical Studies*, 19, 75, pp. 199–212.

BALL, S.J. (Ed.) (1990) *Foucault and Education: Disciplines and Knowledge*, London, Routledge.

BISSERET, N. (1979) *Education, Class, Language and Ideology*, London, Routledge and Kegan Paul.

BLUM, J. (1978) *Pseudoscience and Mental Ability: The Origins and Fallacies of the IQ Controversy*, New York, Monthly Review Press.

CAGAN, E. (1978) 'Individualism, Collectivism and Radical Education Reform', *Harvard Educational Review*, 48, pp. 226–266.

DALE, R. and ESLAND, J. (1977) *Schooling and Capitalism*, Milton Keynes, Open University Press.

DEPARTMENT OF PUBLIC INSTRUCTION (1928) *State Education in Queensland*, Brisbane, Queensland Government.

FOUCAULT, M. (1977) *Discipline and Punish: The Birth of the Prison*, Ringwood, Penguin.

FOUCAULT, M. (1982) 'Afterword', in DREYFUS, H.L. and RABINOW, P., *Michel Foucault: Beyond Structuralism and Hermeneutics*, New York, Harvester Wheatsheaf.

GOOD, T. and BROPHY, J. (1973) *Looking in Classrooms*, New York, Harper and Row.

GOODMAN, R. (1968) *Secondary Education in Queensland 1860–1960*, Canberra, ANU Press.

GOULD, S.J. (1981) *The Mismeasure of Man*, Harmondsworth, Penguin.

HAINE, H.E. (1961) *Classroom Psychology*, Brisbane, Jacaranda Press.

HARGREAVES, D.H. (1967) *Social Relations in a Secondary School*, London, Routledge and Kegan Paul.

HENRIQUES, J., HOLLWAY, W., URWIN, C., VENN, C. and WALKERDINE, U. (1984) *Changing the Subject: Psychology, Social Regulation and Subjectivity*, London, Methuen.

HENRY, M., KNIGHT, J., LINGARD, R. and TAYLOR, S. (1988) *Understanding Schooling: An Introductory Sociology of Australian Education*, London, Routledge.

HOSKIN, K. (1979) 'The Examination, Disciplinary Power and Rational Schooling', *History of Education*, 8, 2, pp. 135–146.

HOSKIN, K. (1982) 'Examinations and Schooling of Science', in MACLEOD, R.M., *Days of Judgement*, Driffield, Nafferton Books, pp. 213–236.

HUNTER, I. (1988) *Culture and Government: The Emergence of Literary Education*, Houndmills, Macmillan.

HYAMS, B.K. and BESSANT, B. (1972) *Schools for the People?*, Hawthorn, Longman.

JONES, K. and WILLIAMSON, K. (1979) 'The Birth of the Schoolroom', *Ideology and Consciousness*, 6, pp. 59–97.

KAMIN, L.J. (1974) *The Science and Politics of IQ*, Harmondsworth, Penguin.

KAPFERER, J.L. (1990) 'Expert Advice: The Mystification of Common Sense', *Discourse*, 10, 2, pp. 36–50.

LEWIS, J. (1987) 'So Much Grit in the Hub of the Education Machine', in BESSANT, B. (Ed.), *Mother State and Her Little Ones*, Bundoora, La Trobe University Press, pp. 140–166.

MCCALLUM, D. (1985) The Theory of Educational Inequality in Australia, 1900–1950, PhD thesis, University of Melbourne.

MCCALLUM, D. (1990) *The Social Production of Merit: Education, Psychology and Politics in Australia, 1900–1950*, London, Falmer Press.

MEADMORE, D.A. (1990) A Socio-historical Analysis of the Manifestation of the Ideology of Intelligence through Schooling, MEdStud thesis, University of Queensland.

MILLER, P. (1986) *Long Division: State Schooling in South Australian Society*, Netley, Wakefield Press.

QUEENSLAND (1914) and (1926) *Report of the Secretary for Public Instruction*, Brisbane.

QUEENSLAND. DEPARTMENT OF EDUCATION (1966) *Kedron Park Teachers' College Calendar*, Brisbane.

QUEENSLAND. DEPARTMENT OF EDUCATION (1987) *Queensland Primary Testing Program: Administration Manual for Year 7 Tests*, Brisbane.

QUEENSLAND. DEPARTMENT OF EDUCATION, *Education Office Gazette*, 28, 7, 1926; 65, 8, 1963, pp. 224–226; 66, 7, 1964, p. 229; 93, 16, 1991, p. 176.

ROSE, N. (1979) 'The Psychological Complex: Mental Measurement and Social Administration', *Ideology and Consciousness*, 5, pp. 5–68.

ROSE, N. (1988) 'Calculable Minds and Manageable Individuals', *History of the Human Sciences*, 1, 2, pp. 179–199.

ROSE, N. (1990) *Governing the Soul: The Shaping of the Private Self*, London, Routledge.

ROSE, S., LEWONTIN, R.C. and KAMIN, L.J. (1984) *Not in Our Genes: Biology, Ideology and Human Nature*, Ringwood, Penguin.

ROSENTHAL, R. and JACOBSON, L. (1968) *Pygmalion in the Classroom*, Eastbourne, Holt, Rinehart and Winston.

SIMON, B. (1983) 'Educating in Theory, Schooling in Practice: The Experience of the Last Hundred Years', in MURRAY SMITH S. (Ed.), *Melbourne Studies in Education 1982*, Melbourne, Melbourne University Press.

STANAWAY, G. (1991) 'National Plan to Lift Literacy of School Leavers', *Courier-Mail*, 3 September.

SUTHERLAND, G. (1984) *Ability, Merit and Measurement: Mental Testing and English Education, 1880–1940*, Oxford, Clarendon Press.

TURNER, B.S. (1988) 'Individualism, Capitalism and the Dominant Culture: A Note on the Debate', *Australian and New Zealand Journal of Sociology*, 24, 1, pp. 47–64.

TYRRELL, I. (1970) 'The Failure of State Secondary Education Reform in Queensland 1900–1914', *Queensland Historical Review*, 3, pp. 4–13.

WILLIS, P. (1977) *Learning to Labour*, Farnborough, Saxon.

WYETH, E.R. (1955) *Education in Queensland*, Melbourne, Australian Council of Educational Research.

Part 2

Observations Abroad:
International Perpectives on Integration

Chapter 3

The Politics of Integration: Observations on the Warnock Report

Len Barton and Maeve Landman

The issue of integration is an important one. It provides an opportunity for raising serious questions about the kind of society we desire and the nature and functions of schooling. Furthermore, it gives us a concrete example of the complex and contentious nature of educational discourse and practice.

Such discourse is the subject of intense struggles in that the participants often adhere to competing objectives and operate from within unequal power relations (Fulcher, 1989a). Part of the struggle involves disputes over the meaning of key concepts such as 'partnership', 'standards', 'discipline' and 'integration'. How we approach this activity and the interpretations we construct will be influenced by the values we are committed to. In acknowledging the existence of multiple discourses in the field of education and the often antagonistic relationships between them, Ball (1991) contends that 'discourses are, therefore, about what can be said, and thought, but also about who can speak, when, where and with what authority.' He continues: 'Words and propositions will change their meaning, according to their use and the positions held by those who use them' (p. 17). These ideas, according to Ball, have their antecedents in the work of Foucault (1977) and are part of a wider interest in the relationship between knowledge and power. In relation to integration this perspective provides a possibility for highlighting the nature and intensity of the struggles involved over definitions, effective policy and practice. It offers a way of exploring these relationships between actors in different arenas and levels of the system (Fulcher, 1989a).

This chapter outlines some of the influences and debates which have shaped segregated policy and practice in England and Wales. The contentious issue of 'integration' is examined, and the position of the Warnock Report (1978) provides the central focus of our analysis. We do not attempt to examine more recent developments emanating from the 1988 Education Reform Act; this has been the subject of other papers (see, for example, Barton and Oliver, 1992).

Segregated Provision

Various arguments have contributed at different historical periods to providing the impetus and maintenance of segregated schooling, particularly for those pupils with severe learning difficulties. While these are not in any order of priority, they include the following perspectives. First, this population is viewed as immature, childlike and thus in need of *protection* from hostile and damaging aspects of the environment. These include mainstream schools and the impersonal nature of their size, their emphasis on academic learning and competitiveness, and the exposure to the cruel and taunting activities of their 'normal' peers. The obverse side of this coin is that, first, segregated schooling is much more benign. Second, the teachers in these schools are depicted as *possessing particular qualities*, including, dedication, love and patience. It is these which make such teachers special and more fitted to meet the 'special needs' of these pupils. Third, the justification has also included the significance given to the *special curriculum* provided within special schools. Finally, support is offered on *administrative/ efficiency* grounds. The centralizing of specialist equipment, support services and specialist teachers is seen to be a most effective deployment of resources. Thus this form of provision is depicted as being in the best interests of these children and young people.

Part of the difficulty with the discourse supporting segregated provision is that it depoliticizes the issues involved and does not engage with the wider socio-economic context in which discussions concerning schooling need to be located. Increasing numbers of disabled people are expressing their criticisms of segregated provisions (Rieser and Mason, 1990; Oliver, 1990; Barnes, 1990). These refer not only to issues of low expectations and overprotective attitudes on the part of staff but also to the contribution these schools make to the powerful means of legitimating stereotypes often based on ignorance. Morris (1990) illustrates this conviction in the following remarks:

> People's expectations of us are informed by their previous experience of disabled people. If disabled people are segregated, are treated as alien, as different in a fundamental way, then we will never be accepted as full members of society. *This is the strongest argument against special schools and against separate provision.* (p. 59, emphasis added)

Being excluded from daily interactions with their contemporaries means their knowledge of the social world is limited and hardly constitutes a good preparation for participation in society (Fish, 1985).

Sociologists have been critical of those arguments which depict 'benevolent humanitarianism' as the sole grounds for government responses in the form of segregated provision (Barnes, 1990; Tomlinson, 1982; Ford *et al.*, 1982; Barton and Tomlinson, 1984). From a systems perspective they have maintained that such provision has been an essential means of removing objectionable, unwanted pupils and thereby enabling the mainstream system to function more effectively. This form of interpretation involves a consideration of the socio-economic, race and gender composition of the pupils in special schools. This approach is receiving increasing sociological and historical support in other countries (Soder, 1984; Lewis, 1988; Carrier, 1986; Skrtic, 1991).

Some educational psychologists have also offered critical commentaries on special schools. Much of their work has been based on a desire for a truly comprehensive system of school provision (Dessent, 1987; Booth, 1983). The continuation of segregated schooling is attributable mainly to the weaknesses of current policy on comprehensive schools; Dessent (1987) also contends that:

> Special schools do not have a right to exist. They exist because of the limitations of ordinary schools in providing for the full range of abilities and disabilities among children. It is not primarily a question of the quality or adequacy of what is offered in a special school. Even a superbly well organised special school offering the highest quality curriculum and educational input to its children has no right to exist if that same education can be provided in a mainstream school. (p. 97)

This perspective is a good example of the level of commitment that some analysts bring to this issue. It also relates to a particular meaning of integration. Supporting this perspective, Booth (1981) maintains that integration is about questions of power and of enabling pupils to have greater participation in the life of the school. This involves challenging notions of selection and ability and being engaged in the establishment of schools which do not exclude children. He believes in 'schools for all'. This approach links '. . . the notion of integration to both a comprehensive principle and a principle of the equality of value of the participants in schools' (Booth, 1989: 7). This relates to broader questions of social justice and equity. Certainly this approach provides an opportunity of viewing 'special educational needs' as *unmet needs*, and this raises questions, for example, about the curriculum, teacher expectations and styles. Attention is directed away from within-the-child concerns to the social context and the creation of disability.

Warnock Report

In 1974 a government appointed committee was established with the following terms of reference:

> To review educational provision in England, Scotland and Wales for children and young people handicapped by disabilities of body or mind, taking account of the medical aspects of their needs, together with arrangements to prepare them for entry into employment; to consider the most effective use of resources for these purposes; and to make recommendations. (DES, 1978: 1)

The Chair of the committee was Mary Warnock, a Senior Research Fellow from Oxford University. The committee's findings were published in an official report in 1978, which became more popularly known as the Warnock Report (DES, 1978).

Opinions differ strongly as to the extent and nature of the significance of the report. It was, however, historically unique by virtue of being the first Committee of Enquiry into the 'Education of Handicapped Children and Young People'. As a major review of existing provisions and practices, its influence was to be felt in various ways. It challenged, for example, medical notions of handicap and introduced the concept of a 'continuum of educational needs'. It confirmed the perspective that the purpose and goals of education for all children are the same. Education was thus viewed as a matter of right and not charity. Finally, it emphasized the centrality of service provision and the role of multi-professional teams in this process. Particular aspects of future legislation reflected these and other insights from the report.

Within the academic world the report has acted as a stimulus for debate, critique and research. Several important criticisms have been made of the report. These include the predominantly professional make-up of the committee resulting in the membership including a former pupil of a special school and the one token parent member. Professional definitions and priorities are thus maintained to have taken precedence over issues of human rights (Kirp, 1983). Second, Lewis and Vulliamy (1981) are critical of the significance given to psychological presuppositions and categories, and of the emphasis on administrative systems, includ-ing the creation of an elaborate bureaucracy staffed by more 'experts'. They also maintain that the committee neglected seriously the issue of social factors in the creation of learning difficulties. Last, criticism has focused on the limited consideration given to the question of the curriculum and the conservative and pol-itically expedient values involved (Wood and Shears, 1986).

The definition of the curriculum is central to the provision of a just and equitable education system and thus to arguments for integration. The Warnock Report is remarkable for the inadequacy of its coverage of the curriculum. What it does offer is a view of the curriculum as content, though no attempt is made to specify detail; on this view curriculum development of children and young people with special needs is seen as:

i)   setting of objectives;
ii) choice of materials and experiences;
iii) choice of teaching and learning methods to attain the objectives; and
iv) appraisal of appropriateness of the objectives and the effectiveness of the means of achieving them. (DES, 1978: 206)

In this — which is given as the universal nature of the curriculum — it is seen to be a value-free, non-political entity, with accurate objectives as central to access. What follows is an enduring concern for administrative and organizational arrangements for ensuring that '. . . every attempt should be made to see that the chosen objectives are as near in scope and quality to those of other children of the same age as is practicable, given the nature and degree of the children's disabilities' (p. 206).

Despite the enthusiasm of commentators for the enlightened view of curriculum offered by the Warnock Report (see, for example, Brennan, 1985), it is argued here that this did not, in fact, take thinking very far forward on the provision of a just and equitable curriculum for children and young people with special educational needs. For the Warnock Committee, justice and equity lay in the availability of resources which would ensure access to 'the curriculum' for all — the metaphor is powerfully revealing. Access was to be gained by the provision of appropriate facilities, according to the educational need perceived to result from disability (on a continuum from mild to severe) for which additional, other resources were necessary.

The Warnock Report advocates an essentially behavioural objectives-based curriculum, in which context and process are fundamentally undervalued. Thus, as Wood and Shears argue in their critique of this approach, it leads to an unacceptable view of the purpose of education:

The aims are taken to refer to end products, that is, what might be achieved by the end of a course in education. . . . Personal autonomy . . . is conflated with 'independence' and seen in a pragmatic way as what a person should be able to do at the end of a course of compulsory education. Autonomy, then, is seen as something which comes along with independence and independence hinges upon being competent in looking after oneself, participating and contributing to society in an acceptable manner, i.e. in a way which conforms to norms of behaviour, convention and law. (Wood and Shears, 1986: 13–14)

The aims, then, are reduced to producing 'near-normal' behaviour: development is compartmentalized in the areas of cognitive, physical, motor, self-help, social and leisure skills. The curriculum becomes a taxonomy of what the child should do: '. . . target behaviours are drawn from norm referenced skills sets and are those which it is thought children with severe learning difficulties need to acquire, rather than indicators of particular levels of development' (Wood and Shears, 1986: 17). Now, even if one can accept curriculum as content as a sound orthodoxy, the fact of this version, reduced to curriculum as performance, cannot be other than offensive, a denial of justice and equity.

Several criticisms have been made of the behavioural objectives approach (Quicke, 1982; Goddard, 1983; Wood and Shears, 1986). In a valuable discussion on 'Curriculum Principles for Integration' Swann (1983) contends that the behavioural approach '. . . assumes that it is the children rather than the curricula which need a remedy' (p. 120). Also, by concentrating on basic skills, a reduced curriculum is offered, and then it is one which is highly individualized. Little opportunity is provided for collaborative learning. While there are some short-term benefits from this approach, Swann maintains that it '. . . offers more opportunities for a process of segregation than for the reverse' (1983: 121).

The question of the position of the Warnock Report in relation to integration is a contentious one; opinions clearly differ. We would concur with Booth (1981) that it is difficult to derive from the report any unambiguous support for a fundamental shift in educational policy on this issue. Part of the reason for this relates to the strong lobby by supporters of segregated provision. Indeed, Wilson (1981) notes that: 'The *bulk* of the evidence submitted to the Warnock Committee clearly favoured the retention of special schools as part of a broader spectrum of special provision' (p. 7, emphasis added). Warnock's failure to address the question of integration in relation to curriculum issues was a lost opportunity to challenge exclusive forms of discourse and practice and to contribute to the realization of a more equitable, or at least less divisive, system of educational provision. For Fulcher (1989b) the Warnock Report represents a conservative political perspective in which there is a celebration of the centrality of professionalism and a form of discourse on disability that serves to deflect rather than engage issues of justice and equality. In a comparison of four government policies on integration and mainstreaming, including Britain, she concludes that 'integration is controversial because it is about discipline, curriculum and pedagogy' (p. 21). Because of a failure to frame the issue in these terms, the outcome of such policies has been, for example, an increase in bureaucratic infrastructure, an escalation of the numbers of pupils 'tagged disabled' or 'integration children', and a form of discourse which obfuscates the fundamental problem of the institutional grounds for exclusion (Fulcher, 1989b).

Integration

Integration means different things to different people. In the light of our previous analysis it could be viewed as being merely about bringing disabled children from special into ordinary schools and is principally concerned with bricks and mortar. Thus integration is often used to refer to desegregated provision. However, post-Warnock provision does cover a range of practices including off-site units, on-site units, special classes, withdrawal and in-class support. If one considers the structure of educational provision as a whole, integration within it takes many forms. One form of provision, for example, that evolved as a response to 'disturbed' and 'disturbing behaviour' and other needs was the *on-site unit*, attached to a particular primary or secondary school, though sometimes serving several. In the review of provision to meet special educational needs undertaken by the Inner London Education Authority a total of 121 such units were counted as follows (ILEA, 1985):

Primary nurture groups	37
Withdrawal units primary	21
Opportunity classes primary	13
Units in secondary schools	50
Total	121

The ability of LEAs to interpret differently the requirements of the 1981 Education Act, the existing provision and practices at the point of implementation of the Act, the widespread inequalities of planning and investment contributed to the maintenance and development of a complex array of varied policies and practices within and across LEAs (Croll and Moses, 1989). In a recent Department of Education and Science sponsored national survey conducted by a team of researchers (Goacher *et al.*, 1988), these differences in policy and practice were confirmed. It also maintained that decisions taken by professionals in the process of determining the special educational needs of a pupil often resulted in making a special school placement, reflecting largely administrative concerns.

In its report the Warnock Committee (1978) acknowledged that the implementation of its recommendations would be contingent upon the supply of 'adequate resources', and in conclusion it acknowledges that 'we have throughout our work been acutely aware of the financial constraints on central and local government. Indeed, our terms of reference required us "to consider the most effective use of resources"' (p. 325). The Committee then expresses its optimistic vision: 'We assume that adequate resources will be made available for the implementation of present policies...' (p. 325). Such optimism is romantic and reflects an inadequate understanding of the extent and endurance of existing inequalities of social and economic relations in society. The assumptions informing the Warnock Committee's anticipations of future developments have a hollow ring of political ineptitude. Yet this is symptomatic of a more general issue.

If one looks at the report as an historical record, it seems quite remarkable that the committee seemed impervious to the need to contextualize its deliberations within the framework of the educational system as a whole. This is related not only to the pursuit of a truly comprehensive school system but also to a range of research findings and their influence on such developments (Lewis and Vulliamy, 1981). The failure of the report to approach the curriculum as central to the question of the purpose of schooling needs to be seen against the background of these more general limitations. This form of tunnel vision is a reflection of the compartmentalized mentalities related to professional interests which have historically informed much of the policy and practice within special education.

The 1981 Education Act, which was clearly influenced by the Warnock Report, was not resource-led. This in itself was a reflection of the lack of political will on the part of government to engage with the practical realization of 'schools for all'. The lack of clarity with regard to the question of integration in the Warnock Report is reflected in the loopholes which the Act provided, thus enabling segregated policy and practice to continue. Thus, according to the Act, local education authorities must ensure that certain conditions are satisfied before a child with special needs is educated in an ordinary school. One of the conditions needs to be compatible with '(b) the provision of efficient education for the children with whom he will be educated' (Section (2) of the 1981 Education Act). Such discretionary possibilities were used to maintain and in some cases extend the segregated forms of provision in England and Wales.

Conclusion

We are not advocating that important changes have not taken place in the immediate post-Warnock, post-1981 Act period. What we do maintain is that changes relating to integration have been essentially localized, piecemeal and lacking any clear national policy. Many LEA equal opportunities policies, where they include disability, do so in a bolt-on inadequate manner (Leach, 1989). Moreover, many cases of integration have involved the least difficult or objectionable pupils being those easiest to manage. Sadly, homogeneous and disabilist assumptions have underpinned the conceptions of pupils in some of these initiatives, particularly in relation to children with Down's syndrome. Finally, education, including the curriculum, in so-called integration settings has tended to be specialized and fundamentally different from that of their so-called 'normal' peers (Swann, 1983).

For disabled analysts like Oliver (1992), integration is not an end in itself. He is critical of models of social and educational change that underpin a great deal of thinking on integration. It is not, he maintains, merely about ideas, but involves a bitter struggle, progress from which requires a new vision: 'At the end of the day, the kinds of change needed to achieve the new vision of integration are changes that can only be achieved through *politics*; through groups getting together and changing the political system.' Not only does this approach raise serious questions about, for example, the nature of society, but also it challenges the notion that integration is something that professionals can give to disabled people. It is part of the ideological struggle which disabled people must engage with if they are to be freed from their chains of oppression.

Len Barton and Maeve Landman

Full inclusion in society is a matter of profound concern. It is a human rights issue involving participation, choice and empowerment. Issues of social justice and equity are thus central to the question of integration. For us, the issue is a means to an end which Branson and Miller (1989) have encapsulated powerfully in the following way:

> ... integration must be a ... programme — oriented towards its own destruction, aiming to destroy the very categories which are seen as needing to be 'integrated' into the 'normal' world. If the disabled are 'normal', so much an accepted part of our world that we take their presence, their humanity, their special qualities for granted, then there can be no 'integration' for there is no 'segregation', either conceptually, in terms of categories, taxonomies, or actually, in terms of institutional separation. (p. 161)

For this to be achieved, the process of struggle will be fundamentally political with no quick or easy answers to the complex issues involved. The contribution that the Warnock Report made towards this end has been, to say the least, disappointing.

Acknowledgment

We are grateful to Jenny Corbett for her helpful comments on an earlier draft of this chapter.

References

BALL, S. (1991) *Politics and Policy Making in Education: Explorations in Policy Sociology*, London, Routledge.
BARNES, C. (1990) *Cabbage Syndrome*, Lewes, Falmer Press.
BARTON, L. and OLIVER, M. (1992) 'Special Needs: Personal Trouble or Public Issue?' in ARNOT, M. and BARTON, L. (Eds), *Voicing Concerns: Sociological Perspectives on Contemporary Education Reforms*, Oxford, Triangle Books.
BARTON, L. and TOMLINSON, S. (Eds) (1984) *Special Education and Social Interest*, London, Croom Helm.
BOOTH, T. (1981) 'Demystifying Integration', in SWANN, W. (Ed.), *The Practice of Special Education*, Oxford, Blackwell.
BOOTH, T. (1983) 'Integrating Special Education,' in BOOTH, T. and POTTS, P. (Eds), *Integrating Special Education*, Oxford, Blackwell.
BOOTH, T. (1989) 'Challenging Conceptions of Integration', in BARTON, L. (Ed.), *The Politics of Special Educational Needs*, Lewes, Falmer Press.
BRANSON, J. and MILLER, D. (1989) 'Beyond Policy: The Deconstruction of Disability', in BARTON, L. (Ed.), *Integration: Myth or Reality?* Lewes, Falmer Press.
BRENNAN, W. (1985) *Curriculum for Special Needs*, Milton Keynes, Open University Press.
CARRIER, J.G. (1986) *Learning Disability, Social Class and the Construction of Inequality*, New York, Greenwood Press.
CROLL, P. and MOSES, D. (1989) 'Policy and Practice in Special Education: The Importance of the 1981 Education Act in England and Wales', in BROWN, R. and CHAZAN, M. (Eds), *Learning Difficulties and Emotional Problems in Children and Adults*, Calgary, Deseling.

DEPARTMENT OF EDUCATION AND SCIENCE (1978) *Special Educational Needs: Report of the Committee of Enquiry into the Education of Handicapped Children and Young People* (Warnock Report), London, Her Majesty's Stationery Office.

DEPARTMENT OF EDUCATION AND SCIENCE (1981) *Education Act*, London, Her Majesty's Stationery Office.

DESSENT, T. (1987) *Making Ordinary Schools Special*, Lewes, Falmer Press.

FISH, J. (1985) *The Way Ahead*, Milton Keynes, Open University Press.

FORD, J., MONGON, D. and WHELAN, M. (1982) *Special Education and Social Control: Invisible Disasters*, London, Routledge and Kegan Paul.

FOUCAULT, M. (1977) *The Archaeology of Knowledge*, London, Tavistock.

FULCHER, G. (1989a) *Disabling Policies? A Comparative Approach to Education Policy and Disability*, Lewes, Falmer Press.

FULCHER, G. (1989b) 'Integrate and Mainstream? Comparative Issues in the Politics of These Policies', in BARTON, L. (Ed.), *Integration: Myth or Reality?* Lewes, Falmer Press.

GOACHER, B., EVANS, J., WELTON, J. and WEDELL, K. (1988) *Policy and Provision for Special Educational Needs: Implementing the 1981 Education Act*, London, Cassell.

GOODARD, A. (1983) 'Processes in Special Education', in BLENKIN, G. and KELLY, A. (Eds), *Primary Curriculum in Action*, London, Harper and Row.

ILEA (1985) *Educational Opportunities for All?* (Fish Report), London, ILEA.

KIRP, D. (1983) 'Professionalisation as a Policy Choice: British Special Education in Comparative Perspective', in CHAMBERS, J. and HARTMAN, W. (Eds), *Special Education Policies: Their History, Implementation and Finance*, Philadelphia, Pa., Temple University Press.

LEACH, B. (1989) 'Disabled People and the Implementation of Local Authorities' Equal Opportunities Policies', *Public Administration*, 67, pp. 65–77.

LEWIS, I. and VULLIAMY, G. (1981) 'The Social Context of Educational Practice: The Case of Special Education', in BARTON, L. and TOMLINSON, S. (Eds), *Special Education: Policy, Practices and Social Issues*, London, Harper and Row.

LEWIS, J. (1988) 'So Much Grit in the Hub of the Educational Machine: Schools, Society and the Invention of Measurable Intelligence', in BESSANT, B. (Ed.), *Mother State and Her Little Ones*, Bundoora, La Trobe University Press.

MORRIS, J. (1990) 'Progress with Humanity? The Experience of a Disabled Lecturer', in RIESER, R. and MASON, M. (Eds), *Disability, Equality in the Classroom: A Human Rights Issue*, London, ILEA.

OLIVER, M. (1990) *The Politics of Disablement*, London, Macmillan.

OLIVER, M. (1992) 'Intellectual Masturbation: A Rejoinder to Soder and Booth', *European Journal of Special Education Needs*, 7, 1, pp. 20–28.

QUICKE, J. (1982) *The Cautious Expert: An Analysis of Developments in the Practice of Educational Psychology*. Milton Keynes, Open University Press.

RIESER, R. and MASON, M. (Eds) (1990) *Disability, Equality in the Classroom: A Human Rights Issue*, London, ILEA.

SKRTIC, T.M. (1991) *Behind Special Educational: A Critical Analysis of Professional Culture and School Organisation*, Denver, Colo., Lowe Publishing Company.

SODER, M. (1984) 'The Mentally Retarded: Ideologies of Care and Surplus Population', in BARTON, L. and TOMLINSON, S. (Eds), *Special Education and Social Interests*, London, Croom Helm.

SWANN, W. (1983) 'Curriculum Principles for Integration', in BOOTH, T. and POTTS, P. (Eds), *Integrating Special Education*, Oxford, Blackwell.

TOMLINSON, S. (1982) *A Sociology of Special Education*, London, Routledge and Kegan Paul.

WILSON, M. (1981) *The Curriculum in Special Schools*, London, Schools Council.

WOOD, S. and SHEARS, B. (1986) *Teaching Children with Severe Learning Difficulties: A Radical Appraisal*, London, Croom Helm.

Chapter 4

Special Educational Needs in a New Context: Micropolitics, Money and 'Education for All'

Anne Gold, Richard Bowe and Stephen J. Ball

If, as we argue, notions of social justice in relation to special educational needs (SEN) provision in mainstream secondary schools can only be represented through a whole school SEN policy, how will that policy be affected by the Education Reform Act (ERA)? We trace the precarious nature of social justice within special educational needs provision through the last 120 years, and examine it in its present context. Will the micropolitics of schools, the forces of the market-place, and the demands of the National Curriculum endanger what is already a very rare species — an effective whole school special educational needs policy?

An Historical Context

In an examination of social justice around the education of children with special educational needs, it may be useful to begin with an historical perspective of the provision for such students. This perspective provides an explanation of terminology, the ideologies and the attitudinal legacies around special educational needs today. Heward and Lloyd-Smith (1990) point out that:

> it has taken nearly a century of compulsory school attendance for the education of children with special needs to capture a small sector of the political high ground in education and for new policies reducing segregation and categorization to begin to be implemented. Its precarious hold on that high ground and the future of the new policies now appear even more vulnerable in the face of the new Education Reform Act. (1990: 34)

The report of the Committee of Enquiry into the Education of Handicapped Children and Young People (Warnock Report) (DES, 1978) begins with the historical background to special education for the handicapped, tracing pre-1870 developments of schools for the blind, deaf, physically handicapped and mentally defective through Forster's Education Act in 1870. This Act did not specifically include disabled children among those for whom provision was to be made, but for the next thirty years committees and commissions strove to define, and provide education for, various different categories of disabled children. The preferred term was 'defective', and was applied to feeble-minded as well as physically handicapped children.

After 1902, and the establishment of a two-tier system of local education authorities for elementary and secondary education respectively, the statutory foundation of special educational provision was consolidated and continued in broadly the same form until 1944. Compulsory provision extended to all the categories of handicapped children which had so far been recognized. According to Warnock:

> The intention of the 1944 Education Act, fulfilled by regulations made by the Minister in the following year, was to extend greatly the range of children's special needs for which authorities would be obliged to make specific provision, either in special schools or in ordinary schools. The Handicapped Pupils and School Health Service Regulations 1945 defined 11 categories of pupils: blind, partially sighted, deaf, partially deaf, delicate, diabetic, educationally sub-normal, epileptic, maladjusted, physically handicapped, and those with speech defects.... The categories (though not the detailed definitions) have remained unchanged since 1944 except that in 1953 diabetic children ceased to form a separate category and have since then been included with the delicate. (DES, 1978: 20)

Although the provision of education for some of these students could take place in ordinary schools if it was available, the reality was that it rarely did — provision in ordinary schools failed to develop on the scale envisaged.

Unfortunately, students who were put into those categories became labelled by them, and expectations of their learning were defined by those categories. By the 1970s there was growing dissatisfaction with segregation both within mainstream schools (in remedial departments) and in special schools (Galloway and Goodwin, 1979; Wilson and Evans, 1980; Brennan, 1979). The labelled students who became self-fulfilling prophecies often did not learn very much in terms of overt curricula because of the environments into which they were categorized. Special schools will perhaps always be necessary for some children, but because of the very nature of most of these institutions — small, the staff dedicated to nurturing, sometimes training or socializing — they could not easily offer full access to the curriculum. So those who were sent to special schools could not easily be reintegrated into mainstream schools. In a microcosm of that situation, those who were in remedial departments in mainstream schools were not easily integrated into the rest of the school.

It is perhaps necessary to examine here the attitudes to students with special educational needs which were held by such people as the majority of teachers, employers or social gatekeepers before the Warnock Report was published. Moore and Morrison summarize those attitudes succinctly: 'Categorizing or assessing children into special education disguises the reality that they are not wanted in the ordinary schools' (1988: 34). Whatever the fundamental philosophies behind the provision of education for students with special educational needs, the reality was that of a marginalized group of labelled people. Because of that margin-alization, access to education, to jobs, to the mainstream of society was much more difficult. In fact, the employment perspective was noticeably to the front in the terms of reference given to the Warnock Committee by Margaret Thatcher, then Secretary of State for Education and Science, in 1973:

> To review educational provision in England, Scotland and Wales for children and young people handicapped by disabilities of body or mind, taking account of the medical aspects of their needs, together with arrangements to prepare them for entry into employment; to consider the most effective use of resources for these purposes; and to make recommendations.

Many educationists were deeply disappointed with the Warnock Report and the subsequent Education Act in 1981. The criticisms centred on the lack of resources to meet the suggested changes, and the looseness of the legislation which allowed loopholes to occur in which individual local education authorities could interpret the Act very differently.

Nevertheless, this was the first time that the language of social justice could be seen to apply to this marginalized group of people. Warnock recommended a radical rethinking of the education provision for children and young people with special educational needs. The report recommended the abolition of the categories of handicap, thus getting rid of the labelling which kept children so often in their special schools. It recommended that the planning of services for special educational provision should encompass 20 per cent of the population at some time during their school career, thus widening the group from a very small one that it was easy to ignore to one which comprised one-fifth of the school population.

Perhaps more importantly, the report changed the language describing special education from looking at the child or young person in a deficit mode to seeing the whole person, with a description of the provision necessary to allow him or her to function within the mainstream. It recommended, for example, that children who were previously described as 'remedial' or 'educationally subnormal' should be described as 'children with learning difficulties'; and it introduced language that brought with it expectations of excellence, such as 'educational opportunities of quality'.

Warnock should be seen in context, as the first large body of work to challenge the 'otherness' of special education provision. Also it provided the stimulus for a massive outpouring of literature and research relating special needs to mainstream provision. Special educational needs became a key component of teacher education courses both pre- and in-service. However, altogether it may be that Warnock did no more than provide a short interregnum between periods within which different forms of marginalization held sway.

Special Educational Needs Provision in the 1990s

The Education Reform Act (1988), and specifically National Testing and the National Curriculum which it introduced, threaten a new kind of exclusion. At first glance the language is still recognizably influenced by Warnock. The Act begins:

1 [2]   The curriculum for a maintained school satisfies
the requirements of this section if it is a balanced and broadly based curriculum which —
[a]   promotes the spiritual, moral, cultural, mental and physical development of pupils at the school and of society; and
[b]   prepares such pupils for the opportunities, responsibilities and experiences of adult life.

It claims to enshrine notions of access to a 'balanced and broadly based curriculum', and demands that those children with special educational needs who require exemption from parts of the National Curriculum should have that exemption examined every six months. This would appear to ensure that educationists are reminded of the entitlement of students with special educational needs to the full curriculum, and seems to seek to keep those students in sight if they are exempted from the curriculum.

However, as with the 1981 Education Act, local authorities, or, even more, individual schools, can interpret the positioning of the provision of special educational needs within the Education Reform Act through their own ideological positions about social justice, definitions of appropriate provision for special needs and institutional priorities.

Heward and Lloyd-Smith (1990) in their article assessing the impact of legislation on special education policy see threats to the rather shaky status quo:

Bringing this powerless and politically unattractive minority [handicapped people] into closer relations with the mainstream after such a lengthy period of rigid categorization and segregation was a difficult task requiring considerable commitment and resources neither of which has been evident in the 1981 Act and its implementation. Consequently, following the pattern of all earlier legislation in special education, implementation has varied widely among schools and local authorities. The [Education Reform] Act is a development which threatens the new directions of special education policy and may reinstate the former assumptions with greater force. (Heward and Lloyd-Smith, 1990: 21)

Furthermore, the Education Reform Act places provision for special educational needs within a financial and a market context as well as a curricular and assessment framework. Special educational needs provisions in school have to be weighed and justified against other forms of staffing and expenditure. Arguments about good practice have now to be viewed in terms of opportunity costs. How will those schools which have decided to take on whole school special needs policies maintain that commitment and keep the department and policy central to the school? With the newly recognized expense of teachers, how will they justify paying Special Educational Needs Key Teachers' allowances?

Outside the school in the education marketplace, will the presence of children with special educational needs attract new pupils? Will schools decide not to have any pupils with special educational needs if their presence affects enrolment? It remains to be seen whether market forces make philosophies about whole school provision for children with special educational needs either too expensive or too problematic.

In this chapter we are concerned with provision for students with special educational needs within mainstream secondary schools. This means that we are addressing the needs of perhaps 19 of Warnock's 20 per cent, the majority without Statements of Special Educational Need, some with Statements, but all in mainstream schools.

In the current educational and political climate special educational needs provision in mainstream schools seems to create a number of tensions and dilemmas. We explore some of these in the remainder of this chapter.

Special Educational Needs and the National Curriculum

The idea of a National Curriculum has, we suggest, a highly complex and problematic relationship to the issue of special educational needs provision in schools, and to the educational experiences of students defined as having special educational needs. Rendered into crude and simple terms, the point is whether the National Curriculum may be viewed as a mechanism for ensuring a set of common educational experiences for all students, including those with special educational needs — a decisive break from the deficit curriculum previously experienced by many students with special educational needs — or as a set of constraints which will inhibit teachers to such an extent that the individual needs of students with special educational needs will either be ignored altogether, or will remain an unattainable ideal within the realities and demands of the National Curriculum classroom.

The National Curriculum Council (1989) in the document, *A Curriculum for All* (Curriculum Guidance No. 2), certainly set high standards for teachers. They define a 'good learning environment' for students with special educational needs as including 'an atmosphere of encouragement, acceptance, respect for achievements and sensitivity to individual needs, in which all pupils can thrive' (1989: 7). They go on to argue that:

> Curriculum development plans, schemes of work, and classroom and school environments need to be closely aligned with the teaching needs and individual curriculum plans of pupils with learning difficulties and disabilities so that maximum access to the National Curriculum is ensured. (1989: 7)

David Galloway (1990), among others, takes a positive and optimistic view of this sort of educational rhetoric and the values it espouses. He argues that '... the National Curriculum, national testing and provision for grant-maintained status may all be seen to have *potential* benefits for pupils with Special Educational Needs' (1990: 51; emphasis added).

Indeed, he goes on to suggest that '... although GERBIL [the Great Educational Reform Bill, or GERBIL as it was known before it became the Education Reform Act in 1988] is in fact the product of a reforming right wing government, an identical bill might equally well have been produced by a reforming government dominated by Marxists' (1990: 51). As regards the National Curriculum specifically, Galloway's key point is that the imposition of a legislative minimum curriculum for all children can go a long way towards ensuring that students with special educational needs are not disadvantaged by the forms of curriculum ex-clusion which currently operate in many schools, '. . . an alternative low-status curriculum that restricts rather than enhances their opportunities', '. . . where proliferation of options is used to shunt pupils of below average ability into a non-examination siding' (1990: 58). Thus, he asserts, 'The requirement that all pupils should have access to the full range of the National Curriculum may make it more difficult for schools to marginalize their pupils with special needs' (1990: 58).[1]

On face value, Galloway has a point. Indeed, the National Curriculum can be seen as a step towards a more comprehensive national education system. But, whatever its *potential* benefits, the National Curriculum must still be examined critically. Although Galloway is dismissive of criticisms of the National Curriculum as so much professional special pleading, there must be real doubts about whether the mix of common provision with '. . . sensitivity to individual needs', set in the context of National Testing, is feasible and realizable in the comprehensive classroom with thirty to thirty-five pupils. It may equally well be that the National Curriculum becomes a set of constraints on good special educational needs practice which makes it increasingly difficult to achieve 'sensitivity to individual needs'. Too much may be expected of teachers given current levels of, or even reducing levels of, resources and support. Thus another recent writer on special educational needs (Ramasut, 1989) takes exactly the opposite position from that of Galloway. She argues: 'It is clear that without amendments to the Education Reform Act, the education of a large minority of pupils will be put in jeopardy. A whole-school approach to meeting special needs (which we discuss below) could be made more difficult to achieve' (Ramasut, 1989: 18). Our point then is that the relationship of the Education Reform Act and the National Curriculum in par-ticular to Special Educational Needs depends not so much on the *potential* benefits of an inclusive common curriculum, as on the context of constraints and possibil-ities within which special educational needs are catered for and responded to in the classroom.

We would suggest that too much is being asked of teachers. In the new ERA the National Curriculum is fixed, heavily prescribed and rests on a strongly nor-mative model of progress in learning. The system of National Testing carries with it a presupposition of classroom, institutional and area comparisons. It is difficult to see comparisons not being made also within schools (between teachers) and within classrooms (between students). The National Curriculum provides a lan-guage of hierarchy and comparison based on levels of achievement. Against all this the teacher must provide *flexibility*, differential pacing, individual classroom support, encouragement and reinforcement. But if problems arise, which will be blamed first: the teacher or the National Curriculum?

Perhaps like so many other writers on special educational needs, Galloway makes good educational practice sound too easy. So much of the 'success' of the National Curriculum rides on the skills, goodwill and guilt of well intentioned teachers. Too little attention is given to the practical, financial market — and to micropolitical factors which inhibit good practice, but which are also a part of the organizational infrastructure imposed on schools by the Education Reform Act. Thus the question of special educational needs and social justice ultimately rests within practice and school provision. How will special educational needs be handled in schools in the new ERA?

Whole School Special Needs Policies and Social Justice

We are arguing that one positive outcome of the demands of the National Curriculum could be that special educational needs provision will be described within a whole school policy which will reflect social justice in an exciting and optimistic way.

In one school, Parkside, we have watched a special educational needs department come out of the portakabin in the playground, where it housed one full-time teacher and several others filling in eighteen periods a week, into a whole school structure of key teachers working to the SEN teacher. The previously marginalized department has been centralized, and all the staff of the school are being encouraged and supported in their integration of students with SENs.

A whole school policy is built on the assumption that 'access for all' implies that all children learn the different parts of the agreed curriculum from subject specialists. The school-based SEN teachers act as a resource to the subject teacher, ensuring that the subject matter and the teaching materials are accessible to those with learning difficulties. This may include notions of differentiation, exploring methods of recording learning other then by writing, and examining methods of pedagogy so that different routes of learning are acknowledged.

Subject teachers are gradually enabled to coordinate the planning for children with SENs in their lessons with support from three sources. One is members of the school SEN department who will offer advice on methods of learning and diagnoses of the particular learning difficulties of the children in the lessons. Another source is the key post holders within their own subjects, whose role may be to remind the department of the presence of children with SENs in their lessons and to explore subject-based materials. The third source should be the in-class presence of support teachers provided by Statements of Special Educational Need.

We look in the next section at how the broader context set for schools by the Act may limit or constrain such whole school policy. The specific issues identified have emerged from ongoing research which examines the struggles of four schools seeking to implement the Education Reform Act alongside maintenance of good practice for students with special educational needs.

The Context

In her review of the National Curriculum Council booklet, *A Curriculum for All: Special Educational Needs in the National Curriculum*, Linda Pound (1990) refers to the worrying failure to tackle the issues of disapplication, the extent to which this might undermine the principle of entitlement for all, and the linked matter of the suitability of the National Curriculum for students with special educational needs. She further points out that:

> Practitioners may also be dismayed by the omission of any discussion
> of the impacts of (a) new procedures for assessing children and for

publishing results, (b) open enrolment procedures, and (c) local financial management, on provision for pupils with special educational needs. (Pound, 1990: 112)

Understandably, in what is a short review she has no opportunity to explore those issues in any detail. We therefore draw upon some of our research to examine some of the new contexts that may inform the success or failure of whole school policies.

Drawing upon the work of Bernstein, we suggest that the intended structure of the National Curriculum, its subject basis and the process of introduction imply a strong classification and framing (Bernstein, 1975). If we look at the attainment targets and levels of attainment in the statutory orders issued thus far (for mathematics, science, English and technology and the proposals for geography and history), we can see a varying level of prescriptiveness. However, overall there are clear distinctions being drawn between subject boundaries and, on the surface, the basis of knowledge is carefully compartmentalized. Teachers and students have minimal control over what is taught and the amount that has to be taught over a given period of time. This crucially affects the organization, teaching and pacing of the learning process.

Although the non-statutory orders and the appeal to consider cross-curricular links indicate a recognition that such rigidity may not be educationally appropriate, it may be some years before this strong classification can be readily broken down. In the case of framing, teachers face the pressure of Standard Attainment Targets (SATs), testing and the publishing of results in deciding how much they try to teach to individual students and the pace at which they do so. In terms of the prescriptiveness of the content, the structure of the curriculum and the pace of the teaching, the National Curriculum may seriously undermine the sort of flexibility teachers will require to respond to student needs and especially to special educational needs. Put crudely, teachers may find themselves responding to the needs of the curriculum and assessment rather than to the students' needs. Some of the flavour of this is apparent in the following comment from the head of the SEN department at Parkside about the possible impact of the National Curriculum and assessment:

> The problem I feel is that departments will turn round to me and say well I don't want that child to go [out for SEN withdrawal] because they're going to miss out on doing a piece of work that's leading up to an attainment target and I don't want them to miss it.... (12 February 1990)

This needs to be contrasted with the positive view that the differentiation set up by the National Curriculum has actually led some teachers to question the whole class approach. The head of special educational needs clearly felt that this had given her a greater opportunity to promote SEN provision with other staff:

> Most staff, in reading their documents, are quite concerned that children have to achieve these different levels of attainment, and they're beginning to realize that there are children within their class with a varied level of attainment, in their class, and how are they going to provide for that? (6 April 1990)

However, in important respects it may not be the National Curriculum that will have the major impact upon SEN provision. Local Management of Schools and its impact upon the relationship of schools to local education authorities, upon the internal dynamics of the school and upon the new relationship of schools to the outside world in the form of educational 'market forces' could well prove far more pervasive. In the case of schools and their local education authorities (LEAs) there are important respects in which individual school policies on SEN provision may be restricted and limited by the new relationship resulting from the ERA. The first hinges upon developments that relate to local authority funding in general, namely, the politics of the Poll Tax and the government's decision to carry out 'capping' on various authorities. Although cuts in LEA funding from central government have usually had some consequences for educational expenditure, the use of a 'formula' means that budget items are preset by agreement with the Department of Education and Science (see below). The fact that the government has also retained the option to extend its powers with respect to capping means that individual school budgets may well become dependent upon a 'politics' that the school is unable to control. The outcome seems likely to make SEN provision open to the vagaries of both LEA expenditure levels and, within that, the levels the formula provides. In both cases this could seriously limit the flexibility a school would be able to exercise in providing for students with special educational needs.

The requirement to devolve expenditures of various sorts from LEAs to schools may also mean the loss of important aspects of the LEAs' strategic role in 'orchestrating a complex range of services in meeting *individual* special needs' (Russell, 1990: 207). The use of devolved monies now rests with school governors, and, as Russell points out, 'the new generation of parent governor-managers may have a sharper view of what constitutes quality in education and optimum targets for their budgets in order to achieve such goals' (1990: 216).

There is also the fact that the formula is applied across the LEA. Although under the Local Management of Schools, schools are expected to control their own budgets and to make their own decisions (in this case expenditure on SEN provision as against other expenditure), the distribution of monies to the schools is done according to a 'formula', which is developed by the LEA and must meet with Department of Education and Science approval. LEAs are not required to follow any particular model of consultation with the schools over this formula, and our research indicates that the degree and forms of consultation vary considerably. Few authorities appear to have involved the schools wholeheartedly in developing the formula; the government imposed pressure of tight timing has been more important here than an LEA commitment to exclude schools. A 'typical' process of 'consultation' has been to issue a series of possible formulas and ask schools to respond individually to the impact of each successive formula. This has minimized the opportunity schools have had to compare how far 'needs' and elements of the formula correspond across schools and has maximized the pursuit of short-term, individual financial considerations. Thus schools have looked at their 'needs' in isolation and as they currently stand. Once the formula is fixed, schools will only be able to negotiate with the authorities for funding on that basis. Consequently, SEN provision in schools will start from the formula and not, necessarily, from the needs of the student. It will be a technical matter of categorizing the needs of the student population according to criteria laid down in the formula. We have already seen examples of various procedures authorities are proposing to decide upon needs which may well take the 'E' out of SEN!

The head of the SEN department at Parkside showed us a circular from her LEA explaining the Local Management of Schools funding for pupils with special educational needs. It proposed that pupils with statements of special educational needs will be funded according to their needs at one of five levels, ranging from 2268 for students with category A needs (moderate learning difficulties, specific learning difficulties including dyslexic difficulties, general learning difficulties, visual impairment and pupils in developmental/diagnostic placements) to 6804 for students with category E needs (hearing impairment, severe learning difficulties — secondary, deaf/blind). 'The deputy Head in charge of finances asked me whether I could get more children statemented so that we could get more money for the school' (13 July 1990).

The question of what students are worth is raised again within the school setting. Although statemented students may well have quite high 'price tags', the remaining 18 per cent may be seen to be something of a liability.

> You are caught ... and this is where LMS [Local Management of Schools] really raises its ugly head, in terms of true educational things. Each child has a price tag on it, and the 6th formers have the highest price tag, so in pure financial terms one obviously is trying to raise the most amount of money you can. But Flightpath staff have always been conscious of our intake being skewed towards the less-able child, and through the years we have developed what has got to be considered one of the best supportive education departments in the Borough. . . . But of course the less-able children tend not to stay on to the 6th form, unless we feel they are really going to benefit from it, and we have an excellent record, through our Guidance department, of ensuring that our children get into employment as well. So you have this conflict of trying to ensure you've got a big 6th form, trying to ensure that you are really doing the best for the individual child, and the introduction of the disabled children. I don't think there's a sort of problem for us in terms of whether it was a bad image or not. I mean I think personally it can do nothing but good for us but one has got to recognize the fact that these children do take a lot of extra time. (Senior Teacher, Flightpath, 23 March 1990)

Schools are thus faced with some genuine dilemmas. Do they promote special educational needs provision in order to attract statemented students with a 'high' worth and then risk gaining an 'image' locally as a low ability school, or try to attract high ability students who will stay on and enhance the school's reputation academically? And what about the category of students that fall into the less well funded 18 per cent? Such dilemmas are apparent in the following comment:

> I've done quite a bit in terms of promoting special needs, for example, because I think we've got more than average special needs in the area that we're serving, so I think that's something that we ought to say is part of our wares. Other people have said to me, 'if you keep advertising special needs, you will turn away brighter kids'. And maybe there's an element of that, but you have to recognize that you are a servant of a

particular area and not try to kid yourself that you're going to become a different type of school if only you could market yourself better. (Senior Deputy, Flightpath, 6 July 1989)

A great deal is going to depend upon the gaps between the worth of different students and their availability in the local area as well as the marketing decisions schools might make. Consequently, the degree to which schools respond to the SENs of individual students is going to be affected by financial decisions (balancing the budget at LEA and school levels), local demography and the vagaries of the 'market', all of which are only marginally within SEN teachers' control.

Within the schools, deciding how the school budget will be spent places SEN provision into an arena of struggle and negotiation that appears on the surface to be about finances. In fact questions of personal status, protecting or promoting 'subject' positions and educational ideologies are all part of the powerful subtext. The head of the SEN department at Parkside was clearly aware of this:

> ... and the schools I went to where people were on a C or a D [allowances] and they were included in the senior management team, were fantastic, 'cos they had a real input and a real say and people listened to them. Whereas here I'm just a department Head, I'm not a policy-maker. I think the B [allowance] just reflects the level of importance. (12 February 1990)

Although she had the 'ear' of the headteacher, it remained apparent that she was, in her words, 'not a policy-maker'. Thus, in the longer term, what is spent on SEN provision will have to be argued against textbooks for a core subject area, or decoration of the entrance hall to enhance the market appeal of the school, or employing a further teacher to decrease class sizes for a practical subject. At this stage she feels very aware of such pressures and constraints: 'I think budgeting and everything is so tight that I can go and demand until I'm blue in the face really for a qualified assistant, full-time, but realistically I'm not going to get it, so you've got to work with what you've got' (1 November 1989).

Furthermore, all of these have to be argued within a shifting power structure which may or may not privilege the position of SEN provision within the school. We believe that a headteacher's personal educational ideology concerning special educational needs provision can be a particularly powerful influence on decision-making about the resourcing and positioning of the SEN department. The headteacher at Parkside explained his thinking behind centralizing the SEN department and developing a whole school policy for special educational needs provision:

> You do things because you have an agenda yourself, and priorities within that agenda, but the good thing about the National Curriculum is that it has highlighted certain areas to make people generally more aware ... special needs have come in out of the cold. ... So if one of the questions you're asking is did I have a master plan, really, then the answer to that would be only insofar as it was one of the issues which I was very firmly determined on dealing with through the curriculum, rather than in any side issues. (6 April 1990)

Anne Gold, Richard Bowe and Stephen J. Ball

Here we have an example of the headteacher as critical reality definer (Rise-borough, 1981), using such language as 'agenda', 'priorities', 'very firmly determined' to describe his commitment to a whole school special needs policy.

In another local school, thinking about resourcing the Learning Support Department has led to a difficult and different policy decision, as reported to the governors' meeting: 'One casualty of cuts has been the loss of in-class support for SEN, it's now all withdrawal and that's the best we can do within the financial constraints' (Senior Teacher, Flightpath, 21 June 1990). They do, however, have a special educational needs department of eight teachers, and a head of department who attends meetings of the school management team.

Thus LMS privatizes the problems and politics of aspects of schooling in such a way that SEN policy becomes part of the wider financial and budgeting dilemmas that may well give rise to a heightened sense of a micropolitics within the school. Consequently, the level of provision for special educational needs and the policies followed will have to be constantly fought for and attended to. One result could be a lack of policy continuity, as SEN finds itself switching and changing to meet a constantly shifting political terrain.

Conclusion

In writing this chapter, we found ourselves rewriting the title — it became 'It Depends. . . .' If, as we argue, social justice within the realms of special educational needs must be translated into a whole school special educational needs policy, then under the Education Reform Act the effectiveness of that policy depends on the strengths and weaknesses of various constraints and possibilities (see Figure 1). The effectiveness depends upon the constraints or possibilities imposed or opened up by the National Curriculum and the attendant testing, attainment targets, published results, but insistence on differentiated work. It depends upon government imposed Poll Tax 'capping', which is different in different authorities, and thus allows some LEAs to spend more on education than others. It depends on the resources available to schools, both demographically as in class sizes and teacher supply, and as a result of the LEAs' formula funding. It depends on how much money statemented students and non-statemented students with special educational needs bring with them. It depends on market forces, and whether schools under local financial management and open enrolment will find that their whole school SEN policies will make them more or less attractive to potential customers. And it depends on the micropolitics of the school: the educational ideology and the value systems of the headteacher, of the governors, of the head of the special educational needs department, and of all subject teachers who give power to or take it away from the effectiveness of any school policy.

Note

1 Galloway's notion of the National Curriculum as a panacea for special educational needs totally ignores the question of 'whose' curriculum is being nationalized. *The National Curriculum* is a particular selection from national culture, as Ken Jones (1979) is at pains to point out. It cannot be assumed that *the* National Curriculum will engage with or reflect the interests of students with special educational needs.

Figure 1. The Constraints and Possibilities Which Could Affect the Social Justice of a School's Special Educational Needs Provision

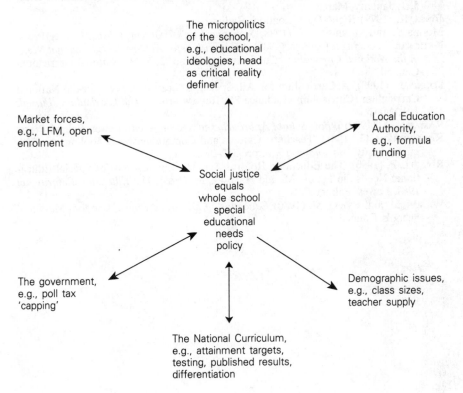

References

BERNSTEIN, B. (1975) *Class, Codes and Control, Volume 3: Towards a Theory of Educational Transmissions*, London, Routledge and Kegan Paul.

BRENNAN, W.K. (1979) *Curricular Needs of Slow Learners*, Schools Council Working Paper 63, London, Evans/Methuen Educational.

DEPARTMENT OF EDUCATION AND SCIENCE (1978) *Special Educational Needs: Report of the Committee of Enquiry into the Education of Handicapped Children and Young People* (Warnock Report), London, Her Majesty's Stationery Office.

DEPARTMENT OF EDUCATION AND SCIENCE (1981) *Education Act*, London, Her Majesty's Stationery Office.

DEPARTMENT OF EDUCATION AND SCIENCE (1988) *Education Reform Act*, London, Her Majesty's Stationery Office.

FREEMAN, A. and GRAY, H. (1989) *Organising Special Educational Needs*, London, Paul Chapman Publishing.

GALLOWAY, D. (1990) 'Was the GERBIL a Marxist Mole?', in EVANS, P. and VARMA, V. (Eds), *Special Education: Past, Present and Future*, Lewes, Falmer Press.

GALLOWAY, D. and GOODWIN, C. (1979) *Educating Slow-Learning and Maladjusted Children: Integration or Segregation?*, London, Longman.

HEWARD, C. and LLOYD-SMITH, M. (1990) 'Assessing the Impact of Legislation on Special Education Policy: An Historical Analysis', *Journal of Education Policy*, 5, 1, January–March.

JONES, K. (1979) *Right Turn*, London, Radius.

MOORE, J. and MORRISON, N. (1988) *Someone Else's Problem*, Lewes, Falmer Press.

NATIONAL CURRICULUM COUNCIL (1989) *A Curriculum for All: Special Educational Needs in the National Curriculum*, Curriculum Guidance 2, York, National Curriculum Council.

POUND, L. (1990) 'A Curriculum for All: Special Educational Needs in the National Curriculum (Curriculum Guidance 2)', Review article, *The Curriculum Journal*, 1, 1, May.

RAMASUT, A. (1989) *Whole School Approaches to Special Needs*, Lewes, Falmer Press.

RISEBOROUGH, G. (1981) 'Teachers' Careers and Comprehensive Schooling: An Empirical Study', *Sociology*, 15, 3, pp. 352–381.

RUSSELL, P. (1990) 'The Education Reform Act: The Implications for Special Educational Needs', in FLUDE, M. and HAMMER, M. (Eds), *The Education Reform Act 1988*, Lewes, Falmer Press.

WILSON, M. and EVANS, M. (1980) *Education of Disturbed Pupils*, London, Methuen/ Schools Council.

Chapter 5

Hanging On by a Thread: Integration in Further Education in Britain

Jenny Corbett

Time and again there was reference to the tenuous foothold which special needs work had within further education. As one co-ordinator observed: 'Usually, special needs is hanging on by a thread within FE.' (Further Education Unit, 1990: 2)

This comment came from a recent study into provision for special needs in colleges of further education (FE) within Britain. The research was instigated by the Further Education Unit (FEU) which was established to develop provision and foster investigations related to further education in the United Kingdom. The implications are that the stability and status of this area of work are in the balance. Such insecurity has long prevailed. In a national survey some ten years earlier Bradley and Hegarty (1981) reported a pattern of uneven provision among colleges in different regions of Britain and a lack of any coherent policy on integration in further education. Their survey had been conducted as a direct response to the conclusions of the Warnock Report (Department of Education and Science, 1978) which suggested that there was a paucity of post-16 provision for young people with special educational needs.

This chapter describes some of the ways in which integration in further education has developed in Britain over the last decade, including illustrations drawn from my own recent experience as a college special needs coordinator. To set the scene, it is useful to record what the Warnock Committee recommended in relation to further education:

— Wherever possible young people with special needs should be given the necessary support to enable them to attend ordinary courses of further education (para. 10.37).
— Some establishments of further education should experiment with modified versions of ordinary further education courses for young people with special needs (para. 10.38).
— Some establishments of further education should provide special vocational courses at operative level for students with special needs and special courses of training in social competence and independence (para. 10.39).

— Within each region there should be at least one special unit providing special courses for young people with more severe disabilities or difficulties which would be based in an establishment of further education (para. 10.40).

— Every establishment of further education should designate a member of staff as responsible for the welfare of students with special needs in the college and for briefing other members of staff on their special needs (para. 10.42).

— A co-ordinated approach to further education provision for young people with special needs should be adopted and publicised by the local education authorities within each region against a long-term plan within which arrangements for individual institutions will take their place. The institutions themselves should publicise their policy on the admission of students with special needs as well as the courses and special facilities which they provide for them (para. 10.43).

— The national colleges which currently provide further education or training for young people with disabilities should in time all become part of their regional patterns of further education for students with special needs (para. 10.44). (DES, 1978: 351–352)

The history of integration in further education since this period illustrates ambiguities arising from contradictory responses to these recommendations. In one respect integration has been dramatically successful. There are undoubtedly many more students with special educational needs in mainstream further education colleges in the 1990s than there were in the 1970s. Their participation in a wide range of course provision is documented in Stowell's (1987) national survey. This is the only research to date which has investigated the numbers of students with special educational needs in further and higher education in Britain, the nature of those courses they attend, the support provided for integration, the extent of staff development and college policy. It clearly records the continued pattern of irregular post-16 opportunities in different regions of Britain and the segregation of students with learning difficulties into special courses. The degree to which these students can be said to be 'functionally' integrated, to use Warnock's terminology, is evidently problematic.

Integration with the Necessary Support

There have always been students with sensory or physical disabilities in further education. As long as they were suitably qualified and able to get into the rooms in which classes were to be conducted, these students have been integrated. It was always they who had to cope with what was available, rather than the college adapt to meet their needs. Consequently, their numbers were insignificant, and they were often exceptionally determined individuals.

Over the last decade efforts have been made by colleges, local authorities and national bodies to provide more support for students with a range of sensory and physical disabilities. An organization which has been influential in fostering support for students with disabilities has been the National Bureau for Handicapped Students, recently renamed the National Bureau for Students with

Disabilities (Skill). In 1983 it published guidance for further education colleges in meeting the needs of deaf students, students with severe physical disabilities and blind students. However, despite an increase in awareness supported by staff development in colleges, what has tended to happen is the establishment of the 'special unit' provision to which Warnock referred.

This has meant that certain colleges in Britain have gained reputations for excellent provision for specific groups of students. So careers officers will guide students who are profoundly deaf to a college which has the established expertise to support them and a student who is in a wheelchair and needs a significant degree of physical help to a college known to offer what is required. Stowell (1987) cautioned of the danger which creating ghetto colleges could cause in restricting student choice. Economic pressures can force local authorities to place the bulk of their special resources in one regional college. It is expensive, for example, to place lifts in all colleges of further education. In London alone there are only a few colleges which have good physical access for students in wheelchairs. As I asked in an Open University diploma course which I designed for lecturers working in further education: 'Would you like to be placed in the position of having to go to the college which offered the best toileting arrangements?' (Corbett, 1990: 51). Hurst (1990), examining the experiences of several students with different disabilities, demonstrated that purely practical issues can take priority over all else and determine the painful process of compromise.

Modified and Vocational Courses

The Warnock recommendation of colleges experimenting with 'modified versions of ordinary further education courses' was reflected in the general hotch-potch of ill-defined and badly managed courses proliferating in the early 1980s. These arose from the lack of appropriate course provision in the colleges and the subsequent establishment of segregated courses for students with 'moderate learning difficulties' coming in from the special school sector. It was these students, who had formerly gone into unskilled jobs on leaving school, who were the first wave into mainstream further education (Newton and Robinson, 1982). Their inclusion suggests a response to Warnock in offering extended educational opportunities. In contrast, it could be regarded as a direct result of economic crisis and the emergence of large-scale youth unemployment. In Nottinghamshire, for example, the virtual collapse of the mining industry from the late 1960s onwards led to North Nottinghamshire College being at the forefront of provision for students with special educational needs (Hutchinson, 1982). This provision was developed to fill the gap left by obsolete courses and to find occupation for underemployed lecturers.

Staff development in curriculum design, teaching approaches and assessment procedures was widely disseminated in Britain, through the collaboration of the Department of Education and Science and research bodies, producing a pack called *From Coping to Confidence* (Bradley, 1985). This pack for teaching students with 'moderate learning difficulties' in further education was followed by curriculum frameworks for students with 'severe physical disabilities' (Hutchinson and Tennyson, 1986) and for students with 'severe learning difficulties' (Dee, 1988).

An emphasis upon profiling and individual teaching programs, which was a feature of these special courses, was also an element of the 'New FE' in British colleges. This was related to curriculum developments like the Certificate of Pre-Vocational Education and the Youth Training programs, in which colleges provided 'off-the-job' teaching. New kinds of students came into further education colleges during the 1980s. These were non-academic students, not following traditional vocational areas characteristic of FE colleges, but brought reluctantly into further education through Youth Training schemes. As the recession led to increased youth unemployment, Youth Training programs proliferated, bringing unfamiliar difficulties and demands to college staff.

Integration in further education has taken many forms over the last few years. It has included the absorption of many older students previously taught in adult education classes and many school students coming in part-time in their last year. It has involved lecturers of academic subjects having to learn to teach new courses in new ways to less able students. As Major (1990: 21) suggests: 'This is fertile ground for disaffection and anger' from both staff and students alike. Within this changing student population, students with a wide range of special educational needs were being integrated.

The Role of the Special Needs Coordinator

The Warnock Report recommended that colleges designate a member of staff to be responsible for the welfare of students with special needs and to brief other members of staff. It was presumably anticipated that the allocation of such a role would come from within the existing college community. However, what almost invariably happened was that special needs coordinators were selected from the special school sector. While this meant that they had detailed knowledge and understanding of specific issues related to special needs, they rarely had any insight into the complex and competitive nature of further education. As I reflected when recording my own transfer from a special school into further education, it took me some time to learn the politics of FE (Corbett, 1987). Colleges are intensely political institutions, in which each department has its own history and hierarchy, each competing for a share in limited resources.

Fulcher (1989: 56) suggests that integration is a complex procedure which can be 'seen as a struggle which occurs at all levels in educational apparatuses'. The way in which integration is initially established in a college will decide the level of participation which can develop within policy-making arenas. All too often those tutors who assume responsibility for students with special educational needs in further education are unused to engaging in any form of ideological struggle. A focus upon individual needs and immediate practical problems narrows their perspective. As the recent Further Education Unit survey found:

> The most common remark made by managers about special needs staff was that they tended to be almost exclusively concerned with their specialism and did not fully understand 'how the FE system actually works'. As one head of department commented: 'They don't know their way around this institution . . . who to ask, or the way to do it. . . .' (Further Education Unit, 1990: 2)

If effective integration involves active participation in a dominant discourse within institutions, it follows that those with responsibility for implementing practice need to understand how the system operates and who and what will make things happen.

Active contributions to policy-making rarely emerge from participants with low status. Special needs coordinators have responsibility without power. They were usually appointed at the lowest grades, with minimal authority to effect change. Yet they are expected to tutor and support students, guide mainstream staff, liaise with outside agencies and offer disability awareness training throughout the college. It is only recently that the issue of status has been raised (e.g., Baillie, 1986) and that some colleges have appointed special needs coordinators to managerial posts. In my current research I am interviewing special needs coordinators in different areas of Britain to gain further understanding of their perceptions of the role they play in FE. What has already emerged strongly is that, where they have managerial roles, they can influence policy to make the overall college more 'user-friendly'. Through flexible teaching approaches, assessment of prior skills and adaptable curricula, they are already altering practice and influencing colleagues: '. . . the good practice that we have in equal opportunities, in terms of the individual curriculum, is showing other people they have a lot of catching up to do' (Interview, July 1991). However, where they are isolated and separate, they lack clout: '. . . my worry about the special needs section is that it is a very dedicated, very committed group of people, but we're far too insular; we are doing it all ourselves. That lets everybody else off the hook' (Interview, June 1991).

It is no surprise either, in terms of power and status, that 'special needs' in FE is still often relegated to a 'caring' department of the college. This might be called 'Community Care' and be involved in training nursery nurses and social service employees, both staff and students being predominantly female. Thus integration becomes a feminist issue in which caring for disabled students is perceived as a female task.

A Transfer of the Special System

At the Annual Conference of the National Bureau for Students with Disabilities in March 1991 the recently retired Senior Inspector (HMI) who had been instrumental in disseminating *From Coping to Confidence* in 1985 and in supporting the establishment of specialist provision in colleges acknowledged that, with hindsight, they should have acted differently. In their efforts to ensure an appropriate and viable curriculum for students with learning difficulties, the inspectorate had helped support what was to become a special system within mainstream colleges.

During the early 1980s an increasing number of colleges in Britain employed specialist staff and ancillary helpers with responsibility for students with special needs. They were usually given a base room or unit, some of which are still bleak huts on the other side of the college playing field. As I have already reflected, where the special needs unit was attached to a department, it was often one with a female ethos associated with caring. In my own case I was placed in the department of Health, Hairdressing and Floristry, where nursery nurses, hairdressers and florists were trained. There were overwhelmingly female students, few male staff and the only woman head of department in the college. She had a son with learning difficulties and felt commitment to the area of special needs. Such physical and social isolation in one specific area inevitably negated a whole college approach. Separateness was reinforced by a special curriculum to be taught by specialist lecturers to discrete groups of students. The pattern familiar in school integration schemes developed. Mainstream staff justified their disinclination to become involved with the students by claiming that they would need specialist knowledge and a familiarity with teaching methods and curriculum frameworks which they were in no position to learn. They preferred to leave it to the 'specialists'. The special curriculum in further education posed a frustrating dilemma. For as long as there were no alternatives available for these students, it was better than their inclusion in classes for which they were ill-qualified. Yet, while it remained in situ, it was an obstacle to functional integration and a full and active participation in the college community. For many students with learning difficulties, still, their inclusion beyond the special curriculum is only into social integration in canteen, sports hall and other aspects of college recreational life.

What, then, should the inspectorate have done in response to the generally chaotic situation in the early 1980s when special needs became an issue in further education? The recommendations in *A 'Special' Professionalism* (DES, 1987) indicate the way in which priorities emerged. This publication arose from the report of the Advisory Committee on the Supply and Education of Teachers in 1984 which offered advice to the Secretaries of State on teacher training and special educational needs. It addressed the training of many different groups in further education, including managers, mainstream staff, special needs coordinators, specialist staff, ancillary staff and local authority officers. It was a publication which reminded colleges of what the Warnock Report of 1978 had said about integration:

> In its original sense integration implies a process involving all parts in creating a new whole through mutual adaptation. In practice many who have pressed the need for integration have been insufficiently critical of the educational provision made in mainstream institutions in terms of its appropriateness for a whole range of clientele, including those with special needs. . . . Functional integration involves joint participation in educational activities where students with special needs attend mainstream courses, either on a full-time or part-time basis, and where they make a full contribution to the life of the college. (DES, 1987: 5)

The need to foster 'mutual adaptation' was seen as critical. This could only come about through staff training at all levels in the college hierarchy. 'Special needs' was not about 'that special course done in the annexe' but was about sharing responsibility and offering appropriate provision. The late 1980s have seen a growth in publications which reflect flexibility in-service training and a broadening of curricular access (e.g., Cooper, 1988; FEU, 1988a, 1988b).

However, once established, a provision is very difficult to remove. In most colleges there are now special needs sections with their own territorial rights. They will have fought to gain precious resources, to recruit part-time staff and to have their own space. In order to promote a whole college sharing of responsibility, such separate sections will need to be dissolved. When or if it occurs, this will be a slow and potentially stressful process. Ironically, it is in those colleges which only responded to special educational needs in the late 1980s where much of the innovative work is now operating. One special needs coordinator on the Isle of Man, for example, when appointed to the college in 1986, declared that he would not establish a special needs section but would work across college departments, sharing responsibility with a wide range of mainstream staff. Having learnt from what he observed in other colleges, he was determined that integration would not mean isolation in a unit provision, nor the development of a 'specialist' mystique.

When reflecting on the mistake of supporting a special curriculum in further education, the senior inspector recognized that, in the circumstances which existed at that stage, it was the only way in to the system. If students with learning difficulties were to be allowed entry into mainstream colleges, support had to be provided for them. Colleges were not responsive to their needs. They came in (sometimes quite literally) by the back door. I charted the progress of integration into further education as:

a) cap-in-hand selected integration: unequal partnership;
b) makeshift provision: unequal sharing of resources;
c) special courses: segregated area of work;
d) staff development: sharing understanding of needs;
e) open access courses: sharing staff expertise and resources;
f) negotiating individual programs: consumers as partners;
g) a legal and administrative right to opportunities. (Corbett, 1990: 15)

We have moved a long way in ten years. In the meantime students have been coming in from special schools to mainstream colleges. What has been their experience of college life?

What Makes Integration Successful for Students?

In examining what leads to successful integration in further education, I am reflecting on those students I taught at a London college between 1983 and 1986. All had come into the large, bustling college from a small, sheltered special school. It was quite a culture shock for most of them. They had spent their years, from the age of 3 to 16, being taught with other disabled children. In that context disability had been the norm. They were then coming, at a vulnerable teenage stage, into a community where their peers where able-bodied, fashionable, beautiful, desirable and full of vitality (or so it seemed). For some of the severely disabled students, it was very difficult to adjust. 'I really fancy that girl but she wouldn't look at me', one student with spina bifida told me as we ate our lunch in the canteen. What could I say? Maybe he was right. Integration can be very harsh. It confronts people with their difference. I saw how students grew through their one or two years in the college. Sometimes it was a painful experience. So much depended upon their personalities. Where a student was extrovert and prepared to have a try at different activities, they were often well integrated into college life. If they were shy and insecure, however, then the extra demands made upon them could be very stressful. My observations led me to realize that it was they who were expected to fit in. The effort had to come from them. I always felt this was unfair, but it was a reality. Where individuals were prepared to make that extra effort, they were rewarded by being seen as 'exceptional' people. In a model of integration which calls for the minority group to adapt, it tends to be the 'exceptional' who survive. Should students with special educational needs have to show that bit extra to succeed?

Where students felt they had been successful on their own terms, it was in relation to the following criteria: they were able to cope with work which was within their capabilities; they made progression which developed their self-esteem; their work in college complemented other aspects of their lives. Three examples illustrate these student experiences.

Michael had muscular dystrophy. He had stayed in a special school even though he could have gone into the mainstream. His parents wanted the more protected environment as he had suffered from earlier teasing when in a mainstream primary school. He was an academically able boy. When he moved into the college, he started on a special, discrete course which I tutored. This was not the most appropriate provision for him, but it was the one way in which he could gain national qualifications in English, science and maths, which had been taught only at a very basic level in the special school. After succeeding in this one-year course, he went on to a two-year course in electronics and microtechnology in the Engineering Department. He was rarely away with ill-health and completed the course with a prize for outstanding application. Michael went from college into open employment in the local council offices. Through offering a degree of flexible support, we were able to ensure that Michael's special schooling did not impede his progress and success in a mainstream course.

Pat had spina bifida and hydrocephalus and was felt to experience some learning difficulties. She was one of the most successful students in developing self-esteem and confidence. Her independence led her to go her own way in the college and not follow the crowd. She used the college facilities and did not hesitate to ask for help when she wanted it. Whereas she had been seen as a loner and something of a recluse at school, she was respected as her own person at college. Moving from the tightly structured intimate setting of a special school, in which there is inevitably a high degree of surveillance, into the more impersonal world of the FE college suited her well. She integrated with floristry students and enjoyed a range of options on her special course. When she left the college, Pat moved into a sheltered workshop where she continues to attend. Perhaps college was just an interlude between two segregated sites. Nonetheless, it gave Pat a chance to gain confidence in her own worth and to be a visible social success.

Arnold was a mature student with cerebral palsy and was unable to read or write. In his 30s, he was still living at home with his mother and came to cookery classes to develop some independence. He surpassed our expectations. There were difficulties, but his motivation was so strong. Arnold never missed a class and always worked very hard, despite only being able to use one hand for mixing food and not being able to read recipes. His mother came to visit and said that Arnold would soon be moving out to live with his brother who would go out to work while Arnold did the housekeeping. Through the course of the year, Arnold made remarkable progress in confidence, dexterity and communication skills and received a distinction in his final assessment. Everything which Arnold was doing at college was supported and reinforced both at home and in the day centre where he spent the rest of the week.

These examples are of successes. Other students dropped out and some experienced failures and frustrations. Even experiences of failure, though, can be valuable. Jane, severely disabled and only able to communicate through her left foot operating a computer, wanted to go in for a public examination in English, which I knew to be very demanding. I tried to dissuade her but she insisted, and I know it was her right to try. She worked very hard to prepare. Years spent in special school with inadequate technical support and a less than rigorous academic program were obstacles. She was a sensitive and creative writer, but had gaps in her early learning. Jane spent all day from 9 in the morning until 5 at night, with only ten minutes break, to write the exam. She failed. It was a distressing and disappointing experience for both of us. Yet, if integration is about competing on equal terms, it is also about the right to experience failure and to develop personal growth and self-knowledge through reflection. Children in special schools can be shielded from failure. Tasks are created to let them experience success. This is valid in promoting confidence, but avoiding possible hurt can foster low expectations. I came to understand that a right to risk failure is a fundamental aspect of an integrated community. It is part of what constitutes true equality of opportunity.

Integration and Equal Opportunities

The 1988 Education Reform Act has brought with it the concept of curriculum entitlement as an 'obligation on providers (or those co-ordinating provision) rather than learners, and as a right to participate in certain learning experiences in addition to working towards particular outcomes' (FEU, 1989: 1). REPLAN (1990), the Department of Education and Science's program to improve the educational opportunities available to unemployed adults, has published a checklist for colleges to encourage them to offer an integrated approach to people with disabilities. This includes questions relating to transport, lifts, toilets and publicity. All too often in the past colleges have said that they do not need to adapt their premises because they have no enquiries from people with disabilities. They have not bothered to let people know that the college is available for them. This new checklist suggests:

> People with disabilities can be very isolated because of their disability or lack of mobility. If the college is going to attract more students with disabilities then, not only must they ensure that facilities and travel arrangements are suitable, but also that their publicity material reaches potential students. This might well involve outreach provision and consultation with local groups and organizations. (REPLAN, 1990: 7)

Both the notion of an entitlement to curricular access and a right to appropriate practical support offer welcome progressions from the 'cap-in-hand' back door integration of the past.

However, equal opportunities in theory usually differ from equal opportunities in practice. I will offer an example of a college which includes special educational needs as part of its overall commitment to equal opportunities. Kingsway College in London tells students: 'We aim to make you welcome regardless of your age, class, colour, gender, nationality, religion, sexual orientation, disability or other need' (O'Grady, 1990: 17). This commitment involves the status of special needs:

> The inclusion of special educational provision in the college's equal opportunities policy is illustrated by the management structure. Vice principal, Sue Sandle, has responsibility for equal opportunities. Reporting to her are a multi-ethnic education coordinator and the co-ordinator for disability who chairs the standing committee for special needs, a sub-committee of the academic board, and also sits on the course monitoring committee representing students with special needs. The co-ordinator for disability — Liz Maudslay — is also a member of the co-ordinating group which considers how equal opportunities can be integrated into the curriculum. (O'Grady, 1990: 18–19)

The special needs coordinator can be seen to engage in interactions which, within Fulcher's (1989) model of different arenas in which struggle for policy-making occurs, have wide implication for the growth of integrated provision.

Yet, while a policy for equal opportunities had developed at one level, there are still anomalies. I reflected on how many of the problems which Liz Maudslay raises in 1990 had also been my concerns as a coordinator in 1986. She notes that the high level of responsibility taken on by general duties assistants is not reflected in their low pay, although integration could not take place without them. It was also my experience that flexible and sensitive assistants were crucial to successful integration, yet they were asked to cope with delicate and difficult tasks for very poor financial reward. She records the fact that, despite efforts to improve access, it is still down to the students themselves to adapt and cope with inadequate compromises. Stair-climbing wheelchairs placed in the college were too difficult and unsteady for some students to use. One student in a wheelchair had to have a course relocated to the ground floor so that she could take part. These modifications show cooperation but, nonetheless, draw uneasy attention to the individual and their needs.

I experienced similar difficulties, with the alteration of venues of classes often causing the maximum of fuss or students having to cope with inconvenient, make-shift arrangements. Areas of college still remain barred, and students with disabilities are made to feel awkward. Liz Maudslay stresses the difficulty with transport, waiting for taxis which arrive late or depending upon special buses delivering the students at a set time. She emphasizes that this reliance upon transport makes the students feel separate from their peers. This was exactly my experience. Waiting for transport with students in wheelchairs, sometimes over an hour, gave me some insight into the frustration they must experience on a daily basis. Clearly, these are all perennial dilemmas, but they are of fundamental importance in evaluating the quality of experience which students being integrated into further education can expect.

An effective policy of equal opportunities has made a considerable impact in the area of staff training in colleges. At Kingsway College this has included promoting a positive image of disability and establishing a strong support structure for mainstream staff. All staff share responsibility for students with special educational needs. Under the 1988 Education Reform Act funding arrangements should enable provision to be expanded and improved. Liz Maudslay feels that the National Curriculum could act as an entitlement curriculum and make students more demanding. My own recent research into what special schools want from link courses with colleges indicated that the schools were asking colleges to provide those aspects of the National Curriculum, like science and technology, which they had difficulty offering within small, all-age schools (Corbett, 1991a). The scope to develop a richer, more integrated curriculum is evident.

Planning for a New Future

The Warnock Report (1978) recommended the establishment of a coordinated approach to provision for students with special educational needs within a long-term plan in each local region of Britain. However, such initiatives can only operate within a stable, confident system. Consistent changes in further education over recent years have culminated in the latest government plan for April 1993, when: 'Each college will become a free-standing corporate institution, funded through a new further education council appointed by the Education Secretary under legislation to be introduced this autumn' (Jackson, 1991: 3). Establishing provision for what is still seen as a peripheral group of students is extremely difficult when the institutions themselves are in a state of flux. Changes are at all levels: in funding, in new National Vocational Qualifications, in learning systems and in relationships with social services.

The 'care in the community' initiative, which is relocating people who have lived in long-stay hospitals, has brought new students into mainstream colleges and has given a specific role to the segregated, special colleges. They are now concerned to create a curriculum to foster independence, but they are coping with the most severely dependent students (Corbett, 1989). Their role is primarily to find appropriate placements in the community (Corbett, 1991b) and to develop links with mainstream colleges. However, these links are proving difficult to create as mainstream colleges rarely provide the level of resources required for students with multiple disabilities.

There are new pressures from the government white paper, *Education and Training for the 21st Century* (Department of Education and Science, 1991), which places emphasis upon outcomes, employability and cost-effectiveness. Recently formed bodies composed of local employers, termed Training and Enterprise Councils (TECs), are having an increasingly significant effect upon integration in further education in Britain. Many training programs specifically designed to support people with special educational needs have been closed by the TECs as they fail to meet the criteria of guaranteed employability. In relation to the 'care in the community' initiative, the severe cutbacks on recreational courses in adult education have limited possible opportunities. This level of integration is evidently not a high priority in the new legislation. The broad educative function which has long characterized British further education is being eroded in the name of 'rationalization'.

I began with a quote from a 1990 publication which suggested that 'special needs is hanging on by a thread within FE' (FEU, 1990: 2). In this chapter I have

Jenny Corbett

discussed some of the ways in which integration in further education has developed in Britain in the last decade. There have been many positive advances during the period. The emphasis has shifted from charitable inclusion to equal opportunities. We can only hope that, in the current upheaval in further education as in all areas of the British education system, this tenuous thread is not severed.

References

BAILLIE, J. (1986) *Burnham: The Biggest Barrier of All?*, London, National Bureau for Students with Disabilities.

BRADLEY, J. (Ed.) (1985) *From Coping to Confidence*, London, Further Education Unit/ National Foundation for Educational Research/Department of Education and Science.

BRADLEY, J. and HEGARTY, S. (1981) *Students with Special Needs in FE*, London, Further Education Unit.

COOPER, D. (1988) *An Opportunity for Change,* London, Skill.

CORBETT, J. (1987) Integration in Further Education: A Case Study, Unpublished PhD, Open University.

CORBETT, J. (1989) 'The Quality of Life in the "Independence" Curriculum', *Disability, Handicap and Society*, 4, 2, pp. 145–164.

CORBETT, J. (1990) *Providing for Special Needs: Policy and Practice*, Milton Keynes, Open University Press.

CORBETT, J. (1991a) *No Longer Enough: Developing the Curriculum in Special School/ College Link Courses*, London, Employment Department/ Skill.

CORBETT, J. (1991b) 'Moving On: Training for Community Living', *Educare*, 39, pp. 16–18.

DEE, L. (1988) *New Directions*, London, Further Education Unit.

DEPARTMENT OF EDUCATION AND SCIENCE (1978) *Special Education Needs: Report of the Committee of Enquiry into the Education of Handicapped Children and Young People* (Warnock Report), London, Her Majesty's Stationery Office.

DEPARTMENT OF EDUCATION AND SCIENCE (1987) *A 'Special' Professionalism*, London, Her Majesty's Stationery Office.

DEPARTMENT OF EDUCATION AND SCIENCE (1991) *Education and Training for the 21st Century*, London, Her Majesty's Stationery Office.

FULCHER, G. (1989) *Disabling Policies?*, Lewes, Falmer Press.

FURTHER EDUCATION UNIT (1988a) *Access to the Mainstream Curriculum*, London, FEU.

FURTHER EDUCATION UNIT (1988b) *Flexible Learning Opportunities and Special Educational Needs,* London, FEU.

FURTHER EDUCATION UNIT (1989) *Towards a Framework for Curriculum Entitlement,* London, FEU.

FURTHER EDUCATION UNIT (1990) *Perceptions of Special Needs in Further Education,* London, FEU.

HURST, A. (1990) 'Obstacles to Overcome: Higher Education and Disabled Students', in CORBETT, J. (Ed.), *Uneasy Transitions: Disaffection in Post-compulsory Education and Training*, Lewes, Falmer Press.

HUTCHINSON, D. (1982) *Work Preparation for the Handicapped*, London, Croom Helm.

HUTCHINSON, D. and TENNYSON, C. (1986) *Transition to Adulthood*, London, FEU.

JACKSON, M. (1991) 'Clarke's Emergency Stop', *The Times Educational Supplement*, 29 March 1991, p. 3.

MAJOR, B. (1990) The Changing Further Education Structure: A Basis for Conscription?' in CORBETT, J. (Ed.), *Uneasy Transitions: Disaffection in Post-compulsory Education and Training*, Lewes, Falmer Press.

NEWTON, J. and ROBINSON, J. (1982) *Special School Leavers*, London, Greater London Association for the Disabled.

O'GRADY, C. (1990) 'Kingsway College: Post-16 Provision', in *Integration Working*, London, Centre for Studies on Integration in Education.

REPLAN (1990) *Abilities Not Disabilities*, London, Department of Education and Science.

STOWELL, R. (1987) *Catching Up?*, London, National Bureau for Handicapped Students.

Chapter 6

From Integration to Inclusion: The Canadian Experience

Bruce Uditsky

In the inclusive classroom the student with a significant disability, regardless of the degree or nature of that disability, is a welcomed and valued member. The student is: taught by the regular classroom teacher (who is supported as needed); follows the regular curriculum (with modification and adaptation); makes friends; and contributes to the learning of the entire class. In the inclusive neighbourhood school the student with a disability participates in all aspects of school life according to her interests and moves year to year with her peers from kindergarten through high school. In the inclusive community the child with a disability participates in the life of the community, has the possibility of a part-time job in the latter years of high school, and considers the opportunity of continuing her education at college/university or the pursuit of a career. While this is not near the reality for the vast majority of children with a disability in Canada, it is a reality for a few and a vision for many. From the dreams of many and the reality of a few a movement grows.

From Exclusion to Integration

Historical Context

A brief historical synopsis is necessary to frame the context for a critical appraisal of integration and in response to develop the concept of inclusive schooling. This analysis, while limited in scope, will serve to illustrate several themes:

1 the struggle for inclusion as a reflection of personal and cultural values not educational science;
2 parents of students with disabilities as the principal leaders and agents of change;
3 educators as allies in the process of change; and
4 inclusive schooling practices as a distinctly different process from integrated schooling.

Any complete historical overview would require an analysis of political, social and cultural values as they affected schooling organization and practices. While this is beyond the scope of this chapter, the reader must nevertheless be cognizant of these factors. For example, to the degree that a culture negates the value of persons with a disability, the social institutions within that culture will reflect those values in its practices and policies (Wolfensberger, 1989). Schools are one of those social institutions.

The move to educate students with significant disabilities in Canadian communities began towards the last half of this century, largely as a result of parental action (NIMR, 1981). Increasing numbers of parents, mostly acting individually, were keeping their children at home, beginning to resist the counsel of professionals to institutionalize. Institutionalization had been proffered, however illogically, as providing greater benefit to children and families than living at home. The family would be relieved of their burden, and the child would be placed under the supervision of professional care and expertise. This rejection of professional advice and the status quo reflected a deepening, although not always easily articulated, perspective of parents — a child with a disability was first and foremost a child (Pivato, 1984). For the child, family and the presence of a home were necessary to well-being. This fundamental difference in world-views between the parents and the professionals with their systems characterizes even now the struggle for inclusion (Jory, 1991). The rationales for segregation are not much different from the rationales in support of institutionalization. The rationales in support of inclusive schooling are directly related to the rationales in support of growing up as a member of a family (Steinbach, 1991).

The Parent Movement

Parents at first wondered if they were alone and began to seek each other out, sometimes, for example, by placing advertisements in local newspapers. As contacts increased, parents began to gather out of common interests and experiences. This eventually led to the development of community living and advocacy organizations on local, provincial and national levels (Neufeld, 1984). One commonality was a belief that their children could benefit from an education; that they could learn and should be in school. Parents often saw some progress from their efforts at home, and, more fundamentally, they believed their children were worth the effort. They were, however, the parents of children who had been deemed by the social authorities (educators, physicians, psychologists) to be ineducable or incapable of benefitting from an education, possibly trainable. When they approached their community school systems, they were naturally rejected (NIMR, 1981; Neufeld, 1984).

Parents were viewed as unrealistic, and failing to cope or adjust to their child's limitations. Educators argued that they did not have the facilities, resources or expertise (except the expertise that children with significant disabilities did not belong in school). The limited resources needed to be spent on those who would benefit the most, and students with significant disabilities would disrupt the education of others.[1] The arguments against further integration have literally not changed in fifty years, regardless of the degree of access to schools acquired by students with significant disabilities (Byfield, 1991; Stolee, 1992; Elliott, 1992). This suggests that the resistance to the inclusion of students with disabilities may have deeper roots than the traditional arguments appear to represent. These roots lie in the long-term systematic devaluation of persons with a disability. This serves to explain why the struggle continues and repeats itself even today (McCallum, 1991).

There were initially no legal requirements compelling public schools to serve students with significant disabilities. In some instances a school system was legally entitled temporarily to exclude a student with 'special needs' until such time as that student's needs could be accommodated. Temporary exclusion was forever in too many school jurisdictions. There was no universal right to education, at least none that had been interpreted by school systems or courts (Gall, 1984). In Canada schooling is a provincial jurisdiction exclusively.

Segregated Schools

Just as parents had resisted the advice to institutionalize, they now resisted the expertise that negated the potential of their sons and daughters. As a consequence of being rejected, but sustaining a belief in the educability of their children, many parents and parent organizations, with the help of community allies, started their own schools (NIMR, 1981). Often with little money, donated space and untrained volunteers, the disabled could learn. Within and between schools students were categorized on the basis of disability. Accordingly, curricula and instructional strategies were developed. These schools did not transcend the categorization and separation according to degree of disability that characterized education in general. The schools, while challenging educational systems on the issue of educability, at the same time engaged in practices that would contribute to future segregated schooling in general.

Over time the schools grew, became formalized and legitimized — subject to government regulations (e.g., teacher qualifications, reviews, approved curricula) and recipients of government funds. Parents had proved their point and more. Some schools would become the responsibility of public systems; some public systems would establish their own segregated systems; and a few schools remained under the auspices of parent/community organizations (NIMR, 1981). This evolution took place over approximately twenty-five to thirty years. The demonstration of educational benefit had been coupled to segregation by default. Segregation, an artifact of a rejecting history, not of educational knowledge (Stainback, Stainback and Bunch, 1989), had been elevated to a higher order good.

Segregated Classrooms

In the 1970s another movement began (Gall, 1984; Stainback, Stainback and Bunch, 1989). New generations of parents were developing their own ideas, concepts which were extensions of what parents before them had dreamed. Like so many past reformers, the radical parents of old became the protectors of the status quo — the segregated school (NIMR, 1981; Neufeld, 1984). Parents of younger children, having had the way partially paved by the previous generation's struggles, perceived their son or daughter as being entitled not only to an education, but also to the delivery of that education in regular schools under the auspices of the public school systems. Parents argued that if their children could learn in a classroom, you could put the classroom anywhere, and logically the best place was in a regular school. They wanted to collaborate in their child's education, not be responsible for the continued management of schools.

By being housed in a regular school, students could be better distributed throughout the community (shorter bus rides). In a regular school there would be an opportunity to be with non-handicapped peers; there would be access to facilities and resources. Integration at this point, for students with significant disabilities, was defined as being in a segregated classroom in a regular school. Resistance to this form of integration, which came from both public schools and private segregated schools, was based on the same arguments as stated previously. However, a number of factors combined to overcome this resistance in addition to the advocacy of parents.

In many urban centres the 1980s would see changing demographics resulting in many public schools in different communities across the country finding themselves with empty classrooms which threatened the viability of a community school. Filling those empty classrooms could keep a community school open. Students with a significant disability were now entitled to government funds and were required to be taught by certificated teachers (members of the teacher unions). Further, public systems were under pressure to fund the education of students with significant disabilities, as students resident in their district. Segregated schools were increasingly expensive to operate. By accepting students previously excluded, monies would remain within the system (some schools would eventually have a quarter or more of their school population labelled and organized around special classes). What is of issue here is that other than child-centred educational principles were at play. Integration founded on these somewhat mercenary factors would be vulnerable to poor practice and quality.

Schools had been providing an education to many students with mild and moderate disabilities, some integrated in regular classrooms and many in segregated classrooms (Gall, 1984). Criticisms of segregated classrooms for those with mild disabilities were forthcoming within the education system. For students with significant disabilities the arguments were about extending the system's responsibility, not about changing the model of education. An increased number of provinces had mandatory legislation (implemented to greatly varying degrees) that supported the education of all children (Gall, 1984; Stainback, Stainback and Bunch, 1989). The Canadian Charter of Rights and Freedoms, which supported equality for persons with disabilities, was reflective of changing community attitudes (Porter and Richler, 1991). Nonetheless, as late as 1987 some jurisdictions still tried to declare students as ineducable (Sobsey, 1987).

Most school systems opened segregated classrooms without addressing or confronting their historical practices and assumptions. A student could travel on a different bus, attend for a shorter day, have an entirely different curriculum, be subjected to aversive procedures, be housed in a separate wing or area of the school, perhaps have a different principal than the one located at the school, have no contact with any non-disabled peers, be located at a school that is age-inappropriate and still be considered as integrated (Knoll and Meyer, 1986). This was the integration that many students with significant disabilities were to experience and that many continue to experience — a practice consistent with the least restrictive placement models, models which legitimized institutionalization, segregation and categorization. Any model based on least restrictive options applied in a context of devaluation would result in the most restrictive options (Taylor, 1988). It was a Kafkaesque system that parents were expected to understand.

In some parts of the country legislation was improved to give students a right to education; however, this did not presume a right to a fully integrated education. In fact some legislation which assured a right to education entrenched segregated classes as the principal means of delivering education (Bill 82, 1980). Many regulatory policies supported and required special classroom placements, to meet standards and receive funding. Coupled with the improved legislation were more formal appeal processes. While a step in the right direction, in some provincial jurisdictions parents chose one of the three panel members, while the school system chose the remaining two (the system never loses). In other provinces the local school board determined the appeal process, and parents might have to face the entire board in opposition to the board's own administration. These appeal processes were at best a formal beginning recognition of the parental right to appeal.

Some systems did not provide segregated classrooms for students with significant disabilities but preferred to contract out this service. Canada has two public school systems: Catholic and non-denominational. Those systems which were smaller and had fewer resources would sometimes send their students with significant disabilities to the classrooms operated by the other public system. In the long term this would be a positive advantage for some of the dispersing systems as they would have less of a segregated system to dismantle. This in itself did not prevent other of these same systems from being resistant to integration even today.

Partial Integration

One of the premises governing the move to include students with significant disabilities in regular schools was the opportunity for contact with non-handicapped peers (Brown *et al.*, 1989). In many instances this was virtually non-existent or so minimal as to be meaningless. One response to this situation was partial integration (Schnorr, 1990). A variety of models evolved from the segregated classroom and its philosophical underpinnings. Individual students might be integrated for various classes from the segregated class or resource room (or some other empty room to which they had been assigned). They might go from their segregated setting to a regular class, return to the segregated class and repeat the process, depending on when and where they were being integrated. For some students this might be an extensive process and for others very limited. In-class support might be provided by a teacher, peers and/or aides. The process of deciding which class to integrate might be based, depending on the school system, on student preference, teacher preference, teacher receptivity, size of the receiving class and/or non-academic nature of the receiving class. Other partial integration models included being individually integrated one day a week (possibly at a different school), integrated mornings or afternoons; half-time in kindergarten and another grade (some students spent years in kindergarten). While being partially integrated, students could still be under the responsibility of the special education teacher. Other models included reverse integration, where a small number of neighbourhood non-disabled students would be placed with a group of disabled students (congregated from different neighbourhoods), often with a higher ratio of students with a disability to students without a disability. In other models students with a disability would be placed in pairs in regular classrooms to share support resources. All of these variations and more continue to exist.

Integration

As before, each step forward, while initially holding much promise, quickly demonstrated the limits of the reform. Many parents and schools were satisfied with the limits of partial integration, assuming that this was as far as things could progress. Others developed a different vision. The early 1980s would bring the next wave of reform-minded parents wanting a more individualized and personal integration — a more complete integration where the student would be a full-time member, as much as possible, in the regular classroom at their neighbourhood school (Stainback, Stainback and Bunch, 1989; Lipsky and Gartner, 1989). Support would be provided within the regular classroom as needed. The student would also participate in regular classroom and school activities as much as possible. Teachers and others would support the possible development of friendships between students with and without disabilities. At those times when a student could not remain in the regular class or it did not make sense to be in the class, the student would have individualized support to engage in an alternative learning activity (Forest and Lusthaus, 1989).

The movement for integration grew stronger and more active. The Canadian Association for Community Living and its provincial member associations made integrated schooling a primary goal (Porter and Richler, 1991). Integrated education workshops were offered at national and local levels featuring prominent educators and parents. National and provincial newsletters and journals published articles on the benefits of integration, often relating personal stories of schools and parents. University summer workshops and courses were offered on community and school integration. In a few provinces Integration Action Associations sprang up as singularly focused advocacy groups. Both Integration Action and Community Living organizations were joined by educators supportive of integration. Videotapes were produced promoting and describing integration. In almost every province there were positive examples of schools and/or school systems that had made a commitment to integration. Some were offering parents choices, and others were dismantling their segregated classrooms. Some provided the option of neighbourhood schooling; some moved gradually and some moved quickly. Many began providing integration at the elementary years and others at any year. Across the country where integration in the regular classroom was denied, parents challenged the system. These challenges and the outcomes are described in a subsequent section.

As noted, provincial legislation and educational policies had gradually improved during the preceding decades. The right to education was more firmly established along with appeal procedures regarding special education placements (McCallum, 1991). Legislation in some parts of the country more clearly supported integration, although patents would still have to resort to the courts (McCallum, 1991). A number of jurisdictions instituted policies supporting neighbourhood schooling and individual integration of students. Many jurisdictions required individual education plans to be developed with parental input. Integration, often in all its varied manifestations, was increasingly considered by government regulation as a legitimate option where appropriate, sometimes the preferred option (although legislation in most instances still did not guarantee a right to a fully integrated education). Provincial rights legislations provided protection against discrimination for persons with a disability, as did the Canadian Charter of Rights and Freedoms (Porter and Richler, 1991). Yet in spite of the examples at systems and individual school levels and the improved legislation, the vast majority of students with significant disabilities remained segregated. Established cultures and social institutions (e.g., schools systems and teacher organizations) do not abandon their values and rituals easily. Most remained actively opposed or passively resistant.

Some school systems claimed that their partial integration models within designated sites were equivalent to full integration. Others took the process a little further by dispersing the students across existing regular classrooms. This could be done where there was a limited number of students to begin with and they happened to be of the right ages to facilitate appropriate dispersal. This was not, however, neighbourhood schooling. It was a model rooted in assessment, placement and categorization. The designated site model typically had an overrepresentation of students with a disability. Further complete participation in the life of the school was difficult, especially after school, given travel needs. Friendship possibilities outside school were inhibited as the students with disabilities did not come from the neighbourhood.

Integration in the regular classroom clearly had positive results (Dreimanis *et al.*, 1990). There were no negative effects on the students without disabilities and potentially even some positive effects (e.g., increased knowledge of individualized accommodation). Teachers and peers were more accepting in practice than had been anticipated. Students with disabilities learned as much or more, being integrated. There were reported diminishments in behavioural difficulties, and peers proved to be effective teachers. Some friendships did develop. Students without disabilities improved their attitudes and could identify positive gains from integration. While integration in the regular classroom was generally positive, simple physical placement in a traditional classroom had some serious shortcomings.

Too often the process of placing a student with significant disabilities in the regular classroom was inexorably linked to all the trappings of segregated special education. Many students found themselves placed in desks that were in various ways separated from the mainstream — to the back, to the side, side-by-side with the teacher's desk or the aide's, behind a barrier or cubicle to minimize distractions. Even on an individual basis within a regular classroom students would be physically separated as a prelude to their social separation. Friendships did not develop to the degree anticipated simply as a result of physical presence. One of the assumed main facilitation methods to integration, the classroom aide, often became an unintentional human barrier (York *et al.*, 1990). In other instances aides became the student's primary teacher. In some schools a student could be full-time in a regular classroom and still be the responsibility of a special education teacher. Curricula would follow the same individual education plan (IEP) as in the segregated classroom. Even following the same IEP process was a way of indicating to all involved that this student was different. Peers who were also seen as possibly the best facilitators of learning and integration were sometimes turned into mini-aides or social workers (Brown and Holvoet, 1982; Kohl *et al.*, 1983). Their role was as helper, not friend. Integrated students would be pulled out for therapy or grouped for instruction. The promise of integration in regular classrooms was not materializing sufficiently for all students. The process of integration clearly needed to be rethought.

Beyond Integration to Inclusion

The Nature of the Struggle

Before the concept of inclusion is described, there is one other developmental factor that requires review. As history does not develop linearly, nor did inclusive schooling. The parent struggles of the 1980s and early 1990s actually transcend the movement from integration to inclusion. These battles differed qualitatively from those of previous decades. For one, they were far more personalized, formal, public and precedent-setting (Batten, 1988; McCallum, 1991). For another, during the course of the struggle the objectives changed. Initially parents' efforts were directed at getting their child integrated in the regular classroom in the neighbourhood school. As the practice of integration was appraised and found wanting, the goal shifted to inclusion. Integration was an end in itself. Inclusive schooling was a process.

While the goals of the struggle shifted, the essence of the struggle remained the same: the *valued presence and participation* of a student with significant disabilities in the regular classroom. Though parents and their allies reconsidered the goals of their advocacy, systems resisted for the same reasons as always (Stainback, Stainback and Bunch, 1989). The change in focus was too subtle. From their perspective the process of including a student with a disability was not the issue; the issue was in reality not wanting students with a disability in the regular classroom and certainly not at the discretion of parents. This is a critical point. The struggle of the 1980s exposed the heart of the matter. The decision to include or exclude was entirely arbitrary and not a function of professional educational knowledge. Exposed was the fact that segregation was an artifact of historical values and in fifty years had no substantive supportive evidence (Dreimanis *et al.*, 1990). It exposed why systems resisted even when research in favour of integration was forthcoming in a relatively short time, given the much longer history of segregation. This exposure plus the results of integration as described above were the two main contributing factors in the development of inclusive schooling.

Integration: An Arbitrary Practice

In requesting the integration of their child, parents experienced a range of responses from open hostility to open acceptance, with a fair degree of apprehension and uncertainty in between. The responses were completely arbitrary and bore no relationship to the student and any accommodations required by the student. Acceptance or rejection depended entirely on: where you lived; which public system you belonged to; and/or the principal, the senior administrator or the written or unwritten policies of the school districts that year. All the mechanisms and pseudoscientific claims of assessment and placement were rapidly called into question. Two children could live in the same community, belong to different public systems and one would be welcome and one would not. The same student rejected in one community would be accepted and welcomed at another. The same student rejected by one principal would be welcomed by another. There was no relationship to the degree of disability, the size of the school or school systems, the age of the student, urban or rural, well resourced or poorly resourced. Values made the difference, and the only difference.

The contrast in receptivity was striking. Across the country one could find school districts prepared and willing either to accommodate or to move to the accommodation of every student as a valued member of the regular classroom (Flynn and Kowalcyzk, 1989; Porter, 1986). Most of these systems were influenced to varying degrees by parent action as well as by individuals in key leadership positions who supported integration as a means to a quality education for all children. In some communities there might not be a school system but individual schools who would do the same. At the same time many parents would find the door to their neighbourhood school closed, if not slammed, in their face (Till, 1990).

The Struggle

Across the country individual parents and families found themselves in uncomfortable and unfamiliar roles. Some were single parents, some the parents of a child with a mild disability, others a severe disability. They came from different walks of life. Some had children entering the school system for the first time, some students were nearing the end of their schooling and had been segregated for years. Very few parents would describe themselves as radicals. They were, however, united in their commitment to their children, in their unerring belief in the equal merit of their child and the necessity that they be educated in the mainstream. They envisaged a life in the mainstream of the community, and school was one of the important avenues to this dream. These parents, sometimes very much alone initially and later with extensive supports, chose to stand in opposition to the regular education and special education empires.

Each had asked for their child to be integrated in a regular classroom in their neighbourhood school and been refused. Most, if not all, the parents had assumed that their school systems would respond in a rational and considerate dialogue. They were unprepared for the degree to which the systems would resist on every level using all the resources available to them. Besides the issue of integration school systems did not want to lose power over student placements. Placements were the domain of professional knowledge and served the vast institution of special education. Wrapped up in the struggle over integration were professional identities, territories, traditions, power and fundamental values about the role of schools in our communities.

The structure of each battle was different as provincial policies and legislation differed. Some parents found themselves in administrative appeal processes that were neither fair nor simple. It was not unusual to take a year to move through the entire process. Each step required preparation, experts, testimony, letters, documentation, hearings, meetings, lawyers, expenses, time, pain, frustration and fear. School systems in their unwarranted opposition, in their refusal even to try to accommodate the child, would pit schools and teachers against child and family. Other parents explored different options, including the courts and human rights commissions (McCallum, 1991). In some instances court cases have dragged on over five years. However, almost every struggle was won. Those students waiting for the resolution of their legal battles have all been integrated in schools that were open. Most were settled without recourse to the courts, and recently in one court case the parents were awarded damages (McCallum, 1991). Advocacy skills and the evidence in support of integration have developed sufficiently to enable parents to win with less and less of a struggle. Nevertheless, unless initiated by parents who are firm in their commitment, integration is not readily offered except in a few places in Canada.

Inclusive Schooling

Inclusive schooling, like integration, suffers from a lack of a coherent definition. The concept is still evolving, and what follows is an interpretation of inclusive schooling. It is quite likely that the term will grow in popularity and ambiguity, rendering it less than useful in the long term. Nevertheless, the term is very useful as a conceptual change agent.

Fundamental to the process of inclusion is a set of principles which ensures that the student with a disability is viewed as a valued and needed member of the school community in every respect. It requires an educational perspective that acknowledges the painful legacy of the past, a broad educational perspective that takes into account the total child and that best teaching practices are applicable to all students, a perspective where parents are truly seen as equal and valued partners in the educational process. These are the values and educational perspectives we almost all want and see as necessary for all children. The following are some of the key components to the practice of inclusive schooling.

Membership. When the parents and students approach their neighbourhood/community school, they are welcomed. The student is enrolled in the appropriate year of education as is any other student. Parents are consulted on the support they feel their child will need. In the inclusive classroom the child with a disability is a fully fledged member (Forest and Lusthaus, 1989). An effort is made to provide the student with a sense of belonging. The regular classroom teacher or teachers are responsible for students' education (Stainback and Stainback, 1989). The student participates in the various roles students may be assigned (giving out supplies, monitor, peer support), goes on field trips, sits among the students, participates in intramurals, supports school teams, attends dances and participates in concerts, and has access to the same options as other students. This is not an exhaustive list but illustrates the concept of embedding the student within the normative educative pathways within the classroom and the school. The student may only be able partially to participate and may require support and adaptation to do so. In some schools a distinct effort is made to create an environment in which all students look out for one another.

Curriculum. There is one curriculum for all students. Whatever the curriculum for that year and school system, the student with a disability participates to the maximum extent possible. In some instances the student may be able to participate as any other student. Other curricular components may require modification: modifications may be simple, as in math where one might be working at a lower skill level; they may be complex, as in science where the objective might be altered from describing why something has changed to pointing to the change (of course, there may be parts of the experiment that the student with a disability could do partially and, if necessary, with assistance). Each modification is individually based, and there is no separate curriculum based on labels. What is functional is being as culturally literate as possible by participating in the cultural basis of the school — the curriculum. Adaptations relate to how the student's participation might be facilitated — for example, using a talking book for language arts, focusing on non-symbolic communication or augmented communication systems. Subsequently, assessment is classroom-based and curriculum-referenced, built from what it is expected the student will learn. Many teachers find this a much more rational curriculum development concept and less time-consuming than traditional IEPs. There is no role for traditional assessments and placement practices.

Teaching practices. Good teaching practices are good for all students (Thousand and Villa, 1989). For example, cooperative learning is an excellent teaching strategy and is very conducive to teaching within the inclusive classroom. The cooperative process not only results in positive learning outcomes, but demonstrates the valued role each can play in learning (Falvey *et al.*, 1989). Experiential or activity-based learning is another effective strategy applicable to all students, including students with a disability. Teaching language arts across all curricular domains and in meaningful contexts is of benefit to all students. Inclusive schooling implies the utilization of effective schooling practices. This is not to suggest that particular instructional strategies for the student with a disability should be abandoned but that they need to be supplemental rather than dominant.

Friendship. All schooling is concerned with the social relationships among students. Relationships are critical to the development of the human capacity within any person. Friends contribute to the shaping of our identity, to our personal security, to our experiences, memories and self-esteem. Friendship is a universal human need. The process of inclusion contributes to the possibility of friendships developing. In addition, inclusion requires a conscious effort to support this possibility by identifying common interests, interpreting students with disabilities, discussing friendship, encouraging collaboration and cooperation, and facilitating participation (Strully and Strully, 1989). Teachers have a lot of implicit knowledge about fostering relationships that needs to be called upon and applied more overtly at times. Relationships need to be seen as reciprocal, without students with disabilities in the perpetual role of helpee. Teachers are powerful role models and need to consider in their own life how to be open to friendships with adults with significant disabilities.

Supports. Supports need to address the needs of the teacher and the classroom, and not be exclusively attached to the student with a disability. Effective teaching supports include collaborative teaming, with parents and administrators included as members of the team (Thousand and Villa, 1990). Teaching is improved in general where teachers have an opportunity to be collaborative, share ideas and support each other directly in the classroom. Consultation models where support is readily available and comes into the classroom are necessary. Team teaching and sufficient time to prepare are assumed. Opportunities must be made for in-service courses and visits to others working on inclusion. Peer support and peer tutor strategies that respond to all students, including students with a disability, are features of supportive classrooms (Stainback and Stainback, 1989). In classrooms assistants are only employed to the degree necessary, and as supports to the entire class. Based principally on teacher judgments, supports should be ready and accessible. Sufficient support is available so that, when appropriate and necessary, the student with a disability can leave the classroom and engage in alternative educational experiences. The emphasis is always on maximizing education within the classroom while at the same time recognizing the challenges and limitations of our knowledge.

Conclusion

Inclusive schooling is still the exception, although examples of including students with the most severe disabilities exist in many communities, rural and urban, across Canada. A few examples of large-scale systems change exist with most efforts at the local school level. Students are making friends and exceeding expectations. Many teachers are eager to address the challenge, and there are many examples of special educators entering the regular classroom as teacher in support of inclusion. Increased sharing is occurring between special and regular educators. A greater percentage of consultation is direct and within the classroom. Inclusion, as with any other aspect of education, is far from problem-free. That is not the objective. The objective is to be in the right educational and values-based context to work on the problems. Inclusion requires effort; it requires support. Friendships and acceptance are not automatic, and when issues arise, they need to be addressed.

Inclusive education may take generations before it is properly understood or practised. Exclusion and segregation were built on centuries of devaluation. Those of us who are parents and teachers have not grown up or been immersed in a culture where inclusion and friendship with persons with a disability is an ordinary and typical life occurrence. We, with this serious long-term deficit, have the responsibility to ensure that this does not happen to our children. Our children need to develop a more inclusive understanding of community. We need to do this in our own lives as well as in our schools. Inclusive education has the potential to contribute to positive generational change, to a more caring culture (Forest, 1988). This, after all, is what we dream for our children.

Note

1   The term 'significant disability' refers to intellectual disabilities which range from moderate to profound.

References

BATTEN, J. (1988) *On Trial*, Toronto, Macmillan.

BILL 82: EDUCATION AMENDMENT ACT (1980) Toronto, Legislature of Ontario, December.

BROWN, F. and HOLVOET, J. (1982) 'Effect of Systematic Peer Interaction on the Incidental Learning of Two Severely Handicapped', *Journal of the Association for Persons with Severe Handicaps*, 7, pp. 19–28.

BROWN, L., LONG, E., UDVARI-SOLNER, A., DAVIS, L., VANDEVENTER, P., AHLGREN, C., JOHNSON, F., GRUENEWALD, L. and JORGENSEN, J. (1989) 'The Home School: Why Students with Severe Intellectual Disabilities Must Attend the Schools of Their Brothers, Sisters, Friends and Neighbours', *Journal of the Association for Persons with Severe Handicaps*, 14, pp. 1–7.

BYFIELD, T. (1991) 'You Won't Help the Handicapped by Handicapping Their Helpers', *Alberta Report*, December, p. 52.

DREIMANIS, M., SOBSEY, D., GRAY, S., HARNAHA, B., UDITSKY, B. and WELLS, D. (1990) *Integration and Individuals with Moderate to Profound Intellectual Impairments: An Annotated Bibliography*, Edmonton, Alb., University of Alberta.

ELLIOTT, O. (1992) 'Minister's Objectives Must be Evaluated', *Staff Bulletin* (Edmonton Public Schools), April, pp. 8–9.

FALVEY, M.A., COOTS, J., BISHOP, K.D. and GRENOT-SCHEYER, M. (1989) 'Educational and Curricular Adaptations', in STAINBACK, S., STAINBACK, W. and FOREST, M. (Eds), *Educating All Students in the Mainstream of Regular Education*, Baltimore, Md., Paul H. Brookes.

FLYNN, G. and KOWALCZYK, B. (1989) 'A School System in Transition', in S. STAINBACK, S., STAINBACK, W. and FOREST, M. (Eds), *Educating All Students in the Mainstream of Regular Education*, Baltimore, Md., Paul H. Brookes.

FOREST, M. (1988) 'Full Inclusion Is Possible', *Impact* (Minnesota University Affiliated Program on Development Disabilities), 1, pp. 3–4.

FOREST, M. and LUSTHAUS, E. (1989) 'Promoting Educational Equality for All Students', in STAINBACK, S., STAINBACK, W. and FOREST, M. (Eds), *Educating All Students in the Mainstream of Regular Education*, Baltimore, Md., Paul H. Brookes.

GALL, R. (1984) *Special Education. Dialogue on Disability: A Canadian Perspective*, Calgary, Alb., University of Calgary Press.

JORY, D. (1991) 'Principles of Change: A Parent's Perspective on the Education System', in PORTER, G.L. and RICHLER, D. (Eds), *Changing Canadian Schools*, Toronto, Roeher Institute.

KOHL, F.L., MOSES, L.G. and STETTNER-EATON, B.A. (1983) 'The Results of Teaching Fifth and Sixth Graders to Be Instructional Trainers with Students Who Are Severely Handicapped', *Journal of the Association for Persons with Severe Handicaps*, 8, pp. 32–40.

KNOLL, J. and MEYER, L. (1986) *Principles and Practices for School Integration of Students with Severe Disabilities: An Overview of the Literature*, Syracuse, N.Y., Centre on Human Policy.

LIPSKY, D.K. and GARTNER, A. (1989) *Beyond Separate Education: Quality Education for All*, Baltimore, Md., Paul H. Brookes.

McCALLUM, S.D. (1991) 'Access to Equality in Education: The Power of Parents', in PORTER, G.L. and RICHLER, D. (Eds), *Changing Canadian Schools*, Toronto, Roeher Institute.

McDONNELL, A.P. and HARDMAN, M.L. (1991) 'The Desegregation of America's Special Schools: Strategies for Change', *Journal of the Association for Persons with Severe Handicaps*, 14, pp. 68–74.

NATIONAL INSTITUTE ON MENTAL RETARDATION (1981) *Orientation Manual on Mental Retardation (Revised)*, Toronto, National Institute on Mental Retardation.

NEUFELD, R. (1984) 'Advocacy: Evolution to Revolution', in MARLATT, N.J., GALL, R. and WIGHT-FELSKE, A. (Eds), *Dialogue on Disability: A Canadian Perspective*, Calgary, Alb., University of Calgary Press.

PIVATO, E. (Ed.) (1984) *Different Hopes, Different Dreams*, Edmonton, Alb., Academic Printing and Publishing.

PORTER, G.L. (1986) 'School Integration: Districts 28 and 29', *Education New Brunswick*, November, 6–7.

PORTER, G.L and Richler, D. (1991) 'Changing Special Education Practice: Law, Advocacy and Innovation', in PORTER, G.L. and RICHLER, D. (Eds), *Changing Canadian Schools*, Toronto, Roeher Institute.

SCHNORR, R. (1990) '"Peter? He Comes and Goes..."?: First Graders' Perspectives on a Part-time Mainstream Student', *Journal of the Association for Persons with Severe Handicaps*, 15, pp. 231–240.

SOBSEY, D. (1987) 'Bill 59: Is this the End of Universal Free Education in Alberta?' *The Spokesman*, December, pp. 6–9.

STAINBACK, W. and STAINBACK, S. (1989) 'Practical Organizational Strategies', in STAINBACK, S., STAINBACK, W. and FOREST, M. (Eds), *Educating All Students in the Mainstream of Regular Education*, Baltimore, Md., Paul H. Brookes.

STAINBACK, W., STAINBACK, S. and BUNCH, G. (1989) 'A Rationale for the Merger of Regular and Special Education', in STAINBACK, S., STAINBACK, W. and FOREST, M. (Eds), *Educating All Students in the Mainstream of Regular Education*, Baltimore, Md., Paul H. Brookes, pp. 15–26.

STEINBACH, A. (1991) 'The Road to Inclusion: One Family's Story', in PORTER, G.L. and RICHLER, D. (Eds), *Changing Canadian Schools*, Toronto, Roeher Institute.

STOLEE, L. (1992) 'Without a Top-down House Cleaning, Dinning's Reforms Just Won't Work', *Alberta Report*, March, p. 31.

STRULLY, J.L. and STRULLY, C.F. (1989) 'Friendships as an Educational Goal', in STAINBACK, S., STAINBACK, W. and FOREST, M. (Eds), *Educating All Students in the Mainstream of Regular Education*, Baltimore, Md., Paul H. Brookes.

TAYLOR, S.J. (1988) 'Caught in the Continuum: A Critical Analysis of the Principle of the Least Restrictive Environment', *Journal of the Association for Persons with Severe Handicaps*, 13, pp. 41–53.

THOUSAND, J.S. and VILLA, R.A. (1990) 'Sharing Expertise and Responsibilities through Teaching Teams', in STAINBACK, W. and STAINBACK, S. (Eds), *Support Systems for Educating All Students in the Mainstream*, Baltimore, Md., Paul H. Brookes.

THOUSAND, J.S. and VILLA, R.A. (1989) 'Enhancing Success in Heterogeneous Schools', in STAINBACK, S., STAINBACK, W. and FOREST, M. (Eds), *Educating All Students in the Mainstream of Regular Education*, Baltimore, Md., Paul H. Brookes.

TILL, L. (1990) *Becky Belongs: Voices Raised in Support of Integration*, Sharon, Ont., Linda Till.

YORK, J., VANDERCOOK, T., CAUGHEY, E. and HEISE-NEFF, C. (1990) 'Does an "Integration Facilitator" Facilitate Integration?' *TASH Newsletter*, June, p. 4.

WOLFENSBERGER, W. (1989) 'Human Service Policies: The Rhetoric versus the Reality', in BARTON, L. (Ed.), *Disability and Dependency*, Lewes, Falmer Press.

Chapter 7

What Is This 'Least Restrictive Environment' in the United States?

Robert A. Henderson

Introduction

Semantics

A common problem found in trying to understand similarities and differences in the educational systems of different countries is the variety of vocabulary employed. At one extreme, different terms are used to mean the same thing, and at the other, identical terms are used to mean very different things. Besides the comparative education problems, authors within the same country are often guilty of creating semantical problems in their writings.

Thus we need to start this chapter by differentiating three key terms: 'integration', 'mainstreaming' and the 'least restrictive environment'. The term 'integration' became a critical educational issue in the 1960s in the United States when the US Supreme Court declared that the principle of 'separate but equal' was no longer valid, and that children of all ethnic backgrounds be educated together in the same age-appropriate schools (*Brown v. Board of Education of Topeka*, 1954). For most American educators, therefore, integration refers to the mixing of black and white students in the same classes in their neighbourhood schools. Since the passage of mandatory special education laws in the mid-1970s, special educators have used the term in reference to students with severe, multiple disabilities who were formerly restricted to residential schools, or segregated, special day schools.

There are three levels of integration in the schools:

1   *physical (or locational) integration*, where the student's special class is physically located in a regular elementary or secondary school building, but no further contact with non-disabled students is attempted on a planned basis;
2   *social integration*, where students with disabilities are permitted to mix with non-disabled students in non-academic activities such as the lunchroom, playground recess, assemblies and the like; they also may be involved in clubs after school;
3   *academic integration*, where the student with a disability is enrolled in a regular class, together with mostly non-disabled students. For the more

severely disabled this may be restricted to music appreciation or art classes; but for the student with no vision it may include the entire range of college preparatory classes, with special education assistance coming in the form of a resource room and assistance for the regular teacher by converting classroom materials to braille, or providing audiotape versions of printed work.

The term 'mainstreaming' became popular after several articles appeared in the professional literature criticizing the effectiveness of special classes for students with mild to moderate disabilities (especially Dunn, 1968). The thrust of this term was that students with minor academic or behavioural problems achieve better academically and socially if they are not labelled and segregated into special classes but left in the 'mainstream' of education — the age-appropriate regular classroom. One must be careful in reading articles in US journals, however, as parents of children being returned to their home and community from a residential institution for the severely mentally retarded have referred to their child being 'mainstreamed' also. In the strict sense the term should apply educationally only when the student with a disability is enrolled in a regular class with only supportive services from special education. In mainstream education the regular teacher is held responsible for that child's education — not the special educator.

The 'least restrictive environment' (LRE) is a principle established originally by the federal courts and later by the US Congress, which insists that, to the maximum extent appropriate, students with disabilities must be educated with children without disabilities. This term is much broader than mainstreaming in that the LRE for a student with a profound or multiple disability might be a self-contained special class located in a neighbourhood elementary or secondary school. The key here is the term 'appropriate', which requires an individually designed educational program (IEP) based on the child's specific educational needs. If the IEP can only deliver the needed resources by means of special classes staffed by a team of special educator and related service personnel (physical therapist, occupational therapist, speech therapist, etc.), then *that* becomes the LRE for that child.

History of Integration in the United States

Unlike most Commonwealth countries, public education was from colonial days a local responsibility in the United States. Even today some 15,000 local school districts exercise considerable control of education in the fifty states. (Only Hawaii — the fiftieth state to join the Union — has maintained a single, state-level educational system.) Such local control is guarded strenuously despite increasing federal and state educational initiatives. Until relatively recent times, local schools (except large city systems) had little to do with the education of students with disabilities.

The history of the delivery of educational services to students with disabilities in the United States reveals a move from total isolation to a majority of such students being served in their neighbourhood schools, a pattern similar to that found almost everywhere in the English-speaking world. The first such institution was the American Asylum (now School) for the Deaf, established in 1817 in

Hartford, Connecticut. Shortly thereafter the Perkins School for the Blind opened in Massachusetts. Residential schools for the mentally retarded followed in the mid-1800s.

Programs in public schools began about the turn of the century as parents living in large city school districts questioned why their child was required to attend a residential school located so far from home. Accordingly, special schools, modelled after the residential ones, were established in many large cities. The depression following the stock crash of 1929 brought a move to tighten the job market by increasing the compulsory school age and eliminating many of the exceptions found in early legislation. This, in turn, forced the public schools both to accept and to keep many students of marginal academic ability, and those with physical or sensory disabilities, especially post-polio cases. To meet this need, schools established special classes, many staffed by teachers without any special training to meet the special needs of the students assigned. By 1950 most states had enacted laws providing for the development of special education programs and providing some state financial support for the additional costs involved.

The United States Congress took action in 1959, providing graduate scholarships for teacher educators who were needed to prepare the special educators (Public Law 85-926). Later this legislation was expanded to provide funds for undergraduate and graduate preparation of teachers as well as leadership personnel. At the state level a mixed picture emerged: some states mandated that local school districts provide special education programs, while other states only permitted districts to take such action. State financial support was similarly varied and delivered via a confusing array of reimbursement systems. In most states special education seemed to have become a separate, parallel educational system for those children who did not 'fit' the regular curriculum (Cruickshank, Paul and Junkala, 1969). In some states legislation limiting public school programs to exclude many children and youth with mental disabilities or multiple handicaps forced their parents to seek private, and in many cases residential, schools for their children.

The civil rights movement of the 1960s and 1970s (for minorities and for women) became the model for parents of children with disabilities to take their case to the federal courts where state legislatures had failed to meet their demands for equity in provision of special educational services.

Legal Aspects

Landmark Federal Court Cases Prior to PL 94-142

It took the federal courts to establish the constitutional rights of all children, including those with disabilities, to an appropriate public education at taxpayers' expense. This may seem strange to a reader who recognizes that education in the United States, as it is in Australia and New Zealand, is a state, not a federal, responsibility. The key difference lies in the individual rights enumerated in the amendments to the US Constitution, which can override state laws or policies which are in conflict with those rights. No such 'Bill of Rights' for individual citizens exists in either the Australian or New Zealand Constitutions (Australian Constitutional Commission, 1988).

The first major decision came in 1954 in a US Supreme Court ruling concerning the segregation of black children into separate schools from those attended by the white majority. The importance of that decision for students with disabilities was the fact that the court addressed the finding to all children in wording its decision:

> Today education is perhaps the most important function of state and local governments. . . . In these days, it is doubtful that any child may reasonably be expected to succeed in life if he is denied the opportunity of an education. Such an opportunity, where the state has undertaken to provide it, is a right which must be made available to all on equal terms. (*Brown v. Board of Education of Topeka*, 1954)

The application of this principle to children with disabilities waited some seventeen years, during which period both the number of children served and the technology of special education made remarkable advances. Then, in a landmark case, parents of retarded children in Pennsylvania sued to force the state to recognize the right of their children to a free appropriate public education. After a single day's testimony the attorney representing Pennsylvania acknowledged the validity of the parents' position, and the case was settled by a consent decree (*PARC v. Commonwealth of Pennsylvania*, 1972). In framing the order to implement the consent decree the court indicated a clear preference for keeping the child with mental retardation as close to his or her neighbourhood school as possible rather than use a special school or residential facility.

In a case brought before the district (trial level) federal court in the District of Columbia (the federal territory encompassing the nation's capitol, Washington), parents of children with a wide variety of disabilities charged the public schools with denial of their children's rights, based on the same constitutional principles as enunciated in *PARC*. In *Mills v. Board of Education* (1972), the right to a free public school education designed to meet the child's specific needs was affirmed for *all* children with disabilities. Similar suits were introduced in several other states, leading Congress to begin work on federal legislation to require that these rights be observed in all states.

Federal Legislation

Two distinct avenues were taken to provide for the rights of students with disabilities. The first was a civil rights measure which essentially requires all agencies receiving federal funds (including the public schools) *not* to discriminate against students with disabilities. This is commonly referred to as Section 504 of the Rehabilitation Act of 1973 (PL 93-112). The second approach was to enact a funding law, promising substantial federal funds to local schools and state departments of education if each would comply with a complicated, extremely detailed law concerning the education of all handicapped children. Public Law 94-142, The Education of All Handicapped Children Act of 1975, has had an enormous effect in making state special education programs more homogeneous than any other aspect of public education in the United States.

The power of this law to require conformity among the several states prompted the article by then Superintendent of Public Instruction in Illinois, Joseph Cronin, 'The Federal Takeover: Should the Junior Partner Run the Firm?' (1976). Since the six basic principles embodied in the statute law were derived from federal constitutional law, the question was really a cry against the extensive regulatory aspects incorporated into the Act which Dr Cronin felt were reducing states' rights to develop and operate special education programs of their own design.

PL 94-142 was designed to ensure a 'free, appropriate public education for all handicapped children.' It contains six substantive and procedural principles drawn directly from the case law of the early 1970s as outlined above.

Zero reject. Based on the assumption that every child, no matter how severely or multiply disabled, can learn something, the local school district of residence must accept responsibility for providing that free, appropriate public education to every child in that district. Further, since so many children had been excluded in prior years, the law requires an extensive 'child-find' procedure to locate and serve such children and their parents.

Non-discriminatory assessment. Based on the findings of some federal courts that minority and non-English-speaking students were being misclassified as mentally retarded and placed inappropriately in special education programs, the Congress insisted that determination of eligibility for special education could only be made by a multidisciplinary diagnostic team which included the parents. Tests used must not be culturally biased, and students with limited English proficiency must be tested in their native language.

Least restrictive environment (LRE). Following the several court opinions, Congress mandated that students found eligible for special education programs or services be placed as close as educationally feasible to a regular classroom in their neighbourhood school. A corollary to this principle is that a continuum of alternative placements be available, from a regular classroom with only special education consultant service to the teacher to a segregated special residential school for the most severely, multiply disabled. As the child's need for more specialized services increases, the movement away from the regular classroom becomes the appropriate LRE for that child.

Individualized education program (IEP). To ensure that schools were conforming to the principles enumerated above, and to provide parents with a vehicle for meaningful participation in decision-making about their child, each child found eligible for special education must have an IEP developed by a team of school personnel and the parents (and the child, if the parents think it appropriate). This program must include information about the child's special educational needs, establish educational goals and specific objectives, specify what services will be provided (both educational and related, such as PT, OT, speech therapy and special transportation) and for what length of time, and how the goals and objectives will be evaluated. The IEP must be re-evaluated at least annually, or at any time the school or parents feel that a major change is required.

Parent participation. Given the previous treatment of parents of a child with a severe disability by the schools, Congress mandated several points at which parents must be permitted to participate as full partners in the decision-making process: at the initial stages of referral for an assessment; during the case conference to determine eligibility for special education; and during the IEP meeting to determine program options and placement alternatives. This degree of parental involvement is unheard of elsewhere in American education. Except for students with disabilities, the school administrator has almost complete authority regarding placement decisions, and parental objections are seldom upheld by the courts. This entry of parents of students with disabilities into educational decision-making may well change the role of principals and other school administrators for all children.

Due process. In keeping with a basic principle of the Bill of Rights of the US Constitution, an impartial due process hearing procedure was established to ensure that parents could challenge a school's decision without resorting to the expensive and time-consuming process of seeking redress in the state or federal courts. Each state is required to train impartial due process hearing officers who are not employed by the state's educational agency to conduct hearings to settle disputes between parents and the schools concerning the education of students with disabilities. Most states have a local hearing and a state-level review procedure. Parents or school districts may still seek review by the courts, but only after the administrative procedures have been exhausted.

These six substantive and procedural principles were designed to ensure that the basic purpose of PL 94-142, a free, appropriate public education for all handicapped children, is carried out. It was the LRE principle that brought so much opposition during Congressional hearings on the bill. Teacher union officials believed that districts would use the principle to 'dump' children with severe disabilities into regular classrooms in order to save money. Even some parents of children with disabilities were worried that the concept of 'mainstreaming' would mean that their child would sit in the back of regular classrooms without being able to participate meaningfully in the learning activities. The framers of the legislation made clear that LRE could only be understood in the context of an 'appropriate' public education. If the student's needs were such that the special education and related services resources could only be provided in a residential school, then that would be the LRE for that child. Stress was placed on the availability of a continuum of placement alternatives, similar to that defined by Maynard Reynolds (1956), and on the requirement that the IEP team re-evaluate the child's placement at least once each year.

This is amplified by administrative law (regulations):

1   that to the maximum extent appropriate, handicapped children, including children in public or private institutions or other care facilities, are educated with children who are not handicapped; and

2   that special classes, separate schooling or other removal of handicapped children from the regular educational environment occurs only when the nature or severity of the handicap is such that education in regular classes

with the use of supplementary aids and services cannot be achieved satisfactorily. (34 CFR 300.550)

(Note the application of the 1954 US Supreme Court decision in *Brown*, which struck down 'separate but equal' schooling for black children, to educational placement of students with disabilities.)

Case Law Following PL 94-142

With such a wealth of explicit language in law and regulation, it may be difficult to understand why it is necessary to utilize the court system to interpret the meaning of the various terms used; however, this is a hallmark of a governmental system based on a balance of powers. Unlike the Westminister system where the executive and legislative branches of government are merged, leaving the judicial branch relatively weak, in the United States decisions of the schools in applying specific legislation such as PL 94-142 can be challenged in the courts, after administrative remedies (due process hearings and review) are completed.

In a series of cases the federal courts have (1) defined 'appropriate' to mean an educational program, based on an IEP which was developed with all parental rights observed, and one which is designed to provide some educational benefit (*Rowley v. Board of Education*, 1982); (2) insisted that 'access' to the public schools was of primary importance, and that the schools must take all reasonable steps to permit such enrolment as opposed to providing home bound services (*Tatro v. Board of Education*, 1984); and (3) maintained the principle of 'zero reject' over a school's objection that the child could not profit from any special education program (*Timmothy W. v. Board of Education*, 1988).

Cases involving disputes as to what constitutes the LRE for a given child have not provided a consistent pattern of decisions. Each seems to depend on a number of factors, including the judges' previous experience and bias regarding children with disabilities, the quality of the expert witnesses on both sides, and the extent to which the schools can demonstrate that they have applied state-of-the-art special education technology in the education of this specific child (see Rothstein, 1990; Turnbull, 1990).

Special Problems in US Schools

Problems in Integration of Students with Disabilities

While it would be nice to think that a federal law with such specific requirements as those contained in PL 94-142 would provide a uniform basis for educating all children with disabilities in the most integrated setting, regardless of which of the fifty US states the child lived in, such a view fails to recognize the differences among states. First and foremost is financial ability to provide for the cost differential between regular and special education. In addition to such factors as family income, local assessed property valuation and other measures of wealth, the distribution of fiscal responsibility for the schools in general, and special education in specific, varies significantly between states. For example, the 1987 per pupil education revenues ranged from \$2160 in Alabama to \$7977 in Alaska, and even greater differences can be found between school districts within some states (National Center for Education Statistics, 1989: 187). Federal funds provided to school districts by PL 94-142 are based on a flat grant per pupil served, and thus do not contribute to fiscal equity among states or districts with high and low wealth available to support local education programs.

A portion of this variability can be traced directly to the cost differences to a local school district in providing very expensive special education programs and related services for profoundly disabled students (e.g., deaf-blind, or severely emotionally disturbed) or contracting with private, residential schools. Some states, using a portion of federal special education funds, provide for a large share of private school costs, thus making it less expensive (from local property tax funds) for the school district to place the child in a segregated, residential facility than to provide an appropriate program itself.

Next comes the state's history of growth and legislation concerning students with disabilities. For example, states like California and Illinois, which were experiencing large growth in public school enrolment in the 1950s and 1960s, found it necessary to pass special legislation enabling school districts and multidistrict special education administrative units to build special education facilities with state financial assistance. Too often these were constructed as segregated, special schools. Confronted with the need to conform with federal and state law regarding the LRE for students with disabilities, financial considerations weigh heavily when placement decisions are made. Hence in those states with relatively new special schools, a larger proportion of the population of students with disabilities is placed in such segregated facilities than in states with a different history. In its 1989 report to Congress on the implementation of PL 94-142, the US Department of Education noted that Delaware places twenty times as great a proportion of its handicapped children in separate schools and residential facilities as does Alaska: 13,000 per million compared with 600 per million (US Department of Education, 1989: 26).

There is also a debate between professional special educators who argue that no child should be educated anywhere except in his or her own neighbourhood school and those who believe that special schools are necessary to provide an appropriate education for students with severe, multiple handicapping conditions (Lipsky and Gartner, 1989; Biklen, Ferguson and Ford, 1989). Some parents have also taken up the cry of 'integration at all costs', believing that the social benefits of physical integration of their child into a regular elementary or secondary program will outweigh the advantages of a special program to provide specific self-help and other training available in a special class or school. Many times, where the dispute cannot be settled at the school level, the courts have been asked to determine whether the child's right to an appropriate education can be abrogated by the parents' insistence that the child be enrolled in a regular classroom.

Parental Demands

Given the power that parents acquired under PL 94-142, it is not surprising that problems in determining the appropriate placement in the LRE have arisen. Three major types are evident. First, some parents of severely, multiply handicapped children insist that the only acceptable educational placement would be a special class in the age-appropriate neighbourhood school. This position has been bolstered by the parent-professional advocacy group, The Association for Persons with Severe Handicaps (TASH), which has championed this concept in publications and meeting agendas. For example, at its sixteenth annual conference, two days of the program were reserved for 'Full Integration Is Possible', and the theme for the December 1990 conference was 'Action for Inclusion'.

Directly opposite are parents who insist that their child be educated in a residential school, even when the local schools have what they believe to be an appropriate program to serve that child. Two major groups seem to be involved: parents of adolescents with severe emotional problems who no longer desire to have the child in their home; and parents of children with severe to profound hearing loss, who themselves have a significant hearing impairment and have never been able to acquire oral or aural communication skills. The latter group presents an interesting argument for segregated (many times residential) schools as being the *only* appropriate placement for their child; that the culture of the deaf is so different from that found in regular schools (and after-school community activities); that children who must communicate with sign language need a school setting in which teachers, administrators and students *all* sign rather than use oral means of communications.

The third group of parents are challenging the validity of special day schools on the basis that such segregation prevents their children from physical and social integration with non-disabled peers. While the courts have been reluctant to overrule educational placement decisions of school administrators, in several cases where excessive costs were not involved a 'transportability' principle was applied. Unless the schools could convincingly demonstrate that there were essential elements of the child's program at the special school which could not be provided in a special class located in a regular elementary or secondary school (i.e., that the program was *not* transportable), some courts have ruled that the least restrictive environment would be that special class, and not the special school.

Differences between and within States

If one remembers that there are some 15,000 local school districts in the fifty states, it is not surprising that differences in delivery of special education services would be present. The first and most obvious difference comes from statistical data obtained from the 1 December child count (on which PL 94-142 funds are based) per state. When these figures are converted to the proportion of public school children being served in special education in each state, considerable differences are evident. For the 6 to 17-year-old age range, Hawaii serves only about 6 per cent of its population in special education programs, while Massachusetts has 14 per cent (US Department of Education, 1989: 7). Further, an examination of enrolment by categories of handicapping condition shows even greater discrepancies between states, with Alaska identifying and serving 0.33 per cent as mentally retarded, while Alabama serves 3.32 per cent. For learning disabilities the range is from 2.11 per cent in Georgia to 7.7 per cent in Rhode Island, and for children with speech impairments only 0.83 per cent in New York, while neighbouring New Jersey serves 4.08 per cent (US Department of Education, 1989: 18).

At least some of the variance can be attributed to the administrative organization required in rural areas. In most states, small districts are required to become members of an intermediate educational unit (IEU) organized to provide comprehensive special education and other services which they could not provide independently. Many times these IEUs are larger (both in enrolment and budget) than any of the school districts they serve. Too often, such size has encouraged the local districts to place complete responsibility on the IEU for the education of students with disabilities, with the result that special education programs become isolated from regular elementary and secondary schools. Sparsity factors complicate the problem in that even when special class programs are placed in regular buildings, bus schedules may dictate different starting and ending times for the special class students, thus preventing much social integration and sometimes even placement in an appropriate regular class when it meets early or late in the school day.

A parallel problem is found when parents elect to have their children educated in local private or parochial day schools. Through dual enrolment in the public school system for special educational services, a student with a disability can receive special education and related services from the public schools while attending the private or parochial schools for the academic subjects. The federal constitutional requirement for separation of church and state in the United States prevents the delivery of any public school program or service in the parochial school, hence the student must be transported between the two systems to take advantage of both. Except for the very wealthy private schools, the cost of special educational services is prohibitive and few offer any, especially since the public schools are mandated to provide them.

Summary and Conclusions

Counterbalancing Forces

The title of this chapter asks, 'What Is This LRE in the United States?', but the answer depends on where you are, and who you ask the question of. The 1980s saw a deluge of national reports critical of public education, the most prominent entitled *A Nation at Risk* (National Commission on Excellence in Education, 1983). In response came educational reform movements and cries for back-to-basics, both designed to improve the academic performance of our public school students in comparison to those in other industrial countries (Cuban, 1990). For example, the state legislature in Illinois passed an educational reform package in 1985 which contained some 169 initiatives. Unfortunately, the so-called reforms resulted in little fundamental change (Sevener, 1991). One which could have had important preventative effect on special education, pre-school opportunities for educationally disadvantaged youngsters, was never fully funded, so that less than one-third of the children who need it are receiving it in 1991 (Illinois State Board of Education, 1991). Similar movements were evident in the other forty-nine states.

The implications of all the national educational reports and their impact on students with disabilities was the subject of the January 1987 issue of *Exceptional Children.* In that issue an article by Lorrie Shepard entitled 'The New Push for Excellence: Widening the Schism between Regular and Special Education' (1987:

327–329) pinpoints the dilemma facing the educational system. On the one hand, teachers and administrators are being held accountable for ever greater academic achievement scores, while on the other, they are being asked to accept more and more students with mild academic and behavioural differences back into the regular class. In short, the emphasis on excellence and higher standards seems to run counter to the needs of students with low academic achievement.

To bolster his self-image as the 'education president', President Bush convened the nation's first educational summit of all the state's governors. This in turn led to the establishment of six national goals for education — none of which directly relates to the education of students with disabilities. Goals 4 and 5 pinpoint the essential aim of moving ahead of other industrial countries in critical areas of achievement:

Goal 4. By the year 2000, US students will be first in the world in mathematics and science achievement.

Goal 5. By the year 2000, every adult American will be literate and will possess the skills necessary to compete in a global economy and to exercise the rights and responsibilities of citizenship. (National Governors' Association, 1990)

In her analysis of the national education reports and special education, Sapon-Shevin (1987) raises the interesting possibility: 'A disquieting suspicion arising from this analysis is that special education was not addressed in the national reports primarily because special education students are not considered worthy or needy of educational attention' (p. 205). She suggests that '... equity and excellence may, in fact, be incompatible given *current political realities*, and that the nation's shift, as reflected in the national reports, is *away* from equity and towards elitism' (p. 205; emphasis in original).

Central administrative organization also came under fire, and building-based management became the catchword of the day. Concurrently, the research literature on effective schools grew, reinforcing the importance of instructional leadership by the principal. All of these changes have an impact on the delivery of special educational services to students with disabilities: some in a positive, others in a negative direction. As parents become more sophisticated in their role as equal partners in the educational decision-making for their child with a disability, principals will need extensive in-service training as an ever greater proportion of such students will be integrated into regular elementary or secondary school programs. The attitude of the principal toward students with disabilities determines in no small part the quality of the school's social and academic integration of these students, yet few principals have had even an introductory course on exceptional children, much less one providing specific guidance on compliance with the radical concepts contained in the state and federal special education legislation described above (National Council on Disability, 1989).

Future Trends

The recent passage of the Americans with Disabilities Act by the US Congress (PL 101-476) extends the civil rights mandate of Section 504 to the private sector, providing access for individuals with disabilities in public transportation, communications and private businesses. A side-effect of this legislation should make community-based educational programs for severely disabled students more feasible, thus furthering their integration into the mainstream of society.

In a similar fashion, Congress recently modified the language in PL 94-142 by passage of PL 101-336, the Individuals with Disabilities Education Act (IDEA). This change in terminology from 'handicapped' to 'disabilities' embodies the concept that advocates have long sought: that while the disability resides in the individual, any handicap must be seen as society's interaction with such an individual in terms of architectural and attitudinal barriers. Also included in this act was an extension of transition services for students leaving school, and a re-affirmation of the need for greater early identification and provision of services for children with disabilities or at risk of requiring special education services when they reach school age.

Despite the wide variance found in implementation of the LRE concept by the 15,000 public schools in the United States, it is safe to predict that the schools will continue on the path of greater inclusion of individuals with disabilities in regular elementary and secondary school programs. Whether this will mean the end of special education, as some have predicted (Lipsky and Gartner, 1989), remains to be seen. There can be little doubt that change will be the order of the day.

References

AUSTRALIAN CONSTITUTIONAL COMMISSION (1988) *Australia's Constitution: Time to Update*, Canberra, Australian Government Publishing Service.

BIKLEN, D., FERGUSON, D. and FORD, A. (Eds) (1989) *Schooling and Disability*, NSSE Yearbook Series, Chicago, Ill., University of Chicago Press.

BROWN V. BOARD OF EDUCATION OF TOPEKA (347 US 483, 1954).

CODE OF FEDERAL REGULATIONS (CFR) 34 CFR 300ff.

CRONIN, JOSEPH (1976) 'The Federal Takeover: Should the Junior Partner Run the Firm?' *Phi Delta Kappan*, 57, 8, pp. 449–501.

CRUICKSHANK, W.M., PAUL, J.L. and JUNKALA, J.B. (1969) *Misfits in the Public Schools*, Syracuse, N.Y., Syracuse University Press.

CUBAN, L. (1990) 'Reforming Again, Again, and Again', *Educational Researcher*, 19, 1, pp. 3–13.

DUNN, L.M. (1968) 'Special Education for the Mildly Retarded: Is Much of It Justifiable?' *Exceptional Children*, 38, 1, pp. 5–22.

ILLINOIS STATE BOARD OF EDUCATION (1991) *State, Local and Federal Financing for Illinois Public Schools*, Springfield, Ill., the Board, 180 pp.

LIPSKY, D.K. and GARTNER, A.E. (Eds) (1989) *Beyond Separate Education: Quality Education for All*, Baltimore, Md., Paul H. Brookes.

MILLS V. BOARD of EDUCATION (348 F. Supp. 866, 1972).

NATIONAL CENTER FOR EDUCATION STATISTICS (1989) *1988 Education Indicators*, Washington, D.C., US Department of Education.

NATIONAL COMMISSION ON EXCELLENCE IN EDUCATION (1983) *A Nation at Risk: The Imperative for Educational Reform*, Washington, D.C., US Department of Education.

NATIONAL COUNCIL ON DISABILITY (1989) *The Education of Students with Disabilities: Where Do We Stand?* A report to the President and the Congress of the United States, Washington, D.C., the Council, September.

NATIONAL GOVERNORS' ASSOCIATION (1990) *Educating America: State Strategies for Achieving the National Education Goals: Report of the Task Force on Education, 1990*, Washington, D.C., the Association.

PENNSYLVANIA ASSOCIATION FOR RETARDED CHILDREN (PARC) V. COMMONWEALTH OF PENNSYLVANIA (343 F. Supp. 279, 1972).

PUBLIC LAW 85-926 (1959) The Leadership Personnel for the Education of Mentally Retarded Students Act.

PUBLIC LAW 93-112 (1973) The Rehabilitation Act of 1973.

PUBLIC LAW 94-142 (1975) The Education of All Handicapped Children Act.

PUBLIC LAW 101-336 (1990) The Americans with Disabilities Act.

PUBLIC LAW 101-457 (1990) The Individuals with Disabilities Education Act.

REYNOLDS, M.C. (1956) 'A Framework for Considering Some Issues in Special Education', *Exceptional Children*, 28, 7, pp. 367–370.

ROTHSTEIN, LAURA F. (1990) *Special Education Law*, New York, Longman.

ROWLEY V. BOARD OF EDUCATION (458 US 176, 1982).

SAPON-SHEVIN, M. (1987) 'The National Education Reports and Special Education: Implications for Students', *Exceptional Children*, 53, 4, pp. 300–307.

SEVENER, D. (1991) 'Revisiting the 1985 Education Reforms: Is the "Old School Bus" Running Better?' *Illinois Issues*, 17, 5, pp. 14–16.

SHEPARD, L.A. (1987) 'The New Push for, Excellence: Widening the Schism between Regular and Special Education', *Exceptional Children*, 53, 4, pp. 327–329.

TATRO (1984) BOARD OF EDUCATION V. TATRO (104 S.Ct 3371, 1984).

TIMMOTHY W. (1988) BOARD OF EDUCATION V. TIMMOTHY W. (EHLR 559:487, DSC 1988).

TURNBULL, H. RUTHERFORD III (1990) *Free Appropriate Public Education: The Law and Children with Disabilities*, 3rd ed., Denver, Colo., Love.

US DEPARTMENT OF EDUCATION (1989) *Eleventh Annual Report to Congress on the Implementation of Public Law 94-142: The Education for All Handicapped Children Act*, Washington, D.C., US Government Printing Office.

Part 3

Politics and Pedagogy:
Inclusive or Exclusive Schools?

Chapter 8

Implementing Policy:
Some Struggles and Triumphs

Bob Semmens

This chapter provides a series of personal observations and experiences which demonstrate that people do not change just because they are expected to change. Ideology, territory and tradition all play a part in the story of implementing the integration policy in Victoria. It has not been a simple process. Fulcher (1989) clarifies why this might be so when she disputes the traditional top-down model of policy made by government and implemented by its bureaucracies. Instead she proposes that policy is made at all levels — school councils, teacher unions, regional committees and in the classroom. Integration of students with disabilities provides evidence of the Fulcher proposal because, while there is a well publicized statement of government policy, what has followed in various arenas looks more like a series of power struggles and policy reformulations than policy implementation. The Fulcher proposal makes sense of the fact that, contrary to government policy but under the banner of integration, some schools are identifying 'integration students' (often called 'integrands') and singling them out for special tuition outside the regular classroom. So the integration (inclusive curriculum) versus special education (disability programs) struggle was not won through top-down imposition of a reforming policy on a willing bureaucracy and receptive practitioners. The battle has to be re-won at all levels. Enthusiastic supporters of the rights of disabled students have to do much more than wave around a copy of a policy document, for even though the integration policy was developed through a year of tough battles among the major players, other representatives of the major players in other arenas do not always act in accordance with agreements previously reached.

The Fulcher proposal helps to clarify the source of many frustrations in the 'implementation' phase. In reality the integration policy has provided a focus for engaging in debate in various arenas. It has not been a mandate for reform. This chapter presents and analyzes some of the struggles in the various arenas in which I have been involved over the past six years. I begin with the report itself because its limitations have enabled opponents to advance their segregative practices. This is not to argue that a perfectly consistent report would have stopped them from struggling. They had too much to lose as illustrated in the various struggles cited here (see also Chapter 1, this volume).

Limitations of the 1984 Report

The Victorian Government's integration policy is contained in its 1984 Report of the Ministerial Review of Educational Services for the Disabled, *Integration in Victorian Schools*. In summary, the policy states that the aim of integration is to increase and maintain the participation of children with disabilities in regular schooling wherever that is the wish of the parents, because:

1 every child has a right to be educated in a regular school;
2 categorization is personally and educationally unhelpful;
3 school-based resources and services are more conducive to education than specialist arrangements;
4 collaborative decision-making (rather than expert direction) enables all participants to share in decisions and own outcomes; and
5 all children can learn and be taught.

The report encourages schools to change from a focus on identified disabilities of particular students to a focus on how schools organize relationships between teachers and students, principal and teachers, parents and teachers, the school and its council, the school and regional administration and so on. It is argued that such a focus develops a collective responsibility for all children regardless of their ability or disability. Consistent with this system focus, the report recommends: no further expansion of special education facilities; transfer of resources to regular schools wherever possible; and coordination of various sources of funding.

In recognition of the complexities of ongoing policy development and to provide impetus for implementation strategies, a coordination unit was established — the Integration Unit. However, only the director's position was openly advertised, and later, after strong protests, the parent representative's position. The result was that almost the entire staff of the Integration Unit were professionals who had been involved in the former clinical mode of service provision. This may have been an advantage for implementation if positions had been filled by people who were clearly knowledgeable *about* the system, but not *of* the old system.

Perhaps the task of the Integration Unit was impossible anyway because the integration report proposed a new category of specialist (Integration Teacher) and a new category of student (Integration Student). Unfortunately, the prevailing specialist tradition embraced these new categories, and integration implementation at the school level came to be seen largely in terms of add-on resources more than inclusive curriculum. Teacher union pressure built up to such an extent that the Director-General of Education decided to defuse the issue by declaring that while every student had a right to be enrolled at the school of his/her choice, delayed admission (Collins, 1987) was permissible in the case of students with disabilities where a school felt it was unable adequately to resource integration. Thus integration in Victoria, despite its rights-based policy, became little different from the policy of gradualism practised in most other parts of the Western world. Such policies admit students with disabilities to a mainstream school where that mainstream school is ready, able and willing. The 'cascade' model is the ultimate example of this drip therapy approach to integration in that there is a scale of complete institutionalization through to complete regular school participation with maybe ten incremental steps between, and 'appropriate' specialist assessment at each stage.

This resourcing struggle might not have become so intense if the integration report had emphasized inclusive curriculum and linked its recommendations to the ministerial paper on curriculum, known as Ministerial Paper Six (1984). Somehow the integration of students with disabilities came to be seen as a separate issue, an optional issue, for mainstream schools. To assist in raising the profile of integration and to unravel issues and tensions surrounding implementation of the integration report, the Minister established a reference group in 1986. The Integration Reference Group consisted of representatives of parents of students with disabilities, a disabled student, teacher unions, principals, non-government schools, teacher educators and the Integration Unit. Such a committee of advice was recommended in the integration report but the delay in its establishment meant that its role was more reactive than proactive. Nevertheless, it achieved some triumphs from its struggles. For example, it was able to influence the way in which mainstream curriculum documents were written. It also questioned some prevailing special education practices. These struggles were fascinating to me as an academic, although I had been prepared for membership of the Ministerial Reference Group through my efforts to establish a Graduate Diploma in Special Education consistent with the principles of the integration report.

Developing a New Graduate Diploma in Special Education

Two years after the release of the integration report the Graduate Diploma in Special Education was due for review and reaccreditation in the institution where I teach. This one-year postgraduate course had existed for many years and was the only accepted way of gaining registration for teaching in special schools. The wisdom afforded by hindsight suggests that this course was not the way to bring about a curriculum orientation consistent with the thrust of the integration report. Old traditions and beliefs die hard.

These old traditions contained vestiges of the test and treat era, Piaget's stages of cognitive development, child care and welfare, and 'what works' pragmatism. The common thread had something to do with a belief in the power of one-to-one teaching to overcome educational and social deficits. Criteria for retaining aspects of the old course seemed to be in terms of whether available staff liked teaching the material and/or whether it was felt that the students liked it or needed it.

On the other hand, development of an approach consistent with the integration report had its own difficulties because the report contained no statement of education theory. Opponents seized on this as evidence that 'integration is a passing fashion', and that, as academics, 'we are not bound to implement government policy'. Eventually the argument that human rights may be of interest to academics, even though it happens to be government policy, and the fact that the government employs most of our students, led to a compromise. The new course emerged with a core program and electives. The core reflected the tensions between the traditional deficit oriented special education and some aspects of an inclusive curriculum orientation. The electives contained the same mixture, although each was either 'deficit' or curriculum oriented, mainly the former.

Allied to the struggles around redevelopment of the Graduate Diploma in Special Education was the conflict over whether the staff of the Special Education Department should be integrated into other departments of the Education Faculty. Curriculum appeared a likely destination for some, while others may have been more comfortable in educational psychology. The 'traditionalists' felt especially intense on this issue because all they had ever studied, practised and stood for was threatened. They could see their entire careers devalued. Ultimately, the 'reformers' compromised and proposed that the Department be renamed Integration Studies with the situation to be reviewed in two years. The 'reformers' had the numbers and carried the day. In an interesting turn around at a subsequent election for the course committee, the traditionalists got the numbers and thereby gained control of the course. Two years later there is neither an Integration Studies Department nor a controlling course committee. These features in the life of special education at the old Teachers' College were removed in a restructure following amalgamation with the Education Faculty at the neighbouring Melbourne University.

The Graduate Diploma in Special Education survived the amalgamation and, following a further review in 1989 when three strands emerged, it is still largely oriented around the interests of the participating staff. There is an integration strand, a moderately/severely disabled strand and an early childhood strand. This time around I took no active part in the struggle, directing my energy to negotiations with the Ministry of Education to offer a school-based mode of whatever the outcome of this struggle was, because it now seems to me that curriculum development for inclusion of all students has to be negotiated within each school. Shortly, this position will be tested through the development of a partnership for professional development between the university and the Ministry of Education. This could be a triumph after four years of on-again off-again negotiations. The next stage is working in schools, where, as the later section on working as an integration teacher suggests, the integration-segregation debate is far from over.

A related course development issue was my attempt to develop a one-year course for integration aides. This would have gained credits towards a teacher training qualification if participants had wanted to take that option. The idea was to create a potential career path. However, there was some resistance from parents of students with disabilities and from ministerial personnel who felt that access to a credential would professionalize a task that should essentially provide a part-time opportunity for local parents to be involved in a paid capacity for assisting in school programs. This issue is now ripe for renegotiation as many integration aides feel exploited by their workloads and very low wage levels. Access to credentials may be a more acceptable way out than finding another job outside the education system for this group of dedicated people.

In addition to these course development struggles and prior to my experience as an integration teacher, there was a period in which I participated in other arenas at a different level of policy development implementation — through the work of the Ministerial Reference Group on Integration, referred to earlier and detailed below.

Membership of the Ministerial Reference Group

From my perspective one of the triumphs associated with membership of this group was the acceptance of a paper that I wrote entitled 'Including All Students in Mainstream Schools', later published in Roger Slee's book, *Discipline and Schools: A Curriculum Perspective* (1988a). The paper provided an educational rationale for integration and became the basis for a special project which set out to discover and publicize exemplary integration practice. The project was called Learning Initiatives to Include All Students in Regular Schools (see Chapter 12, this volume). The Minister provided some funds for a project officer, and members of the project committee visited many schools to collect data on programs which had been identified by regional managers as outstanding examples of integration practice. The committee felt that some regional managers may define integration in ways that are inconsistent with the Minister's definition, but there were a few excellent schools, and some of their inclusive practices predated the integration report. As one principal said:

> We didn't need the Integration Report to tell us how to include all students. I try not to use their resources because they are delivered in such a way as to identify particular students as different. We expect all students to participate and learn. (Slee, 1988b)

At another school an integration aide declared that her aim was to make herself redundant. Such comments were rare among the general clamour for more and more resources to do the integration task well. It appeared to the committee that many schools were trying to integrate using the traditional special education model of withdrawal and remediation programs — and this approach did not accord with the committee's conception of doing the integration task well. When the learning initiatives report was complete, the Ministerial Reference Group felt that it was too large to release in its present form and few people would read its explanation of education theory and its comparative data. A shorter, simpler version was requested, entitled *Successful Schooling* (Fulcher, Semmens and Slee, 1989).

Another very positive outcome of the work of the Learning Initiatives Project committee is that the members have continued to meet and now form the nucleus of a discussion group which meets monthly to review developments in education, review each other's work, and provide professional support for initiatives which members may be planning.

In addition to the Learning Initiatives Project, the Ministerial Reference Group set up a number of task forces, one of which was on teacher training for integration. After my struggles in attempting to reform the Graduate Diploma in Special Education, it seemed that I had the necessary experience to chair such a task force, and the struggles were re-enacted there. The following account provides detail of the experiences of the task force.

The Task Force on Teacher Training for Integration

The Task Force on Teacher Training for Integration was a widely representative group consisting of parents, teacher unions, principals, academics, non-government schools, professional development and other ministry personnel. The major tension throughout the life of the task force was between those who focused on disability issues as the basis for training teachers for integration and those who wanted the major emphasis on inclusive teaching strategies. After a few months of unproductive debate a small subgroup prepared some materials on inclusive teaching strategies, together with examples and reference lists. The material was clearly presented and persuasive, and was adopted as the major part of the task force report.

The report recommended that the prepared chapters on mixed ability classes, cooperative learning strategies, school organization and classroom management become the basis for professional development for integration and that teacher training institutions be requested to include study and practice in those areas. Further, the report recommended that study leave for training in special education/ integration be granted only for tertiary courses which demonstrated a preference for inclusive curriculum theory and practice. This latter recommendation has not yet been implemented one year after submission of the report, although some progress has been made towards changing selection procedures for study leave. Professional development courses have been established within clusters of schools, and these focus on inclusive curriculum strategies.

Participation in this task force was one of the more notable triumphs of all the arenas in which implementation of integration policy had been attempted. Initially, the going was hard, and it seemed at times that policy which was already five years old was being hammered out anew, but the difference in this arena was the presentation of a well documented case for inclusive curriculum strategies. Thus the data became the focus for debate, and task force members were less able to argue from entrenched personal positions. Perhaps in this particular arena it was also easier for task force members to loosen their grip on entrenched positions because their main task was to make recommendations that would have an impact on teacher training and professional development personnel more than resources or career paths of task force members. Such an interpretation of the work of the task force is not entirely accurate because it fails to acknowledge that it is a very competent piece of work and it has led directly to the Ministry of Education establishing an extended series of in-service programs for clusters of schools in various parts of the state. It also led me to follow through on the issue of whether work in various arenas for integration was having an impact on teaching practice, and I decided to find out through direct experience. After all, many of my special education students had commented that the rhetoric sounded fine, even idealistic, but would not work in practice. The following account of the triumphs and struggles in a secondary school indicates that integration policy and practice have to be rewritten at the school level. Schools are simply not the end of the implementation line. Policy is also developed in schools.

Working as an Integration Teacher

Due to the generosity of the principal of 'Inner City' Secondary College, the integration teacher, and my employer, the Institute of Education at Melbourne University, I was able to negotiate an exchange of duties with the 'Inner City' integration teacher. This enabled me to gain firsthand experience of the integration teacher role and attempt to evaluate why integration appeared so difficult in schools. Part of the problem can be explained by the large number of struggles going on in other arenas at other levels of the Education Ministry. The other part of the problem is that the same struggles are being re-enacted in the schools. Policy formulation is occurring at the same time as implementation. Policy stated six years ago in the integration report has not been read or understood by many teachers. It has to be redeveloped in the context of each school.

'Inner City' Secondary College is no exception, although it shares a characteristic common to many schools in lower socio-economic areas which was not accounted for in the original integration report (1984). This characteristic is that almost the entire school population is alienated from schooling. Integration of students with disabilities into a school environment which has a very limited sense of community or belonging is like grasping in the dark and hoping for the best.

This situation made it necessary to negotiate integration in terms of a whole school curriculum, which, although a huge task, has advantages over the limited perception of many schools that integration is an add-on remedial program more the province of welfare than of curriculum. It was important to develop a strong public alliance between integration staff and the curriculum coordinator to establish integration as a curriculum issue and to bring it into the mainstream of school decision-making processes.

Early in the year staff agreed to establish school goals, and the direction of the goals was to include all students. While there were times when some staff were prepared to sacrifice principle for peace and move in the direction of excluding troublesome students, the general commitment to inclusive curriculum was maintained.

Another strategy which helped to maintain staff vision was the process of identification of indicators of successful comprehensive schooling which reflected the school goals. These indicators were adapted from the work of Ramsay *et al.* (1983), and daily observations of the school at work were recorded and evaluated in the light of the indicators at the end of the year. The role of participant observer, more than external observer or committee member, provided an opportunity for action and interaction in integration policy development and implementation in the college. It also demonstrated that the struggle to implement change is continuous. 'Winning' a debate, circulating a 'good' paper, starting a new project, or gaining the support of some colleagues are not signs that the end is in sight. The next day brings new challenges and possibly reversals. The intensity of these engagements is not felt, for example, through membership of a task force where completion of the report is at least the end of a stage, which is followed by a period of waiting and hoping for recommendations to be accepted and implemented. Nevertheless, the following observations from evaluation of 'Inner City' Secondary College suggest that substantial progress was made in the course of a year towards an appreciation of successful comprehensive schooling and definition of the future direction of the college.

Having agreed upon a set of school goals at a two-day in-service early in the year, the staff delegated to the curriculum committee the task of proposing how the goals might be achieved. The following is a summary of the curriculum committee's response.

Aim 1   Success for all students — achieved through aims 2–8.

Aim 2   Relevant curriculum — achieved through:
  a)   understanding ministerial policy and curriculum documents;
  b)   dialogue with Ministry re appropriate curriculum delivery for 'Inner City' students;
  c)   requiring adequate resources and facilities for teaching and learning at 'Inner City' Secondary College.

Aim 3   Balanced curriculum — achieved through:
  a)   involvement of parents and students in planning, implementation and review of curriculum;
  b)   inclusion of all students in all aspects of school life.

Aim 4   Environment for active membership of the college community — achieved through:
  a)   pastoral (planning) groups;
  b)   student association;
  c)   student-led activities;
  d)   lunchtime activities;
  e)   negotiation skills in classroom activities.

Aim 5   Environment which values people — achieved through:
  a)   code of behaviour;
  b)   integration program;
  c)   welfare program;
  d)   English as a second language program;
  e)   accessibility of resource centre to all staff and students.

Aim 6   School ethos — achieved through:
  a)   aims 2, 3, 4, 5;
  b)   emphasizing the unique characteristics of the college and its community;
  c)   developing after-school programs and activities with the local community.

Aim 7   Multicultural appreciation — achieved through:
  a)   teacher interest in different cultures/languages/values of the college community;
  b)   supporting multicultural activities in the local community;
  c)   inclusion of multicultural components in college curriculum.

Aim 8   Participatory college governance — achieved through:
  involvement of students, parents and local community in all of the above.

Action for achievement of college goals was spelt out more precisely in the development of a three-year plan later in the year. The plan specifies short-term and longer-term goal achievement (see Appendix 1). It began with a mission statement and concluded with a timetable for college improvement. In summary, the mission statement set out the importance of having a sense of direction and purpose to deal with Education Ministry constraints and the need for local community support at the same time as the college maintained its commitment to a high quality curriculum for all students. The three-year plan committed the college to remaining a comprehensive school for years 7–12, and to strengthen links with other schools, tertiary education institutions and local industry. Consequently, students would see that the college's emphases on technology studies, computer education, hospitality, tourism and business studies are connected to real labour market and further study options. The mission statement goes on to assert that:

> this (vocational) area of excellence is not the college's total educational provision because skill development and career preparation will be taught in the context of the cultural understandings (democratic decision-making, multiculturalism, the arts, and recreation programs) required of a comprehensive curriculum in an inclusive environment. The total years 7–12 curriculum will aim to keep all students eligible for as long as possible for all available options. Assistance in these developments will be expected of the Education Ministry's consultants and arrangements are also being made for exchanges of teachers with local industry personnel for three to six month periods.
>
> Staff development within the college will focus on implementation of college goals and part of this process will involve establishing indicators for successful achievement of goals. For this purpose task groups will be established with terms of reference, timelines and suggested outcome indicators.

Observation of the college at work suggests that the existence of the mission statement brought some life into the college goals — moving from a fairly standard list of goals towards acceptance of their meaning in terms of a dynamic direction for the college. The three-year plan has helped to clarify that direction. The leadership and support of the principal is another major factor in modelling democratic decision-making processes through involving all parties affected by an issue in its resolution. For example, assessment of student progress involves the student, all teachers concerned and the parents. The focus of assessment is on what has been achieved by the student, how she/he has gone about her/his learning and how discussion of this process can assist the student with further learning. As these and other processes become more firmly established in the College, confidence in negotiation will increase, and it is hoped that action-learning projects will take place outside the meagre college site and engage the generally middle-class residents who have moved into the area over recent years but who have so far avoided, ignored or denigrated the college.

The optimism generated by the development of goals and tasks was good to experience. Engaging with the local community and local industry is important for the viability of an educational institution. Yet in the case of 'Inner City' College these developments are almost entirely teacher-driven. At times when teachers are worn down by the large numbers of resistant students, optimism and professionalism are hard to maintain. In some ways it is easier for the integration teacher, for example, to take on the Regional Director for requiring that a student's disability be labelled (July 1989 Memorandum) in any application for additional education resources than it is to do battle with colleagues who are engaged in the same optimistic struggle for the college, but who persist with devising schemes for withdrawal programs for students with disabilities. While confronting the Regional Director runs the risk of eroding external support which is essential for the survival of the college, struggling with a minority of hostile colleagues is personally debilitating.

Such a situation appears to have developed in 1990. When the Curriculum

Coordinator moved to other areas of responsibility in the college, the precarious nature of the developments during the preceding twelve months became obvious. Staff who had appeared to support the stated goals and tasks began to waiver and lose direction, and students who had become more interested in schooling started to get out of control again. Disoriented staff tended to blame students and look for punitive ways to deal with the situation. There is now a desperate need for staff to regroup, steady up and recommit themselves to achieving the college goals. The tension is reflected in a memorandum about a professional development plan from the integration teacher to the college principal:

MEMORANDUM ON PROFESSIONAL DEVELOPMENT PROPOSALS: THEIR IMPLICATIONS FOR COLLEGE POLICY

Another member of staff gave me a copy of the Professional Development submission 'Curriculum Enhancement via Computers'.

a) Should not this submission have been tabled at Curriculum Committee and Staff Forum? Today was the first time that I have seen it!
b) The proposal is against our current school policy on Integration and, I believe, against the school goals we adopted at the in-service early in 1989.
c) The proposal is based on a deficit, remediation model and is exclusive rather than inclusive.
d) I am alarmed that five of our most senior people in the School would be prepared to put forward such a proposal. I think this shows that there is a school philosophy which contradicts the Integration Policy.
e) It is perfectly legitimate to have a philosophy based on the remediation model, but the school can't have another model based on the right of students *not* to be segregated. The two models are incompatible. Only one model can prevail in a school.
f) I think this sheds some light on the recent discussions at the Curriculum Committee. Obviously some people genuinely believe that the school should adopt the remediation model. The school will very rapidly have to make a decision which model we are going to pursue. Otherwise it will put all of us in an intolerable situation, where the Integrationists are trying to develop inclusive strategies, while the Remedialists are looking for solutions where students are taken out of classes for attention to their alleged deficits.
g) I think this also explains why the recommendations from the Support Group Workshop at the 1990 in-service were published inaccurately. No consensus was reached on 'providing individual and private tutoring where necessary'. In fact this proposal was vehemently opposed since it is not based on an inclusive approach using co-operative strategies in the classroom. Similarly there was no consensus on the proposal to 'avoid mixing ESL students with Integration Students'. Again this sifting and sorting of students is contrary to the inclusive philosophy of mixed-ability groups. It is also against

the School Integration Policy which does not countenance labelling or stigmatization.

h) I think we have a very serious problem with the two competing philosophies. The school has to make a decision about which philosophy is to prevail. The School Leaders need to make a strong stand in favour of one or the other of the philosophies. Otherwise the tensions apparent in having two contradictory philosophies will continue to exist.

i) It is far better for the school to whole-heartedly throw itself behind one or the other of the philosophies, rather than continuing on paying lip-service to both. We must make a decision and if people are uncomfortable with the outcome then they will have to look for a school that has a philosophy they can support.

Signed: Integration Teacher.

Now that the gauntlet has been thrown down, confrontation appears inevitable. Who knows whether the frustrated reformers will ever emerge triumphant. What appears more important is how the situation for students with disabilities can be salvaged. A major priority is to get all parties involved in something they all want to do, and there appears to be general support for continuation of the Professional Development Program. Introducing some carefully chosen facilitators into the situation may be very helpful and contribute to achieving the three-year plan in the area of professional development. There will be some spin-offs in terms of staff relationships and staff-student relationships through development of cooperative teaching strategies outlined in the three-year plan.

Second, the principal could assume the role of Curriculum Coordinator so that the most important area of college life is given the prominence it requires and is taken out of the politics of the staff room. The principal can delegate other, less pivotal duties in order to take on the role of Curriculum Coordinator.

Third, the college can gain support of other schools and the teacher unions in developing a case for a single social justice grant to schools so that various groups of disabled and disadvantaged students are not labelled by various designated funds. In exchange, schools would be required to demonstrate how they would go about including all students in the regular curriculum. While this proposal may set up some other struggles, schools like 'Inner City' Secondary College would be recognized for their sustained efforts to include all students. The fact that these efforts appear to be coming adrift at present should not be seen as due to inherent weaknesses in the school structure and curriculum. Rather, it has been due to the incredible pressures of working in isolation — almost unsupported by the Minister, alienated by the local community, and resisted by a large proportion of its students.

In the meantime selective secondary schools prosper even though their practices are contrary to Ministry policy. Clearly, the development of Ministry policy at the head office is only one level of policy development. When this is recognized, schools like 'Inner City' Secondary College will not be left alone to implement policy which has to be renegotiated in that arena in the 'goodwill' time of teachers who already have their time more than occupied in maintaining a safe environment in which to teach.

Bob Semmens

Conclusion

As Fulcher (1989) argues in *Disabling Policies*, the policy and implementation dichotomy is far too simplistic. The politics of opposing educational philosophies and self-interest have to be renegotiated in a variety of arenas at every level of the education bureaucracy. In the various struggles outlined in this chapter neither the appeal of the human rights movement, nor the exposition of education theory provides sufficient impetus to overcome individual concerns about possible changes in professional status and territory as a consequence of the implementation of the integration report (1984). Upon reflection over the last eight years since the report was released, it appears to me that while there have been many struggles and some minor triumphs, there has also developed a greater acceptance of students with disabilities moving into regular classrooms. Personal struggles and desires for personal triumphs in an advocacy role should not mask the real gains of the group for which one is advocating. Taken together, all of the individual struggles have contributed to some progress towards achieving the purpose of the integration report (1984), that is, to include all students in the regular classroom. This progress has been supported by other events such as the preceding International Year of the Disabled, mainstream curriculum developments and publicity for research on inclusive teaching styles. The most positive prospect for students with disabilities is that their struggle is now on the education agenda — at all levels.

References

COLLINS, M.K. (1987) *Delayed Admission to School of Parent's Choice*, General Manager's Memorandum to Regional Directors of Education.
FULCHER, G. (1989) *Disabling Policies?*, Lewes, Falmer Press.
FULCHER, G., SEMMENS, R. and SLEE, R. (1989) *Successful Schooling*, Unpublished report to the Minister of Education, Victoria.
MINISTERIAL PAPER SIX (1984) *Curriculum Development and Planning in Victoria*, Melbourne, Victorian Government Printing Office.
MINISTRY OF EDUCATION-VICTORIA (1984) *Integration in Victorian Schools: Report of the Ministerial Review of Educational Services for the Disabled*, Melbourne, Victorian Government Printer.
RAMSAY, P., SNEDDON, D., GRENFELL, J. and FORD, I. (1983) 'The Characteristics of Successful Schools', *SET*, 1, Melbourne, Australian Council for Educational Research.
SLEE, R. (Ed.) (1988a) *Discipline and Schools: A Curriculum Perspective*, Melbourne, Macmillan.
SLEE, R. (1988b) *Learning Initiatives to Include All Students in Regular School*, Unpublished report to the Portfolio Policy Coordination Division, Ministry of Education, Victoria.

Appendix 1. College Plan

Ministry Policy	School Goals	Current Means	Tasks for 1990	Tasks for 1991	Tasks for 1992
1. Excellence in education and training, specifically through: computer education, literacy and numeracy, language, review of (music) primary, environmental education, professional development.	1. A quality education, giving all students the opportunity to be successful.	Indirectly through pursuing all other means.	Professional development to focus on District: 1. provision of computer education, business studies, technology, hospitality and tourism, and general education at VCE level — *Start*: Dec. 1989 *Complete*: Dec. 1990 2. provision of literacy and numeracy programs consistent with inclusive teaching styles — *Start*: Feb. 1990 Ongoing.	Re-evaluate 7–10 curriculum in light of VCE, focus — *Start*: Dec. 1990 *Recommendations*: July 91	Action research evaluation to assess progress — *Indicators*: Broad subject range. Increased role of computer education. Literacy and numeracy through curriculum focus. Student and parent support for curriculum focus. Increase in tertiary and employment placement. Environmental relevance of curriculum focus.

Ministry Policy	School Goals	Current Means	Tasks for 1990	Tasks for 1991	Tasks for 1992
2. Expanding education and training opportunities, specifically through: Integration of students with disabilities. Science, maths, and technology for girls. Language action plan. Equal opportunity action plan for girls. School linked accommodation for homeless youth.	2. Curriculum relevance, responsive to changing technological, economic and environmental needs or society. 3. Provision of balanced curriculum for student development.	Understanding Ministerial policy and curriculum documents; dialogue with Ministry re appropriate curriculum for 'Inner-city' community; adequate resources.	Development links with local industries via schools — industry training initiatives — *Start:* Feb. 1990 *Recommendations:* Nov. 1990. Strengthen ties with RMIT, Moorabbin TAFE, and investigate ties with Footscray and Prahran TAFE — *Start:* Dec. 1989 *Recommendations:* Nov. 1990. Strengthen relations with school support centre — *Start:* Dec. 1989 *Recommendations:* Apr. 1990. Special focus on 6–7 transition and closer ties with local primary schools. *Start:* Dec. 1989	Staff/local industry exchange positions — *Start:* Feb. 1991. Close working relationships with other schools in Region, e.g. telematics for language learning — *Start:* Dec. 1990. Plan for retention of homeless youth in schooling.	Action research evaluation to assess progress — *Indicators:* Increased participation of students with disabilities. Increased participation of girls in science, maths, and technology. Increased access to language programs. Increased participation of girls in school activities. Articulation of courses, exits and re-entries. Increased retention rate 7–12.

Ministry Policy	School Goals	Current Means	Tasks for 1990	Tasks for 1991	Tasks for 1992
3. Strengthening community confidence in education and training, specifically through: Quality of assessment and reporting to parents. School Council and participation unit. Parent involvement in literacy and numeracy programs in schools. Promotion of community action on literacy.	4. Environment which fosters personal development.	Pastoral Groups, SRC, Student-led activities, Lunchtime activities.	Social justice project — achieving better outcomes — evaluate implications for current means — *Start*: Oct. 1989 *Recommendations*: Mar. 1990	Evaluate implementation of recommendations of social justice project as they relate to school organization and activities — *Start*: Feb. 1991 *Report*: July 1991	Action research evaluation to assess progress — *Indicators*: Parent satisfaction with assessment and reporting process. Increased student attendance in all subjects at all levels.
	5. Caring, supportive environment.	Code of behaviour, integration, welfare, ESL resource centre.	As above.	As above.	Proactive school council. Increased parent involvement in school organization and activities.
	6. Sense of belonging and ownership.	Nil specific.	As above.	As above.	Increased student involvement in school governance.
	7 Multicultural understanding.	Teacher interest in different cultures/ values, languages of school community.	As above.	Inclusion of multicultural components in 7–10 curriculum review — *Start*: Dec. 1990	Involvement of local industry in school. Increased career opportunities for 'Inner-city College' students in industry in local region.
	8 Involvement of parents, students, staff, and local community in school management.	Community liaison.	1. Local industry advisory committee as subcommittee of council. *Start*: Feb. 1990 *Establish*: Dec. 1990		

Ministry Policy	School Goals	Current Means	Tasks for 1990	Tasks for 1991	Tasks for 1992
			2. Review role of community liaison and careers staff — *Start*: Oct. 1989 *Recommendations*: Dec. 1990		
			3. Develop parent association — *Start*: Feb. 1990 *Establish*: Dec. 1990		
			4. Establish school-community management committee — include local council and MPs — *Start*: Feb. 1990 Interim committee: July 1990 Permanent: July 1991		

Chapter 9

Schools and Contests: A Reframing of the Effective Schools Debate?

Gillian Fulcher

> Although the effective schools formulation is intuitively compelling and important in calling attention to aspects of school practice, it remains theoretically and methodologically limited. (Reed, 1991: 153)

> ... social life is inadequately theorized or understood by (moral) reference to good and bad practice. (Fulcher, 1989b: 43)

The effective schooling debate uses terms or ideas which are inherently problematic for theorizing social life. Its central ideas expressed as themes include those of effective (schools), successful (schools), 'characteristics' and good management. A related idea — the debate's basic assumption or epistemology — is that social life is (merely) normative practice: let us speak with this principal, these teachers and that parent, ask these questions, deduce the characteristics of this school. . . .

What can I usefully say, in the morning that is sandwiched between other projects on seemingly disparate topics (one just complete, two others where there is much to articulate), where I lay no claim to having read the 'whole' of the effective schooling debate: though Rodney Reed summarizes with a North American accent (1991: 152–153)? I shall use the chapter first, to outline some of the misgivings which I, perhaps others also, took into the Victorian Ministry's project, Learning Initiatives to Include All Students in Regular Schools, which is described but not properly theorized in *Successful Schooling* (Fulcher, Semmens and Slee, unpublished, but lying somewhere in the Ministry shelves, with a printed cover, *Work in Progress Series* — shelves have their uses). To this project we took our concerns about integration, and in it we entered the effective schooling debate. I shall talk of some silences behind what is called policy formulation and analysis, and of ideas which mask these silences. Then I will discuss ideas about politics, arguing that it is this aspect of social life which needs inserting in concerns which underlie what is called the effective schools debate: those that appear to manage the pedagogic project of not excluding students where others might, or of 'doing better' with some students than other schools might. I shall not be conclusive for political-theoretical reasons which go beyond this chapter's limits.

Silences?

What do I recall of our visits to country schools in 1988? To a migrant, many years from Europe, an urban inhabitant like over 80 per cent of people in Australia, country Victoria both appeals and repels: the evening drive beside the small Goulburn River (I have yet to read *The Country and the City*) conveys a tranquillity which contrasts with a city where movement is difficult but where, as metropolis, there are currents which suggest a knowledge and experience more worldly than those in country towns. Meeting Tony, John, Roger next morning, I recall coffee, divisive but merry talk (French travels or local meanderings?) and two encounters in schools.

At Wubbleyou (I'm sure the name began with W, but rashly, I threw away my 'data' sheets), in a primary school built in the 1970s? (partition construction), in a spacious room, some large (by city standards) women were gathering — warm, cheerful, one or two with children, some from areas beyond this country town (with stories of how the special school bus would not pick up an 'integrated' child) — and a principal (or was it vice?), and the four Ministry representatives (for the day) from the Learning Initiatives to Include All Students project. These women showed, in their talk and gesture, their solidarity and their past victories: a paediatrician had said, 'Your child will never talk' — of whom her classmates, unknowingly, had said, 'When . . . can speak five words, we'll have a party.' And had. Which these women still celebrated in their talk. Was the room we met in in the primary school or the special developmental school? They were some ten metres apart. Did it matter, as one of the representatives said, that these children did not spend all their school day in the primary school classroom?

The afternoon saw us at a secondary school. In a formal room — the principal's office? — we met more formally: was there a parent advocate, an integration teacher, someone meant to be on the sole parent's side? The woman parent was mostly silent, concerned, answering when questioned. As the afternoon's classes ended and students passed the window, Tony remarked on the shining faces, neat hair — the look of the 1970s, no longer those of their city counterparts. Later we ambled on school paths, in yards, among beds of brilliant roses circled by brown hillsides and eucalypts of northern Victoria. The morning had brought encouragement and the afternoon despondency, briefly set aside by a garish beauty at odds with its surroundings.

Back in the metropolis, approaching 4 million inhabitants, our project resumed its place, took on again the ideas of governance — of management, of system change, of principles for policy, of consensus decisions (in committees) and of 'social justice'.[1] These official ideas were an important influence on our endeavours.

In the next few weeks, was it in the Inclusive Schools subcommittee, or in one of the other three the Ministerial Standing Committee had set up so that it could advise the Minister on Education for Pupils with Impairments and Disabilities (SCAEPID), that a woman colleague and I, unable to get our dissenting view put in the subcommittee report, wrote an extension note on the necessity for dissent, drawing *then* on Amy Gutmann's work on democratic educational practice?[2]

In the following year, in 1989, it was my task mainly to redraft our subcommittee's 'report' so that parents and teachers might read it. The Rialto building, then the highest of Melbourne's several skyscrapers, housed the Ministry policy and portfolio division on level 23: glass walled, it overlooked the flat horizon of the bay, its suburbs and docklands. I reported there on Tuesdays. Freed from other tasks, and some distance from written debate on 'policy' (though Rizvi *et al.*[3] were on nearby shelves along with the telephone directories), I edited and crafted our 'report', working the committee's 'findings' into Reynolds' list of factors. Four days a week in another job, and structurally marginal, reporting in this endeavour to the experienced woman head of the division (she, recently from the Commonwealth public service, soon to move to a Commonwealth position in another state), there was no space to import debate on political theory, to question official ideas. Nearby, some friendly colleagues responded to briefs from the Minister and wrote, redrafted papers for a third (?) version of Rules for Integration Groups — some five years on from the 1984 report, *Integration in Victorian Education*, a year-long process, much quicker yet more critical of the status quo than Warnock; the new scribes in this process, between other drafting tasks, submitted their drafts on more rules to the Minister.

These recollections tell a tale which differs from the pretences of much that passes for policy analysis, from academic policy talk. They set the scene for the difficult disciplines, both mental (what are the ideas we should work with as constructive critique but not as recipe?) and political (how can we wrest ourselves from the seduction and protection of the ideas and practices of governance)? There are careers to be made from uncritical splurgings, allies to be won in sharing the vocabulary of management, and loyalties retained by not critiquing the endeavours of government, by not departing from the politics of consensus — by limited critique. That students may not understand much of these uncritical writings, or dismiss them should they know better, is one consequence.

Clearing the Ground

No one who is literate, concerned about Victorian schools, not aligned with the right or the official face of the left,[4] ought to be able to ignore Stephen Ball's (1990) piece on 'Management as Moral Technology', nor Richard Bates' papers in the 1980s on the exclusion in educational administrative frames of a political analysis. Yet they do, and why? In aligning ourselves with management, there are careers to be made, alliances to be formed, and allegiances (with political parties[5]) to be maintained. It is also a discourse which captures (Ball, 1990; Fulcher, forthcoming): we may not know. We may have less time to get to know — since *governance* increasingly regulates its intellectuals — in the Hawke, now Keating government project to 'rationalize' higher education. This is not to say that under different conditions intellectuals can provide recipes.

Similarly, it ought not now, in Victoria in the 1990s, be possible to ignore the failure of the public face of rational policy (see, for example, Rizvi *et al.*, 1987; Fulcher, 1989a).[6] But it is, and why? For reasons just listed, and in part, because to move ourselves from that position is to face the bewildering complexity of doing things differently — of theorizing that doing differently, of facing more difficult choices.

Rational policy in Victoria proffers solutions, via principles. These are our normative guide to practice/implementation: no child is ineducable, every child

Gillian Fulcher

has a right.... (In 1984 these were brave ideals, uttered emotively in review meetings. In that arena, at that time, under those conditions, these brave ideals were a challenge.) Victorian education (and other) policy is framed, underpinned by the idea of principles. The liberal concern with principles (Rorty, 1991) pervades Australian federal and state policy documents and talk, and those of its reformers. Whereas in relatively conservative policy journals in Britain an author states: 'Government social policy is not now — and never has been — based on rational analysis or on any one coherent and consistent set of principles. For better or worse, discussions of what principles should determine social provision are not likely to be very productive' (Piachaud, 1991: 52). In Victoria, in 1984 as now, government integration policy was based on principles: those principles and setting up 'participatory [democratic] decision-making structures' which were to deploy them, were the nearest it got to.... Principles have a place, but next to that place is another space. Rational policy talk and documents deploy the idea of principles and ignore the adjacent space (more on this later). But these principles we took, silently (with misgivings?), to country schools.

It was through the idea of 'system' change that the Australian Labor Party — yes, and then its elected politicians — sought to articulate their political project: to shift it beyond the liberal concern with individuals. Yet the idea of system change is inherently problematic given the politics of social life. Policy is not 'system' (Fulcher, 1988b); integration policy cannot be evaluated by an ecological-systems model, nor by rich databases, nor by looking at the interdependence of elements of the system; nor are schools usefully seen as systems (Quicke, 1982).[7] The idea of system in social life is a retreat from politics. Is the paradigmatic case Talcott Parsons' social theory, more recently Luhmann's? Which in their political silences hide a conservative stance?

These ideas — of managerial frames, of system change, of consensus decisions (of restricting debate and excluding, heaven forbid, the idea of arguing over social policy) — allow ignoring others — the contests which constitute policy, which we know surround integration policy and which we knew, from the start of making official policy, at government level — the 1984 review. How else can we explain the enormous interest, the contentiousness which surrounded, entered and follows that review?

Publicly ignoring the idea of contests allows us to avoid confronting dilemmas, though Sally Tomlinson wrote of dilemmas in special education in 1982, and, with Len Barton, of the politics of integration in 1981. In Victorian schools integration without dilemmas can then become a place — in the regular classroom. By ignoring contests we mask dilemmas. This allows us to ignore contradictions (on these, Georg Simmel, not the first, wrote last century) which underlie dilemmas; integration implies segregation and is inherently contradictory (Branson and Miller, 1989). That ignoring of contests and contradictions promotes, at least encourages, a search for solutions (final?), recipes (do this and that); it suggests we write and rewrite rules (for integration these are now in booklet form), and that problems which may arise in some 'Integration Support Groups' derive from inadequate rules. Knowing that how language is used matters (Fulcher, 1989a) but ignoring contests, we can continually rework our documents, as if these determined practices at other levels. By keeping within the frame of system, of integration as place, of 'success' defined by a list of principles, within the confines of rational policy, we see less clearly the politics outside schools where some women may win

128

against medical edict, and later, in schools where their struggles, if not now, will resume.

Politics 1: Struggles or contests?

How can we articulate a constructive critique from the idea of contests? In part we already have, but in 1992 more needs to be said. I shall draw on Australian academics whose work reflects on Australian politics in the 1990s, especially Barry Hindess, Michael Jackson (yes), Pat O'Malley and Gary Wickham, putting their ideas against ideas and arguments already put to debate the politics of education policy and disability (Fulcher, 1986, 1989a; Branson and Miller, 1989), and exploring further some of the ideas which influenced the local official debate on effective or successful schools as that framed our endeavours. The ideas here enter wideranging debates on politics, democracy, justice. I shall hope, in this brief space, merely not to distort, misread debates whose central issues can not be tackled here and in which I hope to read more widely.

In the late 1980s, against a limited theorizing of social (including education) policy (administrative models predominating or policy dropping out of a focus which reduced struggles to *the* class struggle), and drawing on Demaine (1981), Culley and Demaine (1983) and some of Hindess' (1983, 1986) ideas, it was possible to develop a critique of integration policy using the following ideas (Fulcher, 1985, 1989a): that policy is the outcome of *political states of play* in particular arenas, made at all levels, in *struggles* where social actors (individuals and groups able to make decisions) deploy (available) discourses, under certain institutional conditions (where, say, national policy does not determine what happens at other levels), and in which they seek to achieve their objectives. Struggles take place in *arenas* — in classrooms, in meetings between union representatives and senior bureaucrats, of the review, etc. — these are forums where debate (may) occur(s) and decisions are made (Fulcher, 1986). The idea of state apparatuses was important, too: it sought to shift debate from a concern with the 'state' (which was less easy to identify). In state apparatuses like the educational apparatus, objectives emerge and can be identified in struggles which matter to those actors engaged in them (Culley and Demaine, 1983). In a debate about integration these ideas provided insights into the politics of educational policy.

This frame puts discourse, social actors, institutional bases, levels, policy struggles and objectives as central ideas, where discourse is both tactic and theory, and where discourses are variously available to social actors. As Hindess (1986) argued, social actors engage in discursive social practices, that is practices based on the discourses available to them. An important idea was that of locating *responsibility* for decisions with the *actors who made them*; for Hindess (1986) this idea was politically crucial. Certainly, it was useful in reframing (to some extent) the debate about integration in a critique of social actors in the educational apparatus (Fulcher, 1986).

This frame dissolved distinctions between theory, policy, practice — arguing against the top-down model of policy and the idea of implementation — and putting 'policy' in a wider model of social life as social practice, in which we seek to achieve our objectives, deploying discourse as both tactic and theory about an aspect of the social world we want to influence, and engaging in *struggle*, in *political states of play*, in what Wickham (forthcoming b) calls 'contests'. In 1986 this frame sought to overcome the tensions in social theory when structure 'determined' and agency allowed; it sought to have something to say to policy-makers.[8]

In a recent paper, 'Justice, Democracy and the Demise of Politics', Wickham defines politics as contests, and spells out the implications for social and political analysis:

> By politics I mean contest. . . . This simple definition has enormous im-
> plications for social and political analysis, because the contests which are
> politics have no given actors, no given forms and no predetermined
> outcomes. Any definition of politics which assumes given actors (classes
> for example), which assumes given forms (contests over market
> mechanisms, for example), and/or which assumes predetermined outcomes
> (the triumph of the ruling class or the triumph of market forces, for
> example) is rejected. A little bit of thought will allow identification of
> the many definitions of politics which have to be rejected. (Wickham,
> forthcoming b: 2)

In this paper Wickham rejects the idea of struggle as politics, an idea he had used in earlier work (1987a, 1987b). But what (for the moment) do we gain from the idea of policy as political, as contests or struggles — when we look, for instance, at the effective schools debate?

Reinserting the idea of politics as struggles or contests (more on the differences later) makes sense of both those encounters in schools in the summer of 1988 and much else. It suggests why 'characteristics' are a limited insight into what we might see as 'successful' schools; how the effective school debate is theoretically and methodologically limited (Reed, 1991). These ideas suggest why this endeavour is problematic: because it works with the idea of characteristics (as normative?), because it obscures politics (even when politics is gestured at but collapsed with the normative), whereas 'programs incorporate discourses of success and failure as part of their political character' (O'Malley, 1991: 9). As O'Malley observes of crime prevention strategies, 'what emerges . . . is a political struggle over the definition and the criteria of failure and success. . . . Such debates are endless. They reveal only that the politics of success and failure are just that and can rarely if ever be reduced to any universally accepted scale of efficiency' (O'Malley, 1991: 11).

Thus the apolitical view of success and failure belongs to the rational rather than the political tale of policy.[9] In other places there is public debate on abandoning the rational tale of policy (Garpenby, 1992); in one locality in Denmark, in Hinnerup, both the Ministry of Education (its documents did not say this, but its tactics implied) and those in the support centre (it was clear to see) recognized 'integration' in schools as a *political* project, in which heightened scrutiny of children with disabilities is a dangerously present possibility — the dilemma of increasing control while assisting? In Victoria increased procedural rules for integration groups promote that opportunity; in these contests, 'diaries' can be deployed either way.

Some actors in the Victorian Ministry recognize these contests in their practices, if implicitly, though this is not to say such recognition wins in these contests, nor does the idea of struggles and contests necessarily mean confrontation and heightened conflict. A constructive critique and tactic emerges, as was deployed in unlikely circumstances in a project on peer workers with sight loss (Fulcher, forthcoming).

The idea of politics as contests, or struggles, reframes the debates on democracy. Both Hindess and Wickham have persuasive arguments against ideas of democracy. Wickham argues that: 'The various proposals about democracy ... turn out ... to be riddled with attempts to impose actors on politics, to impose forms on politics and to impose outcomes on politics' (forthcoming b: 20) so that:

> Democracy, in most of its guises, should be seen as yet another effort at providing a universal system of norms at the expense of specific politics ... supposed universal systems of norms are something of a confidence trick. Universal systems of norms, like all universals, can only ever operate or be known specifically, in the specific spatial and temporal locations where they are being read or heard or seen or talked about. ... (Wickham, forthcoming b: 22)

Thus democracy was an idea that emerged in specific conditions: 'a specific spatial and temporal location — it was an invention of Greek scholars in the fifth century B.C.' (Snell, 1953: 90) (Wickham, forthcoming b: 22, citing Held). It was also an exclusive idea (adult male Athenians were citizens, not others), and 'even many Greek thinkers, including Thucydides, Plato and Aristotle were very critical of the idea of democracy' (Wickham, forthcoming b: 12). Wickham cites Hindess,

> For [whom] ... there is nothing inherently democratic in any particular set of institutional arrangements; what works in some situations won't work in others. 'There is therefore no reason to suppose that any single set of institutional arrangements will be most appropriate for all times and all societies.' (Hindess, 1989) (Wickham, forthcoming b: 10)

This makes problematic ideas of participation (without the conditions necessary for that to occur equally) as an attempt to impose a form and predetermine an outcome. Wickham concludes: 'normative treatments of democracy and justice are impediments to realisations of the central role of politics in the different locations where concepts like democracy and justice are usually applied' (forthcoming b: 1) so that, 'Concepts like democracy (and its sub-concepts like citizenship) and justice are, then, best seen as technical concepts in support of the technical concept of government, as technologies of government (forthcoming b: 23). Thus he usefully reminds us:

> what are to count as government itself are the outcomes of politics: government is a technical concept, very much in the way Foucault has theorised it, as Miller and Rose (1990) and Gordon (1991) have most recently captured. Government in any location — nation state, hospital, prison, school, family, etc. — is a technical matter concerned with the ordering and administration of certain populations, no matter how big or small. (forthcoming b: 23)

Wickham's central idea is specificity: specific politics, sites, objectives, mechanisms and calculations. A concern with specific objectives, and struggles or contests in (arenas or) particular sites (not distinguishing these ideas till later), is all that political theory can address (Wickham, 1987a: 155–156). In this focus Wickham, while aptly critical of metanotions such as a just system, rescues a (problematic) idea of justice: 'What are to count as justice in different temporal and spatial locations and what are to count as democracy can only be the outcomes of politics within those locations' (Wickham, forthcoming b: 23). This seems to collapse the idea of justice into politics: as if the process will deliver justice? As in consensus politics? And what then of injustice? Notwithstanding Wickham's adherence to some of Hindess' views on justice, this is how, for the present, I read Wickham. In addition to the problematic idea of justice as outcomes, there seem further problems in Wickham's ideas associated with his focus on specific sites.

Politics 2: Contests in Arenas or Specific Sites?

In his concern with specificity Wickham argues for politics as contests, against imposing forms (democratic structures), or outcomes ('justice') on politics; political effects are political (they cannot be known in advance). He argues for other ideas which centre on that of specificity: specific objectives, sites, mechanisms and the idea of institutional limits: of, for example, knowledge(s) which circulate in specific sites, different (sociologies of education?) in Ballarat from Clayton? A site, 'we might loosely define . . . as an intersection of particular objectives (with the forces trying to achieve them), but a definition, or this particular term itself, is not as important as the task of sharpening the picture gained in constructing the object of any analysis' (Wickham, 1987a: 149–150). Objectives may be local or global. An objective may be control in a classroom, where the conditions include 'certain pedagogic techniques, implementation of certain rules of classroom behaviour, and limiting decisions about curriculum design' (1987a: 150). And, 'control of the world economy can be a specific objective, with definite conditions of operation in procedures of the World Bank, the International Monetary Fund, the, United Nations, a range of inter-nation trading agreements, and so on' (1987a: 150). *Objectives* may conflict: not people or actors. If objectives conflict, as between child-care and the Accord, then objectives may need rearranging. Mechanisms are both groups (he cites, to illustrate, the ALP, the journal *Arena*, and feminist groups) *and* procedures for decision-making. Mechanisms may need reorganizing, not actors. But these ideas provide an oblique critique. They avoid in-house left politics where unions as corporate social actors may be said to have acted in the interests of some workers (some 'citizens'?) and not others — a debate on which Wickham comments (forthcoming b: 19) but Hindess (1991b) enters.

The idea of mechanisms now replaces that of discourse, so that neither actor nor discourse now appears in Wickham's frame (forthcoming a). Without the idea of discourse, language and its effects drop from our gaze, and ideas which connect sites, which might reveal what I call 'politics which reappear' (the position of girls and women, for instance), are absent. In his specific site politics Wickham argues against the idea of general aggregations of politics, but implies that connectedness may be known in a site (forthcoming a: 20–21; forthcoming b: 3). But what ideas will direct our gaze, shape those connnections? Wickham's idea of politics as contests is wonderfully useful — more elegant than the term 'struggle', or that of political states of play (but no different in critique) — as is the critique of democracy and that of a just system. His injunction against the 'careless generalities' in which sociology has so often dealt is useful, as is his assertion of the general tendency of the centrality of politics but not necessarily their primacy (forthcoming b). Beyond these ideas the specific site focus grapples less clearly with the shape of contests and with the actors engaged in them than does a frame based in ideas of levels, arenas, social actors, institutional conditions and discourse.

The idea of discourse connects arenas (managerial discourse — here we go again), institutional conditions and levels (the discourse on . . . reappears); it postulates tactic and theory (both via discourse); social actors are clearly individuals and groups able to make decisions, whereas mechanisms? These are groups *and* procedures. The idea of social actor allows Hindess to draw our attention to the emergence of key social actors — organizations and corporations which are outside a liberal frame of politics but who are now central actors — an idea which does not appear in Wickham's frame. The idea of discourse allows us to unravel objectives (a discourse of disability which talks of 'integration' as the child plus resources, or one which talks of all children as, first, pupils?), to see that actors may be engaged not only here, in this school as arena, but in contests elsewhere. In addition, in this frame we can rescue a less problematic idea of justice.

Michael Jackson's ideas on justice seem better than the logic which Wickham reaches. Jackson argues against Rawls (as do others), against the 'sun-blinded technocratic rationality devoid of politics', and against the modern strategy of justice (in an Australian newsletter this implicates government in Canberra and Victoria[10]), where,

> Nothing could be further from the general strategy of justice these days than the give and take of politics. Not only does this strategy not place a premium on performance, but it also takes the politics out of justice. To call attention to this exclusion of politics, I use the ugly neo-logism, 'depoliticisation'. (Jackson, 1991: 4)

Thus he argues, 'without politics (reality), justice (rationality) is impossible' (1991: 38). The modern strategy of justice relies on promise, not performance. This suggests why some disability groups are now unwilling to be 'consulted', in current Victorian government policy arenas, where justice may be 'promised' but not performed.[11]

Abandoning the metaproject of a 'just system' allows us to retain the idea of justice, but one which differs from Wickham's idea. We can begin as Wickham does, with 'Hindess's elegant, abstract definition of justice as contentless and formless' (forthcoming b: 23), where:

> 'all members of the community are treated according to their deserts' (Hindess, 1989c). It should be carefully noted that this definition provides only the shape of a position on justice. No attempt is made to give it content: not content for 'community', and hence no necessary criteria for membership of communities; and no content for deserts. (forthcoming b: 2)

If we stay with this notion of justice, give some content to Hindess' idea of 'just desserts', bourgeois though this is, and shift from a focus on specific sites to a frame of contests in arenas and levels, we can work with an idea of 'arena-related justice'. The idea of arena-related justice takes Jackson's position — justice without politics is impossible, and Wickham's critique — 'social justice' as a technical concept of governance is, as is the idea of democracy, an attempt to diminish politics (Wickham, forthcoming b: 23). In a contests in arenas at various levels and so on frame, we can take the idea of arena-related justice, coincidentally recognizing the politics which appear in various arenas — the position of women, a discourse of managerialism and so on, without resorting to metanotions like patriarchy or to structural narratives of inequality *or* equality. As Wickham (citing Schmitt) (forthcoming b: 21) argues, equality, or striving for it, necessarily implies inequality. These ideas require an intellectual critique of governance's ideas.

Politics 3: Intellectuals and Contests

Finally, what of intellectuals and contests surrounding education policy in Australia? Are intellectuals implicated in new settlements with federal and Victorian governments? Or is this a carelessly general question? Perhaps not. In Britain Cohen links mainstream educationists with the success of the Thatcher project on education.

> Whatever her personal delusions of grandeur Mrs Thatcher has no special magical powers to turn her policies into practice. The Thatcherite project would not have got off the ground if certain elements in its programme had not won the active support of mainstream educationalists. In fact there has been a convergence of opinion over the last decade on what constitutes 'good education' and 'effective schooling'. (Cohen, 1990: 51)

Whereas Anderson, in a metanarrative (?), suggests that in the 1980s the oppositional position of intellectuals in Britain, which has typified many European cultures, is an anomaly in the historical relations between British intellectuals and government; that, in a European 'home', this anomaly is likely to be renegotiated in unfamiliar dispositions (1990: 155–156).

In Australia what is the recent history of relations between intellectuals and government? Ideas of the male wage-earner's welfare state (Castles, 1985), of Australian laborism (Beilharz, 1986) are outside the critique from frames such as a specific site focus where mechanisms and objectives may need rearranging — but not loyalties? Such a critique is outside a normative stance on schools; it may reappear in a frame which includes the idea of arena-related justice. The heresy of dissent from governance, the almost hushed tones with which Beilharz's and Castles' critiques of governance are met in conferences, is testimony to the rest. Or is this a careless generality? If the idea of consensus is imposed on policy conferences, what then of the idea of debate?[12] On integration policy Branson and Miller suggest 'reformists effectively support . . . the tyranny they oppose with their very opposition to it' (1989: 161). In this historical bin perhaps Fulcher's (1989a) relatively outspoken critique may now belong. Schooling, if not our tertiary politics, suggests we can do better. On these distant shores, affected, as we are, by European waves, Australian intellectuals in the 1990s might heed Cohen's slightly retributive stance, ponder Anderson's (comfortably distanced) warning, perhaps read more on the politics of exclusion.

So, contests in arenas, at all levels, discourses as tactics and theory, etc. and the idea of arena-related justice — but not system, not transcultural justice, not, please, consensus, not the primary concerns and ideas necessary for governance. Stenson's ideas show there is no easy route.[13] Nor can we rearticulate a project by conceptual critique (Wickham, forthcoming a: 3). Projects in schools and elsewhere are contests with all that that implies. We can offer ideas but not those just mentioned. These technical concepts governance requires — but intellectuals . . .?

Notes

1 The idea of social justice has been important to the Victorian Labor Government elected in 1982. By 1988 the idea influenced a range of government practices — documents, units for social justice, theses on social justice.
2 Fulcher and O'Callaghan (1989).
3 Rizvi *et al.* (1987).
4 These are almost meaningless terms in Australian politics where much of the 'left' has gone right. However, see Wickham (1987a) for a definition of the left.
5 See Pusey (1991) on economic rationalism in Canberra, in the public service; this discourse appears to predominate in policy arenas and policy documents, including Victorian government arenas.
6 For a critique of rational policy in other areas, see Fulcher (unpublished).
7 '. . . a reified system [perspective suggests] that it is probable and desirable for system maintenance that a consensus can be achieved (when in fact schools are places where a consensus is not impossible but extremely difficult to achieve and certainly may not necessarily be desirable)' (Quicke, 1982).
8 This was Demaine's (1981) concern.
9 For a more detailed critique, see Fulcher (unpublished).
10 Victoria is 'ahead' of other Australian states in its strategy of social justice.
11 See Jackson (1991) on promise and performance.
12 As occurred at the 1989 National Social Policy Conference, where an associate professor, on behalf of the Minister of Social Security, refuted Francis Castles' (potentially critical) question. The then Minister for Social Security was in the audience.
13 In his 1991 London paper (not to be quoted without permission) on social work discourse and interview.

References

ANDERSON, P. (1990) 'A Culture in Contraflow — II', *new left review*, 182, pp. 85–137.
BALL, S. (1988) 'Comprehensive Schooling, Effectiveness and Control: An Analysis of Educational Discourses', in SLEE, R. (Ed.), *Discipline and Schools: A Curriculum Perspective*, South Melbourne, Macmillan Australia.
BALL, S.J. (1990) Management as Moral Technology: A Luddite Analysis', in BALL, S.J. (Ed.), *Foucault and Education: Disciplines and Knowledge.* London, Routledge, pp. 153–166.
BARTON, L. and TOMLINSON, S. (Eds) (1981) *Special Education: Policy, Practices and Social Issues*, London, Harper and Row.

Gillian Fulcher

BARTON, L. and TOMLINSON, S. (Eds) (1984) *Special Education and Social Interests*, London, Croom Helm.

BATES, R. (1988) 'Administrative Theory and the Social Construction of School', *Discourse*, 8, 2, pp. 110–126.

BEILHARZ, P. (1986) 'The Left, the Accord and the Future of Socialism', *Thesis Eleven*, 13, pp. 5–21.

BRANSON, J. and MILLER, D. (1989)'Beyond Integration Policy: The Deconstruction of Disability', in BARTON, L. (Ed.), *Integration: Myth or Reality*, Lewes, Falmer Press.

CASTLES, F.G. (1985) *The Working Class and Welfare*, Sydney, Allen and Unwin.

COHEN, P. (1990) 'Teaching Enterprise Culture: Individualism, Vocationalism and the New Right', in TAYLOR, I. (Ed.), *The Social Effect of Free Market Policies: An International Text*, London, Harvester Wheatsheaf.

CREEMERS, B. (1989) 'The Future Development of School Effectivess and School Improvement', in CREEMERS, B., PETERS, T. and REYNOLDS, D. (Eds), *School Effectiveness and School Improvement*, Amsterdam, Swets and Zeitlinger.

CULLEY, L. and DEMAINE, J. (1983) 'Social Theory, Social Relations and Education', in WALKER, S. and BARTON, L. (Eds), *Gender, Class and Education*, Lewes, Falmer Press, pp. 161–172.

DEMAINE, J. (1981) *Contemporary Theories in the Sociology of Education*, London, Macmillan.

FULCHER, G. (1986) 'Australian Policies on Special Education: Towards a Sociological Account', *Disability, Handicap and Society*, 1, 1, pp. 19–52.

FULCHER, G. (1988a) 'Policy and Evaluation Myths', *The Age*, 1 November.

FULCHER, G. (1988b) 'Integration: Inclusion or Exclusion?,' in SLEE, R. (Ed.), *Discipline and Schools: A Curriculum Perspective*, South Melbourne, Macmillan.

FULCHER, G. (1989a) *Disabling Policies? A Comparative Approach to Education Policy and Disability*, Lewes, Falmer Press.

FULCHER, G. (1989b) 'Integrate and Mainstream? Comparative Issues in the Politics of These Policies', in BARTON, L. (Ed.), *Integration: Myth or Reality?*, Lewes, Falmer Press.

FULCHER, G. (forthcoming) 'Pigs' Tails and Peer Workers', Prepared, by invitation, in response to Professor Len Barton's paper, June 1991, 'Disability: The Necessity of a Socio-political Perspective', World Rehabilitation Fund (WRF) University of New Hampshire (UNH), International Exchange of Experts and Information in Rehabilitation (IEEIR) Monograph 51 in the WRF-IEEIR series.

FULCHER, G. (unpublished) 'Pick Up the Pieces! What Do Recreation Workers Need to Know about Working with People with Severe Disabilities?', Report prepared for the Department of Leisure Studies, Phillip Institute of Technology, Bundoora, Victoria, February 1992.

FULCHER, G. and O'CALLAGHAN, M. (1989) Extension note to the Task Force report to SCAEPID, *Teacher Education and Staff Development*, typescript, 3 pp., June.

FULCHER, G., SEMMENS, R. and SLEE, R. (unpublished) *Successful Schools: A Report on Learning Initiatives to Include All Students*, Prepared for the Ministry of Education, Victoria, The Education Shop, 1990.

GARPENBY, P. (1992) 'The Transformation of the Swedish Health Care System, or the Hasty Rejection of the Rational Planning Model', *Journal of European Social Policy*, 2, 1, pp. 17–31.

GUTTMANN, A. (1987) *Democratic Education*, Princeton, N.J., Princeton University Press.

HINDESS, B. (1983) 'Power, Interests and the Outcomes of Struggles', *Sociology*, 16, 4, pp. 498–511.

HINDESS, B. (1986) 'Actors and Social Relations', in WARDELL, M.L. and TURNER, S.P. (Eds), (1986) *Sociological Theory in Transition*, Boston, Mass., Allen and Unwin, pp. 113–126.

HINDESS, B. (1989) 'Political Equality and Social Policy', Paper presented at the Social Welfare Research Centre National Social Policy Conference, 'What Future for the Welfare State?', Sydney, July.

HINDESS, B. (1990) 'Liberty and Equality', in HINDESS, B. (Ed.), *Reactions to the Right*, London, Routledge.

HINDESS, B. (1991a) 'Imaginary Presuppositions of Democracy', *Economy and Society*, 20, 2, pp. 73–95.

HINDESS, B. (1991b) 'Taking Socialism Seriously', *Economy and Society*, 20, 4, pp. 363–379.

HINDESS, B. (1991c) 'Power and Rationality: The Western Concept of Political Community', *Thesis Eleven* Conference, 'Reason and Imagination', Monash University, August.

JACKSON, M. (1991) 'Justice and the Cave', *Political Theory Newsletter*, 3, pp. 37–45.

LEVINE, D. (Ed.) (1971) *Georg Simmel: On Individuality and Social Forms*, Chicago, Ill., University of Chicago Press.

LIGGETT, H. (1988) 'Stars Aren't Born: An Interpretive Approach to the Politics of Disability', *Disability, Handicap and Society*, 3, 3, pp. 163–175.

O'CONNOR, A. (1989) *Raymond Williams: Writing, Culture, Politics*, Oxford, Basil Blackwell.

OLIVER, M. (1989) 'Disability and Dependency: A Creation of Industrial Societies?', in BARTON, L. (Ed.), *Disability and Dependency*, Lewes, Falmer Press.

O'MALLEY, P. 'After Discipline? Crime Prevention, the Strong State and a Free Market', Paper presented to the Joint Meeting of the Law and Society Association and Research Committee on the Sociology of Law of the International Sociological Association, University of Amsterdam, June, typescript, 21 pp.

MANN, D. (1988) 'Pedagogy and Politics: Effective Schools and American Educational Politics', in REYNOLDS, D., CREEMERS, B.P.M. and PETERS, T. (Eds), *School Effectiveness and Improvements*, Proceedings of the First International Conference, Cardiff, Rion.

PIACHAUD, D. (1991) 'Social Policy beyond the Social Services', *Policy Studies*, 12, 4, pp. 47–52.

PUSEY, M. (1991) *Economic Rationalism in Canberra*, Cambridge, Cambridge University Press.

QUICKE, J. (1982) 'Whatever Happened to the "Reconstructing" Movement?', *AEP Journal*, 5, 8, pp. 3–6.

QUICKE, J. (1990) 'Beware of Good Intentions', Review of FULCHER, G. (1989) *Disabling Policies?*, *The Times Educational Supplement*, 6 July.

RAMSAY, P., SNEDDON, D., GRENFELL, J., and FORD, I. (1983) 'Successful and Unsuccessful Schools', *Australian and New Zealand Journal of Sociology*, 19, 2, pp. 292–304.

REED, R.J. (1991) 'School Decentralization and Empowerment', *Journal of Education Policy*, special issue on 'The Politics of Urban Education in the United States', 6, 5, pp. 137–165.

REYNOLDS, D. (1982) 'The Search for Effective Schools', *School Organization*, 2, 3, pp. 215–237.

RIZVI, F., KEMMIS, S., WALKER, R., FISHER, J. and PARKER, Y. (1987) *Dilemmas of Reform: An Overview of Issues and Achievements of the Participation and Equity Program in Victorian Schools 1984–85*, Geelong, Deakin University.

RORTY, R. (1991) *Objectivity, Relativism, and Truth*, Philosophical Papers Volume 1, Cambridge, Cambridge University Press.

RUTTER, M., MAUGHAN, B., MORTIMORE, P. and OUSTON, J. (1979) *Fifteeen Thousand Hours: Secondary Schools and Their Effects on Children*, London, Open Books.

SPECIAL EDUCATIONAL NEEDS (1978) Report of the Committee of Enquiry into the

Education of Handicapped Children and Young People, Warnock Report, London, Her Majesty's Stationery Office.

SPICKER, P. (1991) 'The Principle of Subsidiarity and the Social Policy of the European Community', *Journal of European Social Policy,* 1, 1, pp. 3–14.

TOMLINSON, S. (1982) *A Sociology of Special Education*, London, Routlege and Kegan Paul.

WICKHAM, G. (1987a) 'Foucault, Power, Left Politics', *Arena*, 78, pp. 146–158.

WICKHAM, G. (1987b) 'Turning the LAW into Laws for Political Analysis', *Social Theory and Legal Politics*, University of Sydney, Local Consumption Publication.

WICKHAM, G. (forthcoming a) 'Theorising Sociology in the Face of Postmodernism', *Australian and New Zealand Journal of Sociology.*

WICKHAM, G. (forthcoming b) 'Justice, Democracy and the Demise of Politics', typescript, 26 pp.

Australian Policy Documents

AUSTRALIAN LABOR PARTY, VICTORIAN BRANCH (1988) *Social Justice: The Next Four Years*, Carlton.

DEPARTMENT OF THE PREMIER AND CABINET, SOCIAL JUSTICE STRATEGY (1989) 'Guidelines for Partnership Proposals', 4 pp., March.

DEPARTMENT OF THE PREMIER AND CABINET, THE SOCIAL JUSTICE STRATEGY UNIT (1988) *Performance Indicators and the Social Justice Strategy*, A Discussion Paper, August.

MINISTRY OF EDUCATION-VICTORIA (1984) *Integration in Victorian Education: Report of the Ministerial Review of Educational Services for the Disabled*, Melbourne, Victorian Government Printer (CHAIR M.K. Collins).

MINISTRY OF EDUCATION-VICTORIA (1988) *Integration Support Group Procedures for Regular Schools*, Statewide School Support and Production Centre, Ministry of Education (Schools Division).

MINISTRY OF EDUCATION-VICTORIA (1990) *Integration Support Group Procedures for Regular Schools*, Statewide School Support and Production Centre, Ministry of Education (Schools Division).

MINISTRY OF EDUCATION-VICTORIA (unpublished) *Successful Schooling: A Report on Learning Initiatives to Include All Students*, Victoria, The Education Shop, prepared by Gillian Fulcher, Bob Semmens and Roger Slee, 1990.

VICTORIAN ALP 1985 ELECTION PLATFORM, *Social Justice: The Next 4 Years*, Richmond, Industrial Printing and Publicity.

Chapter 10

Integrating the Secondary School Curriculum: Balancing Central and Local Policies

Tony Knight

This chapter outlines how a Melbourne-based inner suburban secondary school (Duke Park Secondary College) and its community redefined the concept of school integration by reclaiming its own voice in developing a comprehensive and common curriculum. The central working premise was that an integrated school is a democratic school. The democratic ethos in this instance is one in which there is a conscious striving to organize all school activities toward mutually agreed goals. The school defined itself in democratic terms through a collaborative effort at problem-solving within a community of diverse backgrounds that included parents, teachers and students. It was an endeavour to develop a sense of balance, that is, a common core of knowledge and understanding, between the demands of a central curriculum and the educational needs of a local community.

In this chapter it is argued that curriculum policy in Victorian schools has been polarized between the years 7–10 and 11–12. Years 11 and 12 have been skewed toward an emphasis on subject-driven work requirements to the exclusion of the needs of young people in the areas of personal, social and career development. The senior curriculum is not connected to policy at years 7–10. There is not a whole school context that caters for an academically and socially diverse senior and junior school population (Batten, 1989; Ainley *et al.*, 1984). Presently what is in place is a top-down, centralized, subject oriented senior curriculum with a built-in assumption that it will have a trickle-down effect on curriculum process and content at junior levels of secondary schooling. It is a kind of 'steering at a distance' model of school management (Kickert, 1991). What is also being observed at years 11 and 12 is the loss of student commitment to general school activities and a drift toward a culture that instead encourages a commitment to possessive and competitive individualism.

The press for senior students is toward the formation of informal social groupings and a resistance toward school administered symbols. These laissez-faire social groupings have become marginal to general learning needs except for the subject-based work requirements of the senior curriculum. Forms of play, sport, performance activities and school decision-making participation are declining choices within the more formal structuring of the senior school curriculum. The increased formalizing of work at senior school level is accelerated by very high youth unemployment, an inflation in scores required for tertiary entrance, powerful competition for declining work and post-secondary study choices, and a large increase in senior school retention rates.

Both student and teacher work have been subsequently affected. Teacher workloads at senior level have altered dramatically as new forms of assessment and surveillance of student work demand very large commitments of time. Senior teachers are caught between new levels of administrative duties and decisions of a more educational nature. One of the side effects to this new layering of teacher work is a retreat from the general education debate, and perceived lack of time to organize other kinds of educational activities. The weighting of schooling concerns these past two years has been at senior level. This has meant an imbalance in the overall debate on a whole school curriculum and certainly a lack of integration between the two levels of secondary curriculum.

An interesting reaction at a structural level to the loss of school social forms has been the introduction of older social rituals (e.g., the debutante ball) or in the new form of corporate sponsored music competitions (e.g., the rock Eisteddfod) (Whitlock, 1991; Fitzclarence *et al.*, 1991; White, 1989). As the general school ethos becomes increasingly fragmented and confused in purpose and aims, there has been a noticeable drift in school staff developing small informal groupings at the expense of overall collegiality and a sense of common purpose. Both students and teachers are being pushed into newer forms of competitive individualism by the demands of new economic and social forms.

Within the context of these concerns, this school and its community set out to construct a curriculum policy that would offer a more integrated and democratic form of schooling and education. It is, in essence, a study of a practical intervention by a school and its community into a specific political context. It must be stressed that, as an exercise in democratic schooling, the inclusion of *all* students in an enabling and challenging curriculum is assumed.

Changing School Context

The context of this study was part of the ideological shift that has characterized schooling in the state of Victoria in the past ten years. There has been since the early 1980s the rhetoric of devolution of control in Victorian schools, implying forms of participatory democracy in the formation of school policy as to curriculum, integration programs and discipline codes. However, during this decade increasing conflict emerged within schools as continued attempts were made at corporate management and accountability schemes, where a centralized form of decision-making power was allied to the idea of representative democracy.

The tension was, in essence, one where the early devolution theory assumed that school communities could in general formulate and implement school policy, while recent centralized mandates argue that teachers and parents are not able to perform, and an administrative hierarchy was to make the important judgments. The answer to the question of which or whose knowledge is important has been increasingly influenced by a professional and intermediate bureaucracy. The tension between early 1980s government policy emphasizing participatory democracy and later forms of representative democracy, and state mandated curricula, has not been resolved. Inside schools teachers reacted with feelings of resentment

over the loss of their voice in what they perceived as important areas of professional decision-making. The loss of a general school culture has also influenced
student behaviour, as mentioned previously.

By the end of the 1980s the school system was residing inside an economy
that ignored large numbers of its young, with a corresponding increase in school
retention rates, especially in year 12, a movement not unrelated to high youth
unemployment rates. The Karmel Report (1973), *Schools in Australia,* argued for
a more devolved system of public education, based primarily on educational
arguments. However, the structural reform movement of the 1980s was less clear
in terms of educational aims. Drawing from a comparative perspective, Brown
and Lauder (1991: 3) make the following comments:

> In ideal typical 'terms' we can suggest that Western industrial so-
> cieties . . . confront choices between trying to adapt rigid hierarchical
> division of labour, and the low skill and low trust relationships which
> characterize 'fordist' societies such as Britain, to new conditions, or shifting
> to systems of flexible production and organization based on flatter hier-
> archies, adaptable and highly skilled workers, and a breakdown of the
> dimensions which currently exist between mental and manual labour
> and learning. The sense of increase about social change in the late twen-
> tieth century has been accompanied by a universal crisis of confidence
> about the aims and purposes of education.

Present educational debates in Australian education also reflect this unre-
solved tension in the interrelationship of the economy, society and education.
One of the major problems emerging from this tension is how to strike a balance
between centralized and school-based decision-making. It is a key issue to be
addressed in this chapter.

Connecting Curriculum Ends and Means

Victorian schools in the 1990s have set in place Ministry frameworks for subject
content and process in years 11 and 12. Years 7–10 have been sidelined in this
curriculum reorganization. Allied with this is strong Ministry legislation to merge,
or close, existing schools under the banner of efficiency and administrative reforms.
These administrative reforms, driven by economic interests, have changed government schools into sites of contestation, and large-scale tensions have developed
within and between school staff.

A result of this emphasis on school process and management oriented change
is a strong incentive to deflect classroom practice away from educational context.
They act as a centrifugal force in spinning school program practice away from an
educational core. Power, for example, in her analysis of 'Pastoral Care as
Curriculum Discourse', makes the case that the 'consolidation of pastoral care
acquired particular significance in response to tensions created through the reorganization of secondary schooling. Pastoral care provided the means by which
the contradictions embedded within comprehensivation could be reconciled'
(Power, 1991: 193). A result of these processes is that there is no integration of
educational experiences within the overall secondary curriculum and between
various school programs (Slee, 1988; Knight, 1988).

Tony Knight

This lack of coherence in the general secondary school curriculum was interestingly described by Powell *et al.* (1985) as the 'Shopping Mall High School', where the central theme is the 'awesome mindlessness and purposeless' of secondary schools, and where curriculum is constructed to offer enough variety to encourage students to stay on in school, and the schooling ethos is the 'centrality of variety, choice and neutrality', particularly at years 7–10.

In general, school programs have become separated from educational meaning, management and therapy oriented programs are set in place under the labels of 'discipline' codes, 'integration' programs and 'pastoral care'. The management dynamic adopted is informed by values of containment, restraint or control, rarely by forms of social cooperation or student self-understanding. This is done in an effort to reconcile the strong and formalized work requirements at senior level and the general aimlessness of years 7–10 (Crittenden, 1991; Simon, 1985; Knight, 1988, 1989).

A result of this lack of curriculum integration is the formation of a dichotomy between intellectual and social development, and educational aims within this assumed dichotomy became subsumed under social policy (Tomlinson and Finch, 1984; Gibson, 1984; Barton, 1986; Fulcher, 1989; Hargreaves and Reynolds, 1989; Lang and Hyde, 1987). The tension for school staff trying to reconcile these fragmented social and intellectual strands has meant considerable stress within the general life of the school (Sarros and Sarros, 1990: 145–152; Otto, 1986).

Student Motivation: Encouragement or Management?

The newer forms of state mandated curricula, and assessment and performance indicators, have raised the level of 'real' work and busy work for both student and teacher. In educational terms it remains to be seen whether these newer forms of schooling represent an overemphasis on schooling process at the expense of educational learning — or, put another way, a triumph of technique and process over educational vision.

Questions remain to be answered as to the connection between social and educational purpose and the more 'competitive' students that are a major intended outcome of the process. The criticism is the familiar ends-means dichotomy. Is there a relationship between the means to achieve student motivation to learn and a form of educational and social legitimacy? Hargreaves and Reynolds (1989: 36–37) ask whether the process is motivation or manipulation? They give a comparative perspective to these points:

> Under circumstances such as these, the enhancement of pupil motivation shifts from being an educational process of positive disposition to learning worthwhile knowledge; to a sociopolitical, state-managed process of accommodation to the realities of economic crisis; of adjustment to diminishing prospects of employment and economic reward and to an educational experience that, for many pupils, can no longer promise social and economic benefits in adulthood. Motivation that is, becomes transformed from a process of educational encouragement, to a strategy of social crisis management . . . there are then, serious objections to

assessment led reform unless it is developed in conjunction with a clear sense of curricula purpose.

Given the convergence of similar concerns in Victorian schools, it became important for the school in this study to include year 11–12 curricular mandates within an overall sense of curriculum purpose.

In summary, this project came about in response to five broad influences which are currently taking hold on school decision-making:

1 the increasing tendency for curriculum reform movements to define the school as an adjunct of the labour market, and the push for state mandated curricula, corporate management pedagogics and accountability schemes;

2 the fragmenting influence of contemporary culture on family life and community cohesion;

3 the influence of the youth culture, in its various forms, on student behaviour in schools;

4 the increasing amount of systematic knowledge and broad general agreement on what constitutes a good school; and

5 the increasing likelihood that government sponsored education — the public school — is at risk of becoming an endangered species in the absence of unifying principles and a sense of purpose.

Developing a School PolZicy

This case study is an example of how a Melbourne secondary high school (an inner urban school of 700 students of mixed ethnicity — twenty languages — and social class) and its community set about to reclaim its voice in what is taught in the school. It not only addressed the broad and general question of 'what knowledge is of most worth'? but, as Michael Apple (1990) has added, 'Whose knowledge is of most worth'?

As implied earlier, these are profoundly political questions (especially within a context of state mandated subject aims), and it was within this framework that the school council (comprising parents, teachers, students and administrators) set about to decide curriculum policy and content. Each individual school in the state of Victoria appoints a school council to hire the school principal (not staff) and decide the curriculum policy formation for the school (Ministry of Education, 1986). Membership guidelines are as follows:

Parents	no *less* than one-third of the school council;
Staff	no *more* than one-third of the school council;
Students	adequate representation in relation to school size and structure;
Principal	is 'ex officio' voting member of the council;
Co-opted Members	up to one-fifth of membership.

Nominations and elections are held for all candidates except co-opted members. The position of president has to be nominated from school council members

Tony Knight

(except member in paid employment at the school) and a general election held for the position.

Duties of the school council concern the following:

selection of the school principal;
educational policy;
buildings and grounds;
cleaning services;
financial management and accountability; and
reporting to the school community.

Decentralization of curriculum decision-making has evolved in Australian schools in a variety of ways, depending upon state differences and differences between school sectors, and within schools themselves. The definition adopted in the state of Victoria was a model that involved parent and community participation in education — in contrast to school- or teacher-based decision-making or regional decision-making boards. The original legislature for school and community participation was founded on the premise that a democracy should advocate participatory as well as representative democratic practice. However, as mentioned previously, there is considerable tension between the original Ministry of Education policy (1986) and the recent movement toward more centralized and corporate forms of decision-making with an emphasis on the discourse of efficiency (Bates, 1987; Yeatman, 1990; Watkins, 1986; Pusey, 1991).

What Makes a Successful School?

There is no shortage of information in educational circles as to what makes a good school. Teachers and schools can draw from well researched and documented evidence. For example, Jones *et al.* (1982) in a six-year Melbourne study confirmed strongly the proposition that teachers working around shared concerns were more effective in changing school practice. Another Melbourne study (Ainley *et al.*, 1987) found that teacher satisfaction with school climate is enhanced when the curriculum is well organized and coordinated. Ramsay *et al.* (1987: 2) in a New Zealand study isolated eight characteristics which seemed to distinguish 'successful' from 'less successful' schools; the first was 'a clearly articulated philosophy or statement of goals'.

It was with confidence that the school planning committee could draw from these local and overseas studies on successful schooling and plan to construct the school aims and objectives as a first priority. Crittenden (1991: 1) makes the following points: there is considerable knowledge and agreement on what makes a good school; 'there are significant differences over the main purposes that schools should be serving, but when the emphasis is much the same, there also tends to be broad agreement on what makes for a good school.' Other studies making similar conclusions include Clark *et al.* (1980); Maughan *et al.* (1990); Joyce *et al.* (1989); Crandall *et al.* (1986); Smith and Tomlinson (1989); Barth (1990); Mulford (1987); Mellor and Chapman (1984); Connelly (1989); Cole (1990); Rowe (1991); Oakes (1991).

A Democratic Framework for Decision-making

Each faculty, parent representatives and student representative council (SRC) were asked to develop a framework for decisions concerning the main objectives for the school. This process involved many debates, much discussion and meetings over a period of six months. The educational goals that were decided upon after lengthy negotiation were defined through a democratic public philosophy that included personal rights and responsibilities, and an education for democratic and public participation.

There was general agreement for a principled theory of education to inform the school policy. Conceptual guidance for this approach was influenced by (among others) Amy Gutmann (1987), who offered the following guidelines:

> The primary aim of a democratic theory of education is not to offer solutions to all the problems plaguing our educational institutions, but to consider ways of resolving those problems that are compatible with a commitment to democratic values. A democratic theory of education provides principles that, in the face of our social disagreements, help us judge (a) who should have authority to make decisions about education; and (b) what the moral boundaries of educational authority are. (p. 11)

This commitment to democratic values led to policy that aimed to develop within the school a sense of community and shared values through social understanding, that is, the concern for others.

The authors of the Queensland Department of Education (1990) blueprint for education department reorganization concluded that there are benefits for students emerging from a decentralized and community-based system of education. The report states: 'School-based decision-making has the potential to reduce alienation from schools, increase job satisfaction of employees, promote participation of all relevant groups, and raise community understanding' (Queensland Department of Education, 1990: 41). There is, however, scant evidence that teachers view the community as a source of authority for curriculum knowledge (Sturman, 1990: 1). They are more likely to be drawn toward central authorities or professional subject groupings within schools, depending on state decision-making practice. It was against this kind of administrative backdrop that this school and community set themselves to intervene in policy and practice.

Bottom-up versus Top-down Reform

Contrary to warnings from Stephen Ball (1987) in his study and consequent rejection of the prescriptive 'top-down' approach to school decision-making — supported by Cuban (1984) in his study of US schools — this model is deliberately a 'top-down' model. (The 'effective school' movement tends to argue for a 'bottom-up' accountability model, that is, students to teacher, teacher to principal, principal to school superintendent and ultimately to national interest). While the 'bottom-up' model gives the impression of being egalitarian, this is not necessarily the case in practice. The model holds teachers and students most accountable to higher forms of authority or bureaucracy; it is seldom the case in reverse. It is very difficult for schools to hold accountable decisions made by system bureaucrats on their behalf? This is particularly true in large centralized systems. In these 'bottom-up' models the school becomes the weakest link. In democratic schooling accountability goes downward; the ultimate determination is made by the student. Being accountable downward is *defending with logic and evidence all requests made of students — to students.* The strength of the school is the quality of the arguments. Participation between student and teacher is intended to bring about a change in definition of self, from a less self-centred person to a more citizen-centred person. In this sense participation is a logical extension of cooperative learning that is featured in some effective schools. However, the form of accountability being advocated, that is 'top-down' decision-making, is not easy on teachers. When asked questions — 'Sir or Ms, Why do I have to learn this?' — this requires teachers to be accountable and to explain how and what they are teaching is important knowledge for students to understand, that is, how it fits into the wider context of personal or social understanding. None of this is easy; defending with logic and evidence to students raises both the level of debate and the level of preparedness required of teachers. Connecting to long-term aims is critical to this relationship and teaching.

Conflict versus Consensus Models

Overall staff collegiality was not achieved in this study. This was, and is, a conflict model in operation, not a consensus model. There are advantages to this model: it allows for divergences in autonomy and collaboration within the staff, and for protection of minority opinion. What the staff workshops achieved was a critical mass of approval, that is, a working group within the staff offered intellectual leadership; and others, while they had differences of opinion, could live with those differences. Fullan (1990) cites good examples of staff differences in autonomy and collaboration and consequent effects on decision-making. The Duke Park model is more in line with Joyce *et al.* (1989: 15), who observed that school change depends on 'about ten per cent of the staff'. The critical mass in this case study was probably about 10 per cent of teachers who were prepared to work continuously on staff development projects. Furthermore, this case study would confirm the observation of Nias (1989) that 'teachers had great difficulty collaborating even when they wanted to work together.'

These studies raise a number of questions as to why, in general, schools are difficult places in which to achieve staff collegiality. Is it because achievement and success in the academic marketplace require individualized and competitive skills of a high order, removed from forms of cooperating and sharing of knowledge? Is this the 'hidden curriculum' that successfully politicized and schooled people bring to the workplace? There is an argument to be made that newer accountability and efficiency schemes have hardened the existing lines. It was never easy to encourage teacher-initiated school-based change; it appears to be more difficult in present times.

However, there is a connectedness to all this if we are to heed the findings of Joyce and Showers (1988), who provide confirmation of the links between staff development, implementation and student outcomes. Their research claims considerable impact of staff development programs on 'student achievement and

Figure 1. A General Framework

a Purpose: long-term, sustainable and achievable objectives
b Challenge: integrating disciplines — establishing sequences within a democratic ethos
   TEACHING AREAS, i.e., humanities, mathematics, science, languages, physical culture,
   arts, that can be applied to the following personal and social aims:

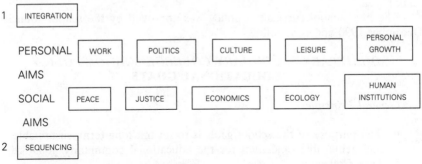

1 INTEGRATION

PERSONAL   WORK   POLITICS   CULTURE   LEISURE   PERSONAL GROWTH

AIMS

SOCIAL   PEACE   JUSTICE   ECONOMICS   ECOLOGY   HUMAN INSTITUTIONS

AIMS

2 SEQUENCING

— moving from local to state to international issues
— connecting issues and historical relationships, i.e., gender, class, race
— moving toward (grades 1–12): economic literacy; cultural and historical understanding; political participation
— schools allow students to test validity of *their* ideas in debate and social practice.

student promotion rates'. The literature on 'successful' in-service programs indicates that one of the factors which bears on whether teachers permanently change their classroom behaviour or not is whether they can see change in their students' behaviour which they perceive is desirable.

Educational Goals: Establishing a Comprehensive and Common Curriculum

The school curriculum debate within the school community· was intensive and extensive. It involved all the school constituents, teachers, parents and students. A general framework was proposed that argued for an integrated curriculum which would link knowledge, cognitive skills, personal development and social aims (see Figure 1).

There is a *developmental* sequencing of educational experiences from grades 1 to 12. The teacher and student would move from local to state to international perspectives during the sequences of debate and research on issues of importance, thereby encouraging students to develop a theory of social and physical causality as to their place in the order and structure of their society. A number of teaching strategies would be involved, including an *enquiry-based* model that would encourage students to understand how social issues relate within each sequence of study and how forms of knowledge, i.e., economic analysis, cultural understanding and political participation, are part of their education. The strength of the model is that it rests upon the quality of the teacher. It relies upon teacher judgment and participation rather than just teacher direction. The

Tony Knight

youth participation projects developed in the community competence arena connect directly with the school curriculum aims. They help to bring a balance between academic excellence and personal skills (Purkey and Aspey, 1988). Each project allows the student to test the power of his or her ideas in school debate and social practice. No program operates as a single entity unconnected to the aims of the school.

The final school curriculum policy was approved by the school council in December 1990 and is as follows.

DUKE PARK SECONDARY COLLEGE SCHOOL POLICY
EDUCATIONAL GOALS

General Principles

- The purpose of the school gaols is to set out long-term, sustainable and achievable objectives for the educational community at Duke Park College.
- These educational goals have been defined through a democratic public philosophy that pays attention to public responsibility, personal rights and democratic tolerance.
- This democratic ethos is one in which there is a conscious striving to organize all school activities toward compliance with mutually agreed goals.
- The school goals aim is to provide every student with knowledge and experience to have equal choice in work, politics, culture, leisure and personal development.
- The school community has agreed upon a comprehensive and common curriculum and its basics include personal and social development, aesthetic understanding, cultural competence, environmental awareness, political literacy and physical education.
- The academic curriculum includes a full range of subjects from year 7 culminating in a comprehensive choice at the years 11–12 Victorian Certificate of Education.
- The school aims are to help teachers to guide and evaluate their own activities and teaching.

Levels of Planning

The Duke Park College educational goals are organized within four planning levels of curriculum:
1 *intellectual aims*
   defined as definitions of worthwhile knowledge and understanding.
2 *skill aims*
   defined as techniques of knowing how to achieve skills, competence, dexterity and abilities.
3 *personal aims*
   defined as forms of personal skill, understanding and responsibility.
4 *social aims*
   defined as forms of community competence and responsibility.

148

General Curriculum Aims

1 Intellectual Aims ... Content

Education for economic literacy and choice of life career.
This would include a knowledge of how to enter the economic world, a knowledge of career perspectives and a knowledge of economics and politics.

Education for responsible analysis and decision-making.
This includes active learning to be a democratic and responsible citizen, and an understanding that school rights carry personal responsibilities.

Education for cultural understanding and participation.
This requires a sense of history as to cultural contributions made by gender, ethnicity, race and social class — culture as a unifying experience. Students as inventors of culture.

Education for inter-intra personal competence.
This requires at least an understanding of how to live with self and others in non-exploitative and non-manipulative relationships. How to live without dependence on drugs or alcohol.

Education for participatory and healthy leisure.
This requires a knowledge of self-sufficiency, skills and enjoyment in personal leisure and participatory sport. An understanding of the place of leisure in contemporary society and its relationship with youth.

Curriculum Implementation

Integrated Curriculum (7–10)

Nine areas of learning listed in VCE (11–12)

Teaching strategies: i.e., enquiry-based, linking subjects with economic, political, cultural, personal and environmental understanding.

The college will draw from a variety of teaching models and methods that include differing emphases on both cognitive and affective domains and the academic, social, behavioural and personal areas of learning.

A problem-solving approach ought to be used in programs where possible.

Programs will encourage students to use a wide variety of resources and to work cooperatively in solving problems.

Students will also be taught and be encouraged to demonstrate strategies for independent and flexible learning. With each area of learning a major program goal will be to train students in the independent use of relevant resources.

Programs will be structured to give students practice in using the range of resources and strategies to complete specific tasks. Homework will be used as a preparation and consolidation of classwork.

Each task and skill should fit into larger context of society and human values.

General Curriculum Aims

2 Skills

Use of language(s)
Numerical techniques
Physical performance
Arts-based competence
Technical skills

Students must be able to think logically and critically so that they bring order to a mass of facts and information, select wisely and make responsible social and personal decisions.

3 Personal Aims

To work toward the application of knowledge and on one's own situation in work, politics, culture and leisure.

To develop the ability for critical self-evaluation of beliefs and attitudes in one's own life.

Provide opportunity for every student to participate in decisions that affect his or her life.

To guarantee rights for teachers, parents and students of expression, privacy, due process.

To increase students' sense of self-esteem and confidence by being active learners and participants.

Curriculum Implementation

All areas of learning will provide students with opportunities to: evaluate arguments, interpret statistical data, sensibly interpret natural phenomena and be able to apply problem-solving techniques to practical situations. Students will be required to explain and justify their opinions and recognize the rationale behind other opinions. An extension of these skills would enable students to develop the notion of generalizability of skills or use of information beyond mastery of technique.

Foster understanding of the different languages and cultural traditions that comprise our society.

Provide equal encouragement of each work unit. Students will

reflect on goals and complete a self-evaluation to ascertain whether goals have been achieved and to identify strengths and weaknesses. This will be done in conjunction with teacher assessment.

Each area of learning will include opportunities for all students to practise a variety of means of expression: these may include written and oral work, public speaking, logical instruction, art forms, performing, model-making. Choice and coaching in competitive sport competition — intra-inter school.

Development of school/class structures that facilitate decision-making for students.

Respect for the rights of others through historical and cultural understanding: race, class, gender, ethnicity.

In-service to reduce sex-stereotyping of career choice for students and to avoid narrow definitions of student ability.

General Curriculum Aims

4 Social Aims

Development of a deliberative democratic character in students.

To define the knowledge and experience necessary to solve critical issues facing society.

Participation in community and school decision-making activities.

Developing an understanding of how diverse environments function, analyzing the effect of human activity, and the role of conservation in their management.

Testing ideas — finding solutions — enjoying school.

Curriculum Implementation

Provide equal encouragement for *all* students and teachers to experiment, take risks and learn to construct knowledge from experience.

School programs will provide opportunities for students to present opinions and consider the views of other members of the community. Curriculum activities will include invitations to guests to participate at the school, and all students will have curriculum experience outside the school in the wider environment.

The program at Mirimbah (outdoor education camp) will continue to introduce students to leadership, survival bushcraft experiences, which are designed to challenge them and increase their self-confidence. Environmental education would include practice in recycling, environmental energy conservation and understanding local ecology.

School projects can be linked with school aims, i.e., recreation/health aides; oral history projects — connecting history and local community; students as tutors; education/work experience; action research projects; parent-student programs; youth service teams, music/media/theatre programs; school governance participation; youth consultation teams; home group exploration of issues; recycling projects.

Integrating Policy, Content and Program

Having settled on the broad aims of curriculum policy, the question of the content has to be worked through. This remains a very contentious debate, as it should be. There are lots of sides to decisions on curriculum content, ranging from discourse analysis, the socially critical school, cultural literacy, feminism and broadsides from Foucault. What is presented here is a framework of questions emerging from the intellectual aims, with a central premise being the teaching of students for democratic and responsible citizenship. The teacher's role is the challenge to provide a *context* for learning. Teachers bring the world into the classroom so that they can help children and youth make sense of a complex and difficult (and often seemingly senseless) world. Examples of questions and concerns developed around the intellectual aims are as follows:

Education and Work

To enable students to seek out occupations and to understand the factors that create or eliminate kinds of work:

- — to understand the relationship between technology, oil prices, inflation, capital intensive work strategies and unemployment;
- — to understand the relationship between education, economy and social change;
- — to embed this analysis into the curriculum so that student work experience programs can be debated and analyzed;
- — to set up alternative arguments regarding how work can be created in a society that is economically feasible, energy conserving and earth respecting;

— the economics they learn to use in solving major problems they also use to solve local and personal problems;

— to understand how work is distributed according to gender, age, ethnicity;

— they participate in the development of job schemes and in the evaluation of them.

Education and Politics

Politics is a major concern of youth.

Many youth are very concerned about power or, more precisely, their *lack of it.*

Power is a major factor in their relationships with parents, school staff, police and other youth:

— it enters into their connections with the work world, their culture, and the way they use leisure;

— it contributes to drug and alcohol abuse;

— one of the places where students learn about the use and abuse of power is school.

To be prepared for *democratic* citizenship students should both experience and research democratic practice.

Schools can make *democracy* a part of daily school life and develop a Code of Behaviour, i.e.:

(a) develop respect for basic rights and responsibilities in the school, years 3–6;

(b) experiment with systems of participatory democracy, years 7–12;

(c) compare adult political problems with classroom difficulties;

(d) engage students in decision-making within the school so that a gradual induction into these skills can link to future adult competence.

Develop a Code of Behaviour with students that would consider:

1 right to free expression;
2 rights to privacy;
3 rights to due process;
4 rights not to be a captive audience;
5 rights to participation in decision-making.

Students can learn to use power legitimately in the community (school) interest — it begins in the classroom and extends to larger systems, i.e., committees and councils, ultimately to the wider society.

If students are to be responsible, then they have to learn and be given responsibilities.

The challenge is how to create a better system.

Education and Culture

Students should learn about culture.

They should be literate, versed in the arts, knowledgeable in science and maths, and have a profound sense of history.

They should be able to appreciate the diversity of culture in Australian society and be able to analyze common cultural themes.

They should be able to analyze and understand the richness and complexity of the world of Australian Aboriginal cultures (within this land occupied by them some 30,000 years ago) and how European settlement initiated a struggle for survival as habitat and hegemony are destroyed, and their struggle for identity and value systems are challenged and often degraded by outside forces.

They should be conversant in more than one language and appreciative of the contributions of the world communities.

Students should understand culture as a dynamic; students should read and appreciate Aristotle and Shakespeare not as passive recipients, but as active philosophers and playwrights — they put their study to use as creators of culture.

They are being asked to integrate the past with the present and to build upon a foundation of accumulated knowledge.

Such culture is not removed from political and economic life; instead, community economics and politics are enriched.

It should connect to a vision of a desirable future.

Education and Personal Life

Schools are in a sense forms of laboratories in personal relationships.

In schools students learn to live harmoniously *or* to abuse each other.

They build a foundation for gender relationships that influences the remainder of their lives.

They learn to relate to ethnic groups (or not to).

They learn about the legitimacy of difference and the contribution of schools to disability.

They learn about tobacco, drugs and alcohol.

It is not easy for today's students to learn how to become healthy and balanced human beings.

Too many are induced or learn to be helpless, exploitive and self-destructive.

Teaching about healthy non-exploitive relationships is a combination of analysis and action.

Curriculum content can be directed to issues raised by students — or by emerging problems.

'Pastoral' care programs do not have a good track record of results (Knight, 1991a). Personal growth needs to be placed within, and integrated to, work, politics, leisure and culture.

Discussions about sex, race or ethnic relationships are not directed to social action but all too often to undisciplined 'sensitivity' or confrontation sessions in which everyone gives vent to feelings.

The measure of the effectiveness of such sessions might be in a 'culture of narcissism' being expounded.

Healthy relationships within the school must be geared to some agreed external criteria, and evaluated by observable evidence of positive changes, and by the elimination of objective and negative conditions, i.e., violence, verbal abuse, exploitive relationships.

The challenges for teachers within these summaries are considerable and complex at each level of pre-school, primary, secondary and tertiary education, but these skills and competences need to become the general rule in schools rather than the exception.

Moving students from being passive recipients of the schooling process to a more active and critical participation in their own learning becomes a central theme. Integrating these five arenas into the general life of the school is not easy. Differing emphasis may be placed at various age levels, but the overall effort is to integrate all school activities within the goals agreed by the school community — to integrate the subject demands of a centralized curriculum within the local demands of a whole school context in order to bring a balance between intellectual, skill, personal and social aims of education.

Summary

One of the assumptions — albeit insufficiently explored — of this project is the relationship between political powerlessness in the broadest sense and school failure. One application of political power is the influence a school and community has over school policy and practice. School policy and practice in turn are crucial determinants of school performance. Policy should determine the long-term sustainable and achievable objectives for the school. This is particularly important to school communities characterized by populations of economically disadvantaged students. For several decades efforts to redress school failure usually fell into one of two main forms: repairing alleged deficits or changing school culture and structures. The school in this case study chose the latter approach. It chose to construct a policy informing a broad and entitled curriculum that aimed to be inclusive of all students in the school irrespective of ethnicity, gender, class background or perceived disability. Evaluation of the program under progress will test the validity of these proposals.

The school and community chose to frame curriculum content within a democratic ethos. It integrated into the ambiance of the school the teaching of moral and ethical concepts in order to influence student behaviour and value systems. To assist this process, the school developed a Code of Behaviour based on rights and responsibilities (Knight, 1985, 1991c). All the school programs, from the cognitive to the affective, will be evaluated according to the general school aims.

Second, this democratic school curriculum is linked to larger complexly interrelated social and community issues — the shape of the political economy, the condition of the environment, the lingering and sometimes festering conditions of race, tribal and ethnic hatred and sexual domination, the ever changing face of international relations, the use and misuse of technology, the failure to include those considered disabled — and unless these issues are an integral part of the educational debate within the school and community, *education* for most will continue to be uneven, most likely illusory.

Third, a strong component to this case study is the influence of a solid core of parent representatives, on School Council, in the deliberation of school policy formation. While the teaching staff struggle to gain a sense of collegiality, this was not the case for the parent group. This group maintained a cohesive presence, brought a pluralist perspective to issues, and provided links to diverse community opinion. They also gave strong support to the willing '10 per cent' of the staff, thus enlarging the group working on policy formation and change in the school. This work offers considerable optimism for the role of parents as decision-makers in schools. Emerging also from this study is a changing notion of parents in schools as partners rather than clients.

Fourth, teacher work is also being redefined in the present climate of educational reform. Stephen Ball (1992) makes the comment: 'In this heterotopia of reform the relationships of teachers with significant others are changed and confused, the teacher as person and professional, is both scapegoat and victim. Professionality is replaced by accountability, collegiality by costing and surveillance.' This project continues as a conflict model. Issues of interpretation and contestation were part of policy formation and are now obvious in the interpretation and implementation of the policy. The role of the 'outsider' — parent and tertiary staff — continues as important. mediator to this process. The democratic principles adopted continue to offer strong guidelines for the resolution of conflict and interpretation of school policy. Students, teachers and community have been invited to a debate. The question they are being asked is: If given the opportunity, what sort of society would you build? Central to this is the question: Who enjoys the rites/rights of passage in such a society, and, in turn, in our school?

Public education of the kind proposed in this model aims to produce citizens considerate of their individual rights and prepared to engage their community responsibilities.

References

AINLEY, J., BATTEN, M. and MILLER, H. (1984) 'Staying at High School in Victoria', Hawthorn, Vic., Australian Council for Educational Research.

AINLEY, J., Reed, R. and MILLER, H. (1987) *School Organization and the Quality of Schooling: A Study of Victorian Government Secondary School*, Melbourne, Australian Council for Educational Research.

APPLE, M. (1990) *Ideology and Curriculum*, 2nd ed., New York, Routledge.

BALL, S. (1987) *The Micro Politics of the School*, London, Methuen.

BALL, S. (1992) 'The Worst of Three Worlds: Policy, Power Relations and Teachers' Work', Keynote address, BEMAS Conference, UK, p. 24.

BARTH, R.S. (1990) *Improving Schools from Within: Teachers, Parents and Principles Can Make a Difference*, New York, Jossey Bass.

BARTON, L. (1986) 'The Politics of Special Educational Needs', *Disability, Handicap and Society*, 1, 3, pp. 173–290.

BATES, R.J. (1987) 'Corporate Culture, Schooling and Educational Administration', *Educational Administration Quarterly*, 23, 4, November, pp. 79–115.

BATTEN, M. (1989) *Year 12: Student Expectations and Experience*, ACER Research Monograph No. 33, Hawthorn, Victoria.

BROWN, P. and LAUDER, H. (1991) 'Education, Economy and Social Change', *International Studies in Sociology of Education*, 1, pp. 3–23.

CLARK, D., LOTTO, L. and McCARTHY, M. (1980) 'Factors Associated with Success in Urban Elementary Schools', *Phi Delta Kappan*, 61, 7, pp. 467–470.

COLE, N.S. (1990) 'Conception of Educational Achievement', *Educational Research*, 19, 3, April, pp. 2–7.

CONNELLY, D.J. (1989) 'Reconciling Purposeful Learning with Increased Participation in the Post Compulsory Years of Secondary School', *Curriculum Perspectives*, 9, 4, October.

CRANDALL, D.P., EISMAN, J.W. and SEASHORE, L.K. (1986) 'Strategic Planning Issues That Bear on the Success of School Improvement Efforts', *Educational Administration Quarterly*, 22, 3, Summer, p. 46.

CRITTENDEN, BRIAN (1991) 'The Ten Million Dollar Question: What Makes a Good School?' *The Melbourne Review*, May.

CUBAN, L. (1984) 'Transforming the Frog into a Prince: Effective Schools Research, Policy and Practice at the District Level', *Harvard Educational Review*, 54, 2, pp. 129–151.

FITZCLARENCE, L., BATES, R., BIGUM, C., GREEN, W. and WALKER, R. (1991) 'Schooling the Future: An Ethnographic Account of Information Culture and Student Experience in the Context of the VCE', Unpublished paper, Deakin University.

FULCHER, GILLIAN (1989) *Disabling Policies: A Comparative Approach to Education Policy and Disability*, Lewes, Falmer Press.

FULLAN, M.G. (1990) 'Staff Development, Innovation and Institutional Development', in *ASCD Yearbook: Changing School Culture through Staff Development*, Ed. Bruce Joyce, pp. 3–25.

GIBSON, R.D. (1984) 'Pastoral Care — For Whom?', in *Secondary School Management in the 1980s: Aspects of Education,* Journal of the Institute of Education, University of Hull, pp. 26–33.

GUTMANN, A. (1987) *Democratic Education*, Princeton, N.J., Princeton University Press.

HARGREAVES, A. and REYNOLDS, D. (1989) *Education Policies: Controversies and Critiques*, Lewes, Falmer Press, Ch. 2.

JONES, D., METCALF, D., WILLIAMS, T. and WILLIAMSON, J. (1982) *A School Curriculum and Self-evaluation Project*, Task Force Report No. 7, Ed. Tony Knight, Melbourne, La Trobe University, School of Education.

JOYCE, B. and SHOWERS, B. (1988) *Student Achievement through Staff Development*, New York, Longman.

JOYCE, B., MURPHY, SHOWERS, B. and MURPHY, J. (1989) 'Reconstructing the Workplace: School Renewal as Cultural Change', Paper presented at the annual meeting of the American Educational Research Association, San Francisco.

KICKERT, J.M. (1991) 'Steering at a Distance', Paper presented at the ECPR joint sessions, University of Essex.

KNIGHT, TONY (1985) 'An Apprenticeship in Democracy', *The Australian Teacher*, 11, pp. 5–7.

KNIGHT, TONY (1988) 'School Discipline as a Curriculum Concern', in R. SLEE (Ed.), *Discipline and Schools*, South Melbourne, Macmillan Australia, Ch. 16.

KNIGHT, TONY (1989) 'A Democratic Apprenticeship in the Primary School. The Best of Set: Discipline', SET Item No. 14, Melbourne, Australian Council for Educational Research.

KNIGHT, TONY (1991a) 'Democratic Schooling: Basis for a School Code of Behaviour', in LOVEGROVE, M. and LEWIS, R. (Eds), *Classroom Discipline*, Melbourne, Longman Cheshire Australia, Ch. 16.

KNIGHT, TONY (1991b) ' "At Risk" Schools: A Problem for Youth', *Principal Matters*, 2, 4, pp. 15–17.

KNIGHT, T. (1991c) 'A School Code of Behaviour: Moving beyond Control Theory', Paper presented at the Annual Conference of the Australian Association for Research in Education, Queensland, 26–30 November.

LANG, P. (1977) 'It's Easier to Punish Us in Small Groups', *The Times Educational Supplement*, 6 May.

LANG, P. and HYDE, N. (1987) 'Pastoral Care: Not Making the Same Mistakes Twice', *Curriculum Perspectives*, 7, 2, October, pp. 1–10.

MAUGHAN, B., PICKLES, A. and RUTTER, M. (1990) 'Can Schools Change', *School Effectiveness and School Improvement*, 1, 3, pp. 188–210.

MELLOR, W. and CHAPMAN, J. (1984) 'Organizational Effectiveness in Schools', *Educational Administration Review*, 2, 2, Spring, pp. 25–36.

MINISTRY OF EDUCATION-VICTORIA (1986) *School Council: General Information*, Interim Manual, Melbourne, Ministry of Education, Council Services Unit.

MULFORD, B. (1987) 'Indicators of School Effectiveness', *Australian Council of Educational Administration*, Monograph Series.

NIAS, J. (1989) *Primary Teachers Talking: A Study of Teaching as Work*, London, Routledge and Kegan Paul.

OAKES, J. (1991) 'Sunshine High School and 9/10/11 Revisited', *Connect*, December.

OTTO, R. (1986) *Teachers under Stress*, Melbourne, Hill of Content.

POWELL, A.G., FARRAR, E. and COHEN, D.K. (1985) *The Shopping Mall High School: Winners and Losers in the Educational Market Place*, Boston, Mass., Houghton Mifflin.

POWER, S. (1991) ' "Pastoral Care" as Curriculum Discourse: A Study in the Reformation of Academic "Schooling" ', *International Studies in Sociology of Education*, 1, pp. 193–208.

PURKEY, N.W. and ASPEY, D.N. (1988) 'The Mental Health of Students: Nobody Minds? Nobody Cares?' *Person-Centred Review*, 3, 1, February, pp. 41–49.

PUSEY, M. (1991) *Economic Rationalism in Canberra: A Nation Building State Changes Its Mind*, Cambridge, Cambridge University Press.

QUEENSLAND DEPARTMENT OF EDUCATION (1990) 'Focus on Schools: The Future Organization of Educational Services for Students', p. 41.

RAMSAY, P., SNEDDON, D., GRENFELL, J. and FORD, I. (1987) 'The Characteristics of Successful Schools', SET No. 1, Item 8, Melbourne, Australian Council for Educational Research.

REYNOLDS, D. (Ed.) (1985) *Studying School Effectiveness*, Lewes, Falmer Press.

ROWE, K.J. (1991) 'Students, Parents, Teachers and Schools Make a Difference', Melbourne, Ministry of Education and Training, Victoria, State Board of Education, Schools Programs Division, December.

SARROS, A.M. and SARROS, J.C. (1990) 'How Burned Out Are Our Teachers', *Australian Journal of Education*, 34, 2, August, pp. 145–152.

SIMON, B. (1985) *Does Education Matter?* London, Lawrence and Wishart, p. 99.

SLEE, R. (Ed.) (1988) *Discipline and Schools: A Curriculum Perspective*, South Melbourne, Macmillan Australia.

SMITH, D.J. and TOMLINSON, S. (1989) *The School Effort: Study of Multi-Racial Comprehensives*, Policy Studies Institute, London, Pinter, p. 302.

STURMAN, A. (1990) 'Devolved Decision-Making and Its Impact on the Curriculum', *Working Papers in Public Education Vol. II*, Melbourne, State Board of Education, Victoria, Ch. 5.

TOMLINSON, S. and FINCH, J. (1984) *Education as Social Policy*, London, Longman.

WATKINS, P. (1986) 'From Managerialism to Communicative Competence: Control and Consensus in Educational Administration', *Journal of Educational Administration*, 24, 1, Winter, pp. 86–106.

Tony Knight

WHITE, D. (1989) 'Theorizing the Post-Modern Curriculum', in STOCKLEY, D. (Ed.), *Melbourne Studies in Education, 1987–88*, Bundoora, Vic., La Trobe University Press.

WHITLOCK, F. (1991) 'Been There, Done That, Groovers', *The Age*, 16 November, Extra, pp. 3–4.

YEATMAN, A. (1990) 'Administrative Reform and Management Improvement', in *Bureaucrats, Technocrats, Femocrats: Essays on the Contemporary Australian State*, Sydney, Allen and Unwin, Ch. 1, pp. 1–12.

Chapter 11

Contests in Decision-making at the School Level

Genée Marks

Because strong interest groups exist in the field, education is always contested. Parents, teachers, students, educational administrators, teacher educators and political parties are among those who all have their own view about what, how and who should be taught. As a consequence, compromise, contest and contradiction mark educational systems. This typical state of affairs functions to provide the impetus for change in classrooms and schools (Kemmis, 1989). The contests within schools and educational systems over inclusion, curriculum and pedagogy are rarely thoroughly resolved, however, and different practices may co-exist in some sort of uneasy truce. Such conflicts may be either tolerated or ignored, but 'beyond that point, attempts are made to secure agreements, frequently through regulation in the form of new system or school policies' (Kemmis, 1989). Recent history suggests that this may well have been the case in the move from segregated special education to integration.

In 1982, when the Victorian Minister of Education set up a committee to review the educational services provided by the state for children with disabilities, it was both a beginning and an end. The parents' movement had for some time been lobbying politicians in an attempt to provoke official action. Integration, however, did not spontaneously come into existence in 1984, when the policy was written. It had been functioning for some time in Victoria, frequently without official sanction, but occasionally with encouragement from various parts of the educational bureaucracy. Little initial support for integration came from the Ministerial bureaucracy.

In the 1950s and 1960s there was also pressure from the teachers' unions to expand the segregated system. This attitude was supported by the state education bureaucracy. The following statement, for example, appeared in the *Educational Magazine* in 1963:

> Enough has been said to illustrate that basic philosophy that underlies the work with handicapped children — that wherever possible they should share the school experiences of other children, but never at the expense of their own welfare or the educational progress of other children. (Newman, 1972: 65)

While this statement may appear superficially to be supportive of the integration of children with disabilities into regular schools, the discourse that informs it is very much of the segregationist model. The language within which this statement is framed has been echoed since in the American Public Law 94-142 (i.e., 'least restrictive environment', 'most appropriate setting'), the Karmel Report (*Schools in Australia,* 1973: 109) (i.e., 'there are clearly children who require special provision for their education beyond that available in an ordinary classroom'), the Working Party on Commonwealth Policies and Decision in Special Education (1985) (i.e., 'most advantageous environment'), and the Victorian Teachers' Union Policy (1989) (i.e., 'least restrictive environment').

It seems unlikely that the impetus for reform in the field of special education came from either the bureaucracy or the teaching service. Lewis (1989) reports that it was really the parents of children with disabilities, supported by the various parents' organizations, who instigated a grassroots social movement for integration. Before the organized action of the parents' organizations, any integration that existed came about through isolated private arrangements in particular schools and between particular teachers and parents.

The parents' movement, however, ensured that the issue was big enough for the Victorian Branch of the Australian Labor Party to include a policy on integration in its platform for the 1982 state election, and the government was committed to the idea once it was elected. The Ministerial Review Committee established working parties to address four main areas:

the rights of children and their parents, and the processes that may require legislation in order to ensure the observance of these rights;

structures and decision-making, at all of local, regional and State levels;

normalization, and the processes of assessment and placement, as well as the necessary support services to facilitate this process; and finally,

parent, teacher, and community education. (Fisher, 1989)

When the review released its report in 1984, there was initial elation among the parent bodies, and fear and trepidation among teachers. Both groups may have reacted prematurely. From the outset, the process of implementing integration was hampered by a marked lack of resources. Furthermore, in May 1985 the Labor Government beat a hasty retreat on integration by implementing a 'delayed admission' process, which meant that while schools must *enrol* local children with disabilities, they did not actually have to *admit* those children. The parents were outraged at the introduction of such a discriminatory practice, and established the Victorian Parent Advocacy Collective (VPAC). This group persistently lobbied the Minister until it established its right to have regular contact with him about integration issues. It has maintained a high profile in the press, in working parties on integration and in its training programs for parent advocates (Reidy, 1989).

The 1984 ministerial review, *Integration in Victorian Education,* attempted to change the entrenched orientation to the education of children with disabilities. Importantly, it rejected the traditional decision-making models that had been the hallmark of special education. Interestingly, the review also rejected the American definition enforced by Public Law 94-142, which stresses the placement of children with disabilities in the 'least restrictive environment', for this notion conforms to a deficit model that was rejected by the review in favour of a collaborative model. The ministerial review contested the terrain of special education, by challenging not only its models but also its definitions. The review addresses not only the problem of *increasing* the participation of children who have previously been segregated out of regular education, but also *maintaining* the participation of children already in the regular setting (in old terminology the 'at-risk' children) (Ministry of Education-Victoria, 1984: 6).

Implementation of the Victorian government policy on integration has been constantly confounded by bureaucracy. Resources have been withheld, and the 'appropriate channels' have discouraged parents from taking action. Fulcher (1987) argues that resources have been used by bureaucracies on its procedures rather than in the schools. She also notes that when the task force on integration presented its recommendations, they were the same as those proposed by the review three years previously! As well, Fulcher accuses the bureaucracy of concealing some of the facts, and only revealing suitable parts of others. It is this sort of bureaucratic contest that has marked the implementation of the integration policy from the outset.

There are many questions that may be asked about the establishment and implementation of the integration policy in Victoria. The field of special education generally is scarified by vested interests of varying sorts. Special education has moved from a medical model of intervention in disability. When the dominance in this domain was wrested by the Education Department from the medical profession, special education moved into an era of consultative intervention. Psychologists and other consultants were called on to remedy the situation. This has been replaced recently with the collaborative model, which, it is claimed, empowers members of the school community and involves them in the participatory decision-making process. In truth, all three discourses still appear to play a role in special education and its current form of integration.

The Policy: Integration in Victorian Education

The perspective of the Victorian review of services for people with disabilities was that the segregation of educational resources either emphasized or generated differences which belied the similarities and denied the rights of students with disabilities. In observing that 'there has been a *gap* between a *written* and *stated policy* on integration and *enacted policy*, i.e., practice', the review naively equated 'practice' with 'enacted policy'. As well, the review argued that 'lack of clearly conceptualised policy', lack of accountability within the system and a lack of enactment mechanisms were seen as contributing to this disorganized and unsystematic situation (Ministry of Education-Victoria, 1984: 91).

From the outset, contestation and resistance have plagued integration policy. Fulcher (1989) highlighted the resistance within the review team itself to the institutionalization of integration. She observed that 'the proponents of democratism did not have an easy time', especially when debating the membership of the participatory decision-making structures that so dominate current policy. Although the ministerial review was presented as a consensus report, 'Extension Notes' that expressed dissension from the majority recommendations were attached by the parent representative and the teacher union representative ten minutes before the report was to be presented to the Minister (Fulcher, 1989).

Looking back now, the Victorian proposals for participatory decision-making structures seem naive politics but they were in line with the Victorian Labor government's general policy and they were, at the time, hotly debated, and much time, energy and group dynamic ploys were expended in attempting to influence these decisions. (Fulcher, 1989)

As well as defining integration the ministerial review established five guiding principles. These are considered to be of paramount importance, as they inform the bureaucratic constructs and processes established by the review. The first guiding principle promotes the right of every child to be educated in a regular school. (As a corollary, they are also seen as having the right *not* to attend a regular school. Segregated special education will not be denied to parents who wish to utilize this system.) Responsibility falls to the government to ensure that regular schools can provide the necessary programs and support for all children, and not just those considered able bodied (Ministry of Education-Victoria, 1984: 13). This emphasis on 'rights' has been seen as epitomizing the discourse that has informed the review.

The second guiding principle demands 'non-categorization' in both legislation and service delivery. Legislation 'should be framed without reference to particular categories of impairment and disability.' The additional or particular educational requirements of a student are to determine the applicability of the Act, rather than the requirement of 'a specific qualifying impairment or disability'. Additionally, while special expertise with specific impairments will not be expected to disappear, 'service delivery should be organised, administratively and conceptually, on a non-categorisation basis.' Cross-category provision is recommended (Ministry of Education-Victoria, 1984: 13).

The third guiding principle advocates the use of school-based resources and services. It was suggested that neighbouring schools should share resources to ensure that shortages do not occur. Personnel, as well, may be shared between schools. Certain services have been regionalized under this principle, and additional educational resources, such as integration aides and teachers, are provided at school level on the basis of perceived need, as determined by regionally based integration committees.

The fourth guiding principle takes its direction from Ministerial Paper Number One (1983) in demanding collaborative decision-making processes. The review defines this as meaning 'equal participation of all those concerned with decisions about a child's education progress' (Ministry of Education-Victoria, 1984: 14).

Finally, the fifth guiding principle affirms 'that all children can learn and be taught' (Ministry of Education-Victoria, 1984: 13). This challenges earlier assumptions about intelligence and educability.

The integration policy claims potentially to empower parents by ensuring their participation in educational decision-making, yet the policy and its supporting documents are formally expressed in a language of control. Parents who wish to facilitate the integration of their child into a regular educational setting are *required* to participate in an Integration Support Group, so that the decision about the integrated child's education may be made collaboratively. This group is expected to meet regularly, and while only mandated by government policy and not law, compliance is enforced by the control of financial resources available from the policy administering bodies. In reality, if funding is to be ensured, parents and schools have little choice but to establish Integration Support Groups for each child classified as having a disability or impairment and being educated in a neighbourhood school.

The composition of the Integration Support Group is described in the review and clarified in subsequent ministerial memoranda, which indicate that each group is to include:

the child's parent(s) or guardian(s);
a parent advocate if a parent wants that support;
the child's class teacher (primary level), or a teacher nominated as having responsibility for the student (post-primary);
the principal/headteacher (primary) or principal/nominee (postprimary); and
the student (where appropriate).

As well, the group may co-opt two people to any *particular* meeting, but not on a regular basis. Included in this latter group are integration teachers and aides, and consultants from the supporting services (Executive Memo No. 144, 1987: 3). If additional people are at the meetings, or members are co-opted without group consensus, then all decisions may be challenged on the grounds that due process has not been observed (Executive Memo No. 144, 1987: 3).

The collaborative decision-making model advocated by the review works on the premise that in the majority of cases it is the system and not the child that requires change. The education system is seen as being fraught with disabling structures that frequently create problems. The collaborative model places the power of information and the responsibility of action with designated participants, who are seen additionally to share decision-making and responsibility. This model is framed to emphasize the value of the unique skills and perspectives of parents, teachers, students and principals, as well as making full use of the expertise of consultants (Fisher, 1987).

The review suggests a number of structures to facilitate collaborative decision-making. These proposals aim both to protect the rights of parents and children, and to ensure a 'democratising [of] the constituency of members of various arenas of decision-making (at school, regional and state levels)' (Fulcher, 1986: 33). The Integration Support Group mechanism, for example, is to be set up for each child who is to be integrated into the school. Initially described by the review as an 'Enrolment Support Group' only, its function was later expanded to include decision-making power once the child was both enrolled and admitted to the school. Thus the facilitation of enrolment is only one aspect of its role, for it is also required 'to determine the educational requirements of the student including curriculum and resource needs', and 'to provide ongoing support for all the participants in the group' (State Board of Education, 1987: 7). Stone has observed: 'There *is* a need . . . to bridge the gap between the idealism of the integration policy, and the realism of integration practice. *The Enrolment and Support Group Guidelines are intended to bridge that gap.* They are an attempt to turn the idealism of the Guiding Principles into a set of workable implementation procedures' (1987: 11–12).

Within the group, while not officially granted greater decision-making power, the principal is charged with particular duties. He or she is required to convene and chair meetings, keep minutes, and at the close of each meeting read the records of all decisions aloud to ensure understanding and agreement (Executive Memo No. 114, 1987: 5). As well: 'It is the responsibility of the Principal to facilitate the collaborative processes by offering support to, and ensuring the equal participation of, parents, teachers and other members of the group (Executive Memo No. 34, 1986: 7). The nature of the principal's power during such meetings may well be problematic.

This chapter examines closely the patterns of discourse within Integration Support Group meetings in an attempt to discover the nature of the interrelationships between the group members. The somewhat naive liberal belief that equality and social justice may be achieved by service delivery along the lines of one or other notion of equality has been perpetually hampered by 'the great behemoth of social welfare programming, lumbering about with its "delivery of services" mentality, [that] spends an inordinate amount just keeping itself fed, protecting its domain from intruders, and squabbling within its own den' (Fried, 1980).

Participation and Collaborative Decision-making in Schools

When reviewing the Australian education system in general, King and Young (1986) take a less than sanguine view, arguing that schools are deceptively encouraging participation. These efforts, rather than generating open access, are actually serving to restrict the means of access, and thus protect the authority of the school. 'Even in the schemes promulgated by departments of education in some states, only a few selected parents have the access to the processes of decision-making' (1986: 161). If the contribution of parents is to be effective and to enhance the structure of participation, then power must be shared with parents.

Such a view of the effectiveness of parental participation in decision-making is depressing, for it suggests that the status quo has changed little in almost two decades. In 1973 *Schools in Australia*, popularly known as the Karmel Report, provided an historical precedent, not only for the concept of integration, but also for the notion of collaborative decision-making. The report asserted that: 'Responsibility should be devolved as far as possible upon the people involved in the actual task of schooling, in consultation with the parents of the pupils whom they teach and, at senior levels, with the students themselves' (White, 1987: 22). The Karmel Committee believed that sharing responsibility and decision-making among people with a vested interest in the resultant decision was a very effective approach to the control of schools. The 'popular issues of participation' were made 'part of a planned official policy' (White, 1987: 23).

Care must be taken, however, not to confuse the idea of participation in educational decision-making with a consumerist view of education, which Sallis (1988: 11) observes, 'is superficially so beguiling, that it must be taken seriously even by those . . . who find it unconvincing or distasteful.' The commodification of education is mistakenly seen to be linked with parental participation. It is suggested that schools, like other suppliers of goods and services, will respond to demands made by the consumers of education. This perspective, Sallis wryly argues, 'is advocated with great sincerity by many academics, with passionate conviction by generations of right-wing politicians, and the popular newspapers love its rallying cry' (1988: 11). It has little to do with participation, however.

Freedom to shop elsewhere should not be confused with a right to run the shop (Sallis, 1988: 18).

Fulcher has noted that the democratization of special education practices in Victoria is part of 'the wider struggle to democratise general education' (1986: 44). The Ministerial Papers, for example, released between 1983 and 1985, address the issues of the devolution of authority, responsive bureaucracy, collaborative decision-making, the redress of disadvantage and discrimination, school determined curriculum, and the school council responsibility for educational policy (Fulcher, 1986: 44). Ministerial Paper Number One (1983), in particular, is directly relevant to the problem of collaborative decision-making and the devolution of authority. It asserts: 'The Government will implement a system in which people affected can participate in the decision-making process and in which all students have the opportunity to develop the knowledge, skills and concepts to participate in a democratic society' (Ministerial Paper Number One, 1983: 4). As well, the paper confirms the government's commitment 'to the implementation rather than the rhetoric, of devolution and broader participation' (1983: 4). Groups charged with collective responsibility are recommended, and such participation is expected to occur at school, regional and state levels.

This commitment was reaffirmed in 1986, when the Victorian Ministry of Education released its controversial document, *Taking Schools into the 1990s* (Ministerial Structures Project Team, 1986), which contained proposals for the reorganization of ministerial structures. This policy document was clearly informed by the rhetoric of Ministerial Paper Number One (1983), when it addressed the government's intentions in relation to the devolution of power within the state education system. The project team responsible for the new document asserted: 'Devolution of power, implemented through collaborative processes and serviced by an efficient and responsible bureaucracy, is seen as a means of improving the quality of education and achieving the Government's educational objectives' (Ministerial Structures Project Team, 1986: 7). The team observed that, in fact, people interviewed felt that the process did not go far enough. When the team's conclusions are examined carefully, however, it becomes obvious that it is concerned that change is occurring at a rate with which teachers and parents cannot cope. 'We are conscious of the voluntary input of parents and teachers and that rapid change can have adverse effects ... For these reasons, the change we propose will involve school communities in more meaningful decisions and occur at a rate which allows parents and teachers to adapt' (Ministerial Structures Project Team, 1986: 9). Rather than develop ways of facilitating change then, or of assisting teachers and parents to cope with change, it would appear that the intention of the Ministry of Education is to slow down the process!

One of the perceived problems with the collaborative decision-making model is its ascribed democratic nature. The multifarious and elusive nature of democracy poses many difficulties. Dahl has written: 'The prey we have been stalking is the proposition that democratic authority requires a variety of forms. The democratic idea is too grand to be trivialised by restricting itself to only one form of authority' (Dahl, 1970: 67). Democracy, popularly defined by its inclusion of all members of a set in all decision-making, can only exist among a very small group of people. 'When decision making involves discussion ... time's limits are inexorable and cruel to equal participation' (1970: 68).

Committee democracy, which is proposed as the model for the Integration

Support Group structure, should in theory allow all group members to participate fully in decision-making (cf. primary or town meeting democracy, where everyone who really wants to speak is given an opportunity, and representative democracy, where individuals elect a representative to speak on their behalf) (Dahl, 1970). Dahl has suggested that 'committee democracy is, typically, hostile to partisanship. For the committee reflects the familiar . . . needs of small and intimate groups' (1970: 74). However, Integration Support Groups frequently are exposed to partisanship, for the groups represented are polarized by their attitudes towards integration.

Methodology

To understand the nature of the decision-making process within integration, and to discover whether Integration Support Groups are truly collaborative, or whether the traditional bureaucratic decision-making models still dominate, a study was made of all Integration Support Group meetings within one year for two different children integrated into the same neighbourhood school. The discourse of these meetings was closely analyzed in order to discover what patterns of language were used, in the hope that any perceived patterns might hold some clue as to whether the meetings were truly collaborative, or not.

Language users make choices when they are making meanings. These choices reflect what the language interaction is about (the field), the interpersonal relationships between participants (the tenor) and the way the text is held together grammatically (the mode). These factors, field, tenor and mode, combine to form register. The cultural environment in which the language is generated (context of culture) generally determines the choice of genres (ordered, verbal activities), and the nature of the specific situation (context of situation) determines register choice. The register used by a speaker may change, while the genre — the order and purpose — may remain constant. If a teacher is greeting a colleague and then later greeting a child, the genre or pattern of the discussion might very well be the same, but the register would vary. This is because the context of situation is different, most particularly in the area of tenor, for the roles and relationships seen between teacher and child are quite different from those we would expect to exist between colleagues. At another level the tenor of language varies, for we talk in different ways to different people. Halliday argues that through interpersonal relationships, 'social groups are delimited, and the individual is identified and reinforced, since by enabling him to interact with others, language also serves in the expression and development of his own personality' (1970, quoted in de Joia and Stenton, 1980: 40). It is through this interpersonal function that language has the most potential to establish and maintain social relations.

One very useful aspect of grammar is *theme* — that which comes first in an English clause and is the point of departure for the message. 'Theme structures express the organisation of the message: How the clause relates to the surrounding discourse, and to the context of situation in which it is being produced' (Halliday, 1985: 148). A study of theme is a very strong tool, for it can provide a window (albeit a very subjective one) into the attitudes and beliefs that may underpin the behaviour of participants in language interactions. Thus, for Integration Support Group meetings, it should be possible to determine whether an ideology that supports collaborative decision-making is really influencing linguistic choices, or whether some other ideology is underpinning the choices made by participants. Theme has the potential to highlight what may really be going on, so it is useful when we want to improve our discourse. Theme highlights at an unconscious level what the language user possibly thinks is important. The choices made by the speaker or writer highlight what it is that they really want to say; and they make these choices from the linguistic resources available to them. When theme is studied, it is possible to discover the kinds of choices the speaker is making so that such choices can highlight the message the speaker wants to convey.

The Structure of the Meetings

Mehan (1983, 1984) tackled a similar research problem in America, where Eligibility and Placement Committees, mandated by Public Law 94-142, make decisions about the placement of students with disabilities. (In contrast to the Integration Support Groups, the Eligibility and Placement Committees are charged with determining the 'most appropriate educational setting' for the child.) While the American system works very much on the deficit model, it is useful, by way of comparison, to consider Mehan's work. It was Mehan's aim to explore the 'relationship between linguistic processes, cognitive activities, and social structures' (1983: 187), and to observe the way different members of the decision-making group approached the meetings with disparate perceptions of the student. He concluded, however, that by the end of the meeting the viewpoint of consultants was usually accepted as the prevailing perception: 'This authority contributes to the assembly of a presentational mode of making decisions in which decisions are presented, not discussed; credentialled, not negotiated' (1983: 187).

It is expected that the differences in theoretical paradigm that inform the American model will have contributed to the apparently widespread acceptance of the position of the professional, in contrast with the empowering rhetoric of the Australian model. What is especially interesting to this research, however, is that Mehan (1983) identified a clear and predictable, although loose, structure among the numerous Eligibility and Placement Committee meetings observed. He noted four phases that were temporally sequenced: the information presentation phase; the decision phase; the parents' rights phase (in which the rights of parents to educational services and the range of evaluative services were explained); and the goals and objectives phase (which was based 'on the discrepancy between the child's actual and expected level of performance)' (Mehan, 1983: 194). Clearly, the American system is *not* based on a collaborative model.

A potential structure for Integration and Support Group meetings is foreshadowed by some of the aspects of the socially democratic perspective discussed in the report, *Integration in Victorian Education* (1984). It argues, first, that shared information is essential if the collaborative model is to be successful. All participants in Integration Support Group meetings have a right to equal access to information about the system. This information sharing begins when the principal, as directed by policy documents, gives the parents a copy of Integration Support Group guidelines at the time of enrolment. As well, all members of the group are granted equal access to the relevant files. It is anticipated that an information sharing phase will play a major role in the Integration Support Group meetings.

The review also discusses the value of shared decision-making, but as Stone (1987) has observed, this must be preceded by a shared goal, which may be either overt or implicit. He suggests that the goal of an Integration Support Group must necessarily be the goal of integration. This, he asserts, 'is to maximize the social and educational participation *of the child in the classroom*' (1987: 15; emphasis in original). Such a shared goal 'is the one stage of the collaborative process which is not negotiable' (Stone, 1987: 15), and is consistent with Ministerial Paper Number Six (1984), which stresses the importance of access and success for all children.

Shared action is seen as the next step in the Integration Support Group structure, and this is coupled with shared responsibility. The group is responsible for carefully considering *all* information about the child (not just that provided by the professionals), deciding upon a course of action, and then taking responsibility for that action by seeking resources, approaching personnel, liaising with school council subcommittees, regional committees and so on. Members are committed to making the decided actions successful: teachers carry out programs as agreed; principals facilitate organizational change; parents follow specific programs at home. It is important that the group meets regularly to ensure that all action is monitored carefully and altered if necessary.

From a superficial consideration of Mehan's analysis, it seems fair to describe the meeting as an interview, in that it comprised task oriented dialogue. In contrast, the Integration Support Group meetings oscillated between being task oriented, when, say, programming issues were considered, and person oriented, when the problems of the child being integrated were specifically addressed. At times they were clearly interviews, but on other occasions they resembled conversations. During one of the meetings, for example, the child's mother and the psychologist discussed Simon's developing skills in oral language:

Mother: I notice he's been using, ah, lots more long sentences instead of just the basic word. We're really getting. . . .
Psychologist: Oh, that's good. Language is very important. That's great. It really is so important. You know, if he can communicate through language, and if he doesn't have to get so physical. . . .
Mother: That's right.

Yet at other times the meeting is clearly task oriented (although these tasks at all times relate to the child and his successful integration into the regular classroom). The teacher, for example, outlines a proposed program to enhance Simon's social and self-help skills. Interestingly too, in this extract the teacher is moving much more towards the lecture mode, in his enthusiasm to deliver a monologue.

Teacher: From the book that Heather brought me, we've come up with three headings: communication skills; self care skills; motor skills and social skills. I'll just go through some of these, and what I hope this meeting, is that if anyone has got any ideas, other things, then we can jot those down, and then we can prepare something formal, so that his time here isn't just spent sitting down doing language and so on. We're preparing him for other things in life. First and foremost probably, was going through practice writing his own name, address and phone number, perhaps teaching him how to use a telephone. These would all be with your approval of course.

Kress and Fowler have studied in some depth the nature of the interview as a style of communication. They observe that it may be described as a peculiar type of conversation 'in that the formal rules of status relation are exceptionally overt, strict, and legitimized by the . . . genre' (1979: 64). The degree to which this is true depends very much on what 'factors relating to pre-existent social statuses' the participants bring with them. A parent who has been brought up to fear or respect people in authority may feel that she does not really have the right to act collaboratively in an Integration Support Group meeting, for example. Such a situation was abundantly clear during Dane's Integration Support Group meeting. Dane's father confided that he found people in authority very intimidating, and that throughout Integration Support Group meetings he felt little short of devastated.

Yet both the expected aspects of the meetings described earlier and the prescribed participants are treated as optional to some extent. In an Integration Support Group meeting at a Melbourne primary school (Kirner, 1987) there was no school principal present, nor, indeed, a principal nominee. While, in the meeting being analyzed for this research, the guidelines concerning participants and structure do seem to have been observed, other Integration Support Group meetings within the school have disregarded guidelines. At one, for example, as well as the permissible participants there was an additional teacher, a third expert and a senior education officer from the region. Another meeting commenced without the parent, who had been delayed. By the time he arrived the 'shared' information phase was finished. It is quite common for ministerial guidelines to be flouted in respect to membership of Integration Support Groups. This remains an issue about which the parent movement is justly concerned.

It was anticipated, however, that when the meetings were examined carefully, the four stages of shared information, shared decision-making, shared action and shared responsibility would be present, along with a greetings phase and a closure phase, during which the principal would be expected to comply with the prescriptions of Executive Memorandum No. 144 (1987: 5) by reading 'the record of the decision to the group to facilitate understanding and agreement'. In reality, certain other unexpected phases showed up in both Integration Support Group meetings studied and in others observed. All groups (including those observed by Kirner, 1987 and Talbot, 1987) included a socializing phase and a premeeting discussion about the child, while waiting for late group members to arrive. As well, the four anticipated 'shared' phases are very difficult to separate, for they do not fall into neat and easily characterized segments (unlike those in the American Enrolment and Placement meetings studied by Mehan). Instead, they tend to be extensively interwoven. At best, it is possible to comment that shared information and shared decision-making tend to be coupled with each other, as do shared action and responsibility. After these interwoven, and in a sense convoluted, phases there is a phase in which 'last minute' thoughts are discussed. The meetings conclude with a farewell phase. In none of the meetings observed did the principal comply with the expectation to read the transcript, although he did send minutes of the meetings to all participants.

To ensure that the prescribed elements of the structure are realized, it is sometimes necessary for whoever is chairing a meeting to probe. A commonplace example of the use of probes is when a shop assistant says to a potential customer: 'Yes, can I help you?' Repair strategies, on the other hand, may be used when an obligatory element is realized, but inadequately. If a customer at the green grocery says, 'I want to buy oranges', the storekeeper may ask, 'What sort were you after?' or 'How many would you like?' These are repair strategies. Finally, realignment may be used to bring the participants back to the business at hand, if participants are diverted for one reason or another (Hasan, in Halliday and Hasan, 1985: 66).

In the Integration Support Group meetings studied, the principal, in his role as convenor, appeared to control the use of such strategies. Early in one meeting, for example, the principal cut short the premeeting discussion with a probe to ensure a movement into the greetings phase:

Principal: Derek, Jane, you know each other. This is Genée.

He used a less abrupt approach very soon afterwards, but it was, nonetheless, a probe, for it signalled a move into the shared information phase.

Principal: What we're really doing is looking at, um, Simon's progress over the last month or so, and um, seeing where he's going. It's probably, we could start and nip around to see what people say he's doing . . . Jane?

On the other hand, towards the end of the meeting, the principal attempted to realign after a failed probe a little earlier in the discussion. Thus, when he said: 'What about a get together?', he was ignored and another discussion ensued. The principal interrupted with:

Principal: When do you want to get together again? We've got, the last week of term's the 26th of May, ah, 26th of June. Do you want to meet again this term?

If the principal's use of strategy is a guide to what elements of the structure are obligatory, it would seem that the socializing phase, the premeeting discussion and the last minute thoughts may be optional. As well, the principal did not probe the farewells phase in this meeting, but this will be considered an obligatory element for obvious reasons.

From the perspective of studying the uneven distribution of power, it is interesting to observe that rarely do any other participants in the meeting use strategies to ensure the successful adherence to the necessary structure. By virtue of his position as convenor, the principal is empowered further: he has the choice of ensuring whether the meeting continues successfully or not. This is a very powerful position in which to be placed. Thus the principal's power in this sense is institutionalized. It is enshrined in the discourse that is intended to empower those members of the group who are not traditionally blessed with power within educational settings! Perhaps it is too cynical to ask whether this additional empowerment of the principal is merely an oversight by administrators and policy planners.

Theme Use as an Indicator of Control

To gain a manageable insight into the way language is used within Integration Support Group meetings, two of the meetings, one for each child, were focused on and the discourse analyzed in depth. The first of these meetings was Simon's second Integration Support Group meeting for the year. At that meeting the school principal, the child's mother, the child's classroom teacher, an integration aide and a psychologist were present, as well as the researcher. The second meeting was Dane's third for the year. At Dane's meeting there were in attendance a number of participants who should not have been present had ministerial guidelines been observed. Apart from the child's father, the principal, the classroom teacher, there were also the integration aide and the integration teacher (who *may* be present as co-opted experts). There was also an additional teacher, who was to replace the classroom teacher when he went on long service leave, and a senior education officer from the Ministry of Education. Had the boy's father been displeased with decisions made during the meeting, he would have been successful in objecting on the grounds of due process not having been observed.

Both the Integration Support Group meetings discussed appear to compare favourably with the Enrolment and Placement meetings described by Mehan (1983), in which he observed that decisions were *presented* rather than debated. One such meeting documented by Mehan (1983: 188) proceeded thus:

Psychologist:	Does the uh committee agree that the, uh, learning disability placement is one that might benefit him?
Principal:	I think we agree.
Psychologist:	We're not considering then a special day class for him?
Special teacher:	I wouldn't at this point //
Many:	= No

Interestingly, while the mother of the child being discussed *was* present at this decision-making phase, she had no input at all. In Simon's Integration Support Group meeting his mother had a strong role to play in many of the phases and certainly made her presence felt when decisions were being made, although the teacher very clearly took control during the action phases in which responsibility was allocated. In contrast, Dane's father played only a very weak role in the meeting, and contributed only very superficially to any decision-making. He was considerably more empowered, however, than the parents seemed to be in the meetings studied by Mehan.

As with any game, or any other human interaction, whoever directs the move is in control. In language, the control of continuatives (words such as 'yes', 'no', 'well' at the beginning of clauses) may be a significant signpost to control of the discourse generally. The control of continuatives specifically is suggestive of control of moves in the text. If the use of continuatives in Simon's meeting is examined, a somewhat conflicting picture emerges. Of the textual themes (those that glue the text together logically, such as conjunctions) used by the principal, nearly two-thirds were continuatives, whereas for the mother only slightly less than a third of her use of textual theme was composed of the use of continuatives. For the psychologist only one-fifth of her textual theme use consisted of continuatives; and the teacher and the integration aide used very few continuatives as a proportion of their overall use of textual theme.

Significantly, in the shared information stages, which incorporate some de-cision-making, the mother used just under half the total number of textual themes used during those phases, followed by the teacher who used only a quarter of the textual themes. These two participants have the greatest and most continuous contact with the child, so it is not surprising that they shared control of the information phases in this way. What is surprising perhaps is that the psychologist used almost a fifth of the textual themes, when she has negligible contact with the child.

In the phases where responsibility and action (as well as some decision-making) are decided upon, the control very clearly shifted. The mother suddenly had very little influence on these processes. She controlled only 7 per cent of textual themes in these phases. It would be fair to say that, although the ministerial review requires *all* stages to be collaborative, the mother was not being granted an opportunity to participate in the stages where actions are decided upon and responsibility allocated. The teacher, on the other hand, used well over half the textual themes used during these phases — a very strong indication that he is in control of issues that directly affect his classroom operation. The psychologist used a fifth of the total textual theme use, which suggests that she believed herself entitled to provide some measure of input into classroom planning and operation. As well, the principal's participation was greater in these phases than in the shared information phases. He obviously still found a great need to be a part of decisions concerning actions and who is to be responsible for them.

Simon's mother also made more frequent use of interpersonal theme than any other participant. She used three times as many interpersonal themes as the principal, psychologist or teacher; and the integration aide used fewer again. Of particular interest to this study is the use of modal adjuncts, which are grammatical choices that signal the uncertainty of the language user (such as 'I mean' and 'sort of'), and an examination of these may be approached from a number of different perspectives. Kress (1985: 54) argues that such language choices signal tentative-ness. He asserts that prefacing utterances with 'I suppose' and 'you know' has a force that suggests that what is said is supposition rather than fact. He extrapolates further to suggest that such modality may be linked with either lack of power or lack of knowledge.

While the mother and the principal devoted about one-fifth of their overall theme usage to interpersonal theme, the nature of the interpersonal themes used was markedly different. Fewer than one-fifth of the interpersonal themes used by the principal were modal, and of these three were assertions, as in: 'Yes, *I know*, what we're really doing is looking at Simon's progress over the last month or so ... *That's beaut* Derek, many thanks. ...' As well, the principal used one ad-junct of opinion when he remarked: 'You can see the differences in these ones that have been here all the time we've had Simon here, and *sort of* all seem to look after them. ...'

A vastly different picture is evident when the mother's use of interpersonal theme is examined, for over 80 per cent comprised modal adjuncts. Many of these choices expressed probability, for example: '*Perhaps* I should get together with Derek ...' and '*Sometimes*, I think, he just does it to bait me. ...' Interestingly, the latter example was, in any case, followed by an expression of opinion, which, along with expressions of assertion, were typical of the mother's language choices. However, she also expressed presumption, such as in '*No doubt* Simon will try whoever it is out thoroughly.' The mother's choice of topical theme made very clear her priorities: during the information sharing phases, for example, she was primarily concerned with her son, his progress and his behaviour. The major deviation from this was when she referred to herself when she was either expressing uncertainty about what she has just stated, for example: '*I* don't know about school . . .' and '*I* was just saying . . .', or when she was referring to something she had done, or was proposing to do. She also made efforts to situate her son's behaviour in time and place by emphasizing the circumstance. Thus, she said: '*at home*, he's on a definite [low]' and '*this morning at home* he threw his pyjamas over to the kitchen' and '*before Easter* he needed a break.' By stressing the circumstances, and putting them first, the mother emphasized their importance. Thus the mother may have been indicating that such a behaviour as that which occurred *this morning at home* was in fact atypical and therefore worth emphasizing. Similarly, she foregrounded circumstance to emphasize that her son's behaviour might be different *at home* from at school, and that things might have been different *before Easter*. In contrast, in the planning phase the mother used 'I' as topic almost exclusively: '*I*'m easy' and '*I* might be able to change it' and '*I* can't', which suggest that it was the mother herself who was of greatest importance during this phase. This seems reasonable, as the mother was attempting to ensure that another meeting was arranged at a convenient time. At the same time, however, she almost seemed willing to compromise her essential role at the meeting, if the other members could not meet when she was available.

The contributions made by Dane's father were far more tentative than those made by Simon's mother, his posture suggesting that he felt very defensive. He frequently had his arms crossed, and when he spoke, he tended to do so through his hand. At other times he wrung his hands and looked clearly frightened by the intimidating nature of the situation. For information to be successfully shared, the principal basically had to interview the parent, and when the parent did offer information, the principal tended to interrupt, interpret for and 'talk over' him. As well, the parent's contributions were typically short, rarely comprising more than a couple of clauses. At no time, and in no phase, did Dane's father take control of the discourse, whereas the teacher quite obviously exerted considerable control over the direction the discourse took.

Unlike Simon's mother in the shared information phase, Dane's father said very little in the comparable phases, and what he did say had to be coaxed out of him. He controlled less than a tenth of the total textual theme used in the information sharing phases, compared with a fifth by the integration aide (who was reticent in Simon's meeting), and a massive two-thirds used by the teacher during this phase. There is very little doubt at all that it was the teacher who was in control of the information sharing phases in this Integration Support Group meeting. This observation is confirmed when it is noted that the father used only two continuatives ('yes' and 'well', both of which occurred in the one clause), and all other structural themes were additive ('and').

In the phases of the meeting where actions were decided upon and responsibility allocated, the teacher was once again clearly in control. He was responsible for 75 per cent of the textual themes used by the group, while the principal controlled only 10 per cent and the integration aide just under 4 per cent. The father also controlled 10 per cent, similar to his contribution during the information sharing phases. While he generally still needed to be coaxed to speak during this phase of the meeting, at one stage he felt so angry that he could no longer control his annoyance, which overrode his usual timidity. He disapproved of a strategy that the teacher was using, and suddenly interrupted, saying:

> I don't know that that's really a good way to do it, myself, not being critical, *but* I think that's creating an aggressive type response. I'd be more inclined to think *that if* you wanted, *if* you left him in the room *and* got the other children telling him not to misbehave, he'd know *that* they were watching him, I'd be inclined to think *that* he'd probably behave, *but* I might be wrong. . . .

It is interesting to observe that even though the father was very angry when he spoke, he was still so unsure of himself that he used very few textual themes (which are in italics). The interpersonal language choices indicate that the father was very concerned that he might have overstepped the mark, and that he would be criticized for interfering in a matter that he clearly viewed himself as not empowered to comment on:

> *I don't know* that that's really a good way to do it, *myself, not being critical*, but I think that's creating an aggressive type response. *I'd be more inclined to think* that if you wanted, if you left him in the room and got the other children telling him not to misbehave, he'd know that they were watching him, *I'd be inclined to think* that he'd probably behave, but *I might be wrong*. . . .

As Kress and Hodge assert: 'the speaker translates uncertainty about status in the power situation into uncertainty about the status of utterances' (1979: 127). Yet within the guidelines for the process of Integration Support Group meetings the father is officially empowered to contribute to such issues. Irrespective of this, however, the father was hedging in order to protect himself from potential attack. If the teacher had attacked, he could have then conceded that he *had* been wrong, and that he should not have spoken!

From an examination of the two Integration Support Group meetings, it becomes apparent that the psychologist had considerably less power than the psychologist in Mehan's (1983) Enrolment and Placement meetings. However, it is clear that the psychologist in the two meetings studied in this report still wielded considerable power. Especially interesting is that as someone trained in the 'human sciences', such as psychology and special education, the psychologist was eager to highlight reasons and consequences. The psychologist's use of words such as 'because' and 'if' occurred equally in the shared information and action phases, was minimal in the premeeting discussion, and did not occur at all in any other phases. She seemed to use language that expresses consequences when she wished to interpret the child's behaviour, or to supply a reason why she approved of an action; for example: 'It really is so important you know, *if* he can communicate through language . . .' and: 'I think that is fabulous *because* you're not just looking at that tight little education of the three Rs. . . .' The psychologist used interpersonal language differently from the other participants in the meetings. She used 'That's great', for example, as a tool for encouraging the other participants to continue their contributions while still ensuring that they also continued to be aware of her existence. As well, she used 'I think' as a way of announcing that she intended to make a contribution, but that she *will* try to be aware that she is expected to avoid being an assertive expert in this meetings. Thus, she said things such as: '*I think* that's what you often find . . .', when the context suggests that what she really was saying was, '*We psychologists know that is often the case.*' Such a ploy characterized the psychologist's speech. In contrast, the principal saw little need to modulate his language. This may reflect his comfort in taking a position of authority. In the past, as well as currently in many other situations, he was expected to hold the power and take control.

The psychologist took a rather different position from the other participants too in the information sharing phases. As she has very little direct contact with the child being integrated, she made little reference to herself. In fact, when she did thematize her own responses, she depersonalized them in a way that typifies psychologists in their role as professionals; for example: 'Perhaps *it's* more a plateau . . .'; '*that's* why you often find . . .'; and '*it's* pretty intensive and hard in a lot of what happens, isn't it?' Rather than referring to the children directly, she tended to thematize their particular disability group, thus: '*you* find with a lot of *these* children, that *they* have a real spurt.' This use of language depersonalizes the child being discussed. It also suggests that all children who have that particular disability behave in the same fashion. Such an assertion is not only untrue; it contravenes the guiding principles used as the basis for the 1984 review, *Integration in Victorian Education,* which stated that labelling and categorizing on the basis of disability were unacceptable.

It is of interest that the only time the psychologist consistently made any reference to herself was during the planning phase, when she attempted to ensure that she could get to the next meeting. This is of special interest, for she was assuming a right to be *at* the next meeting. According to due process prescribed by the Ministry, however, the entire Integration Support Group must agree to invite consultants, and this decision must be made separately for each meeting. No such decision or invitation had been voiced. The psychologist had exhibited, and been granted, an extraordinary amount of power in her assumption that all the group wished her to be present at the next meeting. As a concession to the guidelines, she did ask: 'Do *you* want me to be at that?' and the principal answered: 'Yes, *that'd* be beaut.' However, the principal is not empowered to make the decision for the group, and in any case, the meeting being discussed was the Integration Support Group meeting for a different child, whose group was not even present to make the decision. Later in this phase the psychologist also assumed that she would be at Simon's next meeting, and none of the group members objected. It was treated as a fait accompli. Yet this is a tremendously disempowering action, suggesting that the role and ascribed power of the psychologist have changed little despite the introduction of new guidelines.

In both Integration Support Group meetings the principal clearly tried to take a less dominant role, but his choice of language suggests that he was exercising considerably more power than some of the other participants. Unfortunately, it seems that the principal did not exert his authority strongly enough to ensure successful completion of the anticipated structure. In both meetings the parents were still disempowered during essential stages: in the case of the second meeting the parent had little power in any stage of the meeting; in the first meeting the parent was permitted to share the power, until the time when actions were planned and responsibility allocated. During these phases the notion of collaboration failed badly, and the principal, who had the power to do so, failed to remedy the situation. The principal should ensure that membership of the Integration Support Group is in accord with the Ministry of Education guidelines. Meetings loaded with experts, even if they are sympathetic, are extremely disempowering.

In Dane's meeting the only decision-making phase was extremely brief, and neither the parent nor the integration aide made any contribution to this phase (perhaps fitting their role as the weakest and most disempowered members of this Integration Support Group). In this phase the principal was in control, using nearly 80 per cent of the total textual themes. Of the seven textual themes the principal used in this phase, five were continuatives. It is clear that the principal was comfortable in this decision-making role, which is supposed to be a shared stage of Integration Support Group procedures.

The use of interpersonal theme by the principal, however, included more use of expressions of probability (such as 'probably', and 'perhaps'), of the names of group members, and he frequently asked questions to keep the meetings moving. To a lesser extent he also made interpersonal language choices that affirmed rather than suggested uncertainty. He said: *'That's right*, it was too ...' and 'Yes, *that's true*, well, what are we going to do ...' and 'Yeah, *I bet*, well alright. ...'

In both meetings the integration aide seemed disempowered, although when the parent was fairly weak, as in Dane's meeting, the integration aide seemed willing to adopt more power. The evidence is strong, however, that she still had very limited power within the Integration Support Group structure, and very possibly throughout the school as a whole. What her work entails, both in content and method, is dictated to her by the classroom teachers. As well, she is disempowered by the Integration Support Group structure, which does not list her as an automatically entitled participant, but classes her as an expert who must be co-opted (even though integration aides are untrained and almost powerless within school structures). That the principal assumed she would be present at all Integration Support Group meetings did empower her a little, but at the expense of the guidelines.

For the integration aide, the patterns of meanings built up by the use of conjunctions are very straightforward, comprising mainly simple addition of information, augmented by the occasional sense of time and by scant reference to consequences and causes. She explained, for example, that Simon's day at remedial gym had been altered. When the mother questioned her further, she replied: *'Because* the gym would like Thursdays and Fridays to go out to schools. ...' She thus drew a consequential link between this and what has been said previously.

During the decision-making phases of Simon's meeting the integration aide depersonalized her discourse, and made no mention of Simon at all, as well as only seeing herself as part of a sort of institutionalized 'we' that might mean either the school or the staff. In the information sharing phase, however, the integration aide addressed events to do with remedial gym, and Simon and the integration aide. Throughout the comparable phase in Dane's meeting, however, she chose to stress the people most intimately concerned with that phase. Thus, during the shared information phase, she frequently emphasized 'he', and also made reference to the child by name several times. As well, she referred to adults as 'we', 'Jack', 'you' and 'I'. Infrequently, she thematized the other children ('some kid's'), or inanimate objects ('the last meeting', 'his way'). This pattern typified the integration aide's responses in all phases. It is clear that for the integration aide the players are more important than the game.

It is interesting to observe that considerable power rested with the teachers in both Integration Support Group meetings: both took a very active role during the shared information phase, and both very clearly dominated the phases in which actions were determined and decisions regarding responsibility for actions were made. The teachers indicated a belief that educational action is their domain, and neither the parents were able, nor the principal willing, to challenge this assertion of power. It is possible that it is fear of losing control of this aspect of their work that makes many teachers apprehensive of integration. Perhaps it is not that the teachers do not have the skills to teach children with diabilities, as is so readily argued by teachers and teacher unions, but that they fear that they will have the power over how and what they teach removed from their domain.

During Dane's meeting, for example, the teacher used continuatives extensively, and they were widely varied (for example, 'alright', 'well', 'yes', 'now' and 'no'). Additionally, he appeared to be firmly in control of the patterns of reasoning. As well as extensive use of additive conjunctions, he stressed time and contrasts: '*But, prior to that* I must add, I had three mad days . . ., *when* religious instruction was on . . ., And *thereafter*, it was on for three days . . .' Additionally, the teacher made many comparisons and frequently stressed consequence.

Notably, during the information sharing phases of the meeting, Simon's teacher made language choices to indicate topic in a very similar way to the mother, for he is concerned with both the child's progress and his behaviour. He made limited reference to himself, but also referred to the principal and the integration teacher, apparently to support his own position by calling on authority. In the second information sharing phases he stressed the other children in the grade, and how they react to Simon's behaviour: '*all the kids* in there are very supportive' and '*they* don't retaliate.' He was also very concerned, however, with Simon's enthusiasm for petty theft, and much of what he chose to make topical referred to what had been stolen. The behaviour was referred to as 'it', and was of considerable concern to the teacher, for he said much in relation to 'it': '*It* built itself up to that. . . .'; '*it* seemed to stop very quickly . . .'; '*it* wasn't just every night . . .'; '*it* was every recess and lunchtime. . . .' Despite the petty, and to an extent humorous, nature of the 'crime', the child had upset the teacher, who felt that such misdemeanours must be exposed and stressed.

During the phases where the decisions were being made, actions planned and responsibilities allocated, the teacher's use of topic was almost entirely to stress the role that members of the teaching, administrative and consultative staff would play. The mother, and indeed the child, seemed to be almost entirely overlooked in the teacher's zest for planning curriculum activities, and for ensuring that their execution and recording operate smoothly. Thus the teacher frequently referred to himself, either alone, or in collaboration with other staff: '*I said to Jack* . . .'; '*Pam and I* sat down . . .'; '*We* tried to call it life skills. . . .' This pattern continued throughout the phase. The teacher seemed to have almost entirely lost sight of the fact that this phase too, like all the others, was supposed to be collaborative. As a concession to collaboration, he briefly drew breath in the middle of what was essentially a monologue to say: '*These* would all be with your approval, of course.'

It was not surprising that the mother said almost nothing in this phase. She had been disempowered by the way the teacher excluded her from the decision-making process. The most she felt able to intervene was to say: '*We* should be able to think of some other things . . .' and '*That* could be added.' It is noteworthy that even when she interrupted the mother did not stress herself, for she realized that she had no power in the situation. At best, she hoped that 'we' (presumably the group at the meeting) might be able to make some contribution. The principal came to her rescue to a degree, although not effectively enough to ensure that collaboration was observed, when he suggested that the mother might like a copy of the planned curriculum activities. The mother replied: '*I*'d love a copy. *Lots of vital areas* in it. *It*'s everyday living skills.' Such a minimal amount of input certainly cannot be seen as collaboration.

Dane's teacher too made varied language choices to express topic, depending on the phases of the meeting. During the shared information phases, for example, the teacher made constant use of 'he', but also considerable reference to the rest of the grade: 'And *the kids* have got a fairly good attitude to it too. . . .' It is interesting to observe that in the main the teacher did this when he wished to stress the way Dane either did or did not fit into the grade, the effect he had on the grade, or the attitude of the grade to him. In this phase too the teacher made circumstance topical by thematizing it. He thus referred to 'the last seven days', 'the first thing', 'this morning', 'in the space of half an hour'. Such choices seemed only to be made when the teacher was stressing some unsatisfactory aspect of the integrated child's behaviour.

The teacher's choice of topic use differed in other phases of the meeting. During the very brief decision-making phase he stressed himself twice, and the teacher who would replace him twice: '*I* think it'd be better to work on some strategies for her, because *Janice* was telling me, even though she knows Dane, she . . . *I* wouldn't like her to go through three days such as I had a fortnight ago, *she*'d need some strategy for handling it.' During the action phase of the meeting the teacher still thematized unacceptable behaviour, and the locations or times of such misdemeanours, suggesting that it was with the problems, and not their solutions, that his interest *really* lies. Thus, he reminded the meeting: 'after *the third day* I was exhausted . . .'; 'Usually, *by the time Monday comes around* you start with a clean sheet . . .'; '*One of the problems with that approach* is that he might think. . . .'

As well as this tendency to stress the negative aspects of the child's behaviour instead of possible solutions, the teacher chose frequently to make himself the most important aspect of his language, using 'I' at the start of clauses sixty times during the action phase. It is obvious that for this teacher the way he handles and approaches the problems is secondary to the fact it is *he* who has to do it. Finally, during this phase the teacher often referred to the child being discussed. He was mentioned specifically as 'he' thirty times, and yet he was referred to by name only once.

The Impact of the Policy

Government level policies frequently do not control what happens in schools. As Kemmis (1989) has observed, the formulation of new policy, with its attendant regulations or recommendations, does not necessarily ensure compliance. The implementation of new policies far from guarantees an end to conflict and resistance. Frequently, such policies are vigorously contested. Integration, we have seen, is one such policy. There exists in integration, as in other areas of social life (Kemmis, 1989), 'a permanent tension ... between *contestation and institutionalisation*: between the forces which generate diversity and those which harness it within frameworks of accepted policy and practice.' New areas of contestation have certainly been generated and defined. At the same time patterns of social interaction have been transformed and in many cases institutionalized. There is, however, as Kemmis would suggest, still much room for change.

It has been observed that a social democratic approach to decision-making poses a threat to the school bureaucracy: 'Democracy does not suffer bureaucracy gladly. Many of the values we associate with democracy — equality, participation and individuality — stand sharply opposed to the hierarchy, specialization and impersonality we ascribe to modern bureaucracy' (Thompson, 1982: 235). Hegel, Thompson notes (1982: 241), observed that democracy and bureaucracy may be reconciled by 'the professionalism of the civil service', which would encourage bureaucrats 'to be responsive to the professional opinion of colleagues'. Professionalism is viewed less favourably by other authors, however (e.g., Fulcher, 1986; Tomlinson, 1982), who see it as legitimating claims to an ideology of expertise, and encouraging professionals to work independently of other interested individuals. It is also seen as a way to mystify special education (Tomlinson, 1982).

One espoused intention of the ministerial review was to assist the parents of children with disabilities to take greater control of the decision-making concerning their children's education; to empower them in a domain in which they have previously had very little power. It was an aspiration marked by noble intent. As Freire (1973) argues: 'The important thing is to help men [sic!] (and nations) help themselves, to place them in consciously critical confrontation with their problems, to make them the agents of their own recuperation' (n.p., quoted in Fried, 1980: 8). This, contends Fried, is what empowerment is all about, for, put simply, empowerment means 'helping people take charge of their lives, people who have been restrained, by social or political forces, from assuming such control' (1980: 8). Power is necessary if people are to respond critically to their own needs and problems, and those of their children (such as in the area of special education). 'A people without "power" ... is a people easily tyrannized by political, cultural, or institutional forces' (Fried, 1980: 8).

Conclusions

Potts has looked carefully at how professionals might be affected by integration, and advocates the need to involve parents in decision-making as a 'solution to the problem of professional mystique and unilateral power' (1985: 184–185). She warns that the catchphrase, 'parents as partners', much used in Victoria as in Britain, may carry with it very little equal participation.

The problem with the slogan 'Parents as Partners' is that it implies that parents *are* partners, that things are all right now, and that the improvement has been easy. But making permanent changes in client-professional relationships is far more difficult. (Potts, 1985: 185)

Much of what has been made obvious by this research into discourse patterns during Integration Support Group meetings makes depressing reading. Despite the rhetoric of empowerment made explicit by the review, *Integration in Victorian Education* (1984), and restated in ministerial memoranda since, and despite the very carefully thought out establishment of guidelines, structures and processes designed to ensure that the rhetoric of parental empowerment becomes a reality in the practice of integration, parents in particular are still very clearly a dominated and disempowered group in the decision-making process. As Prunty (1984) observed when discussing the Ministerial Papers (1983, 1985) that inform much of the current discourse about collaborative decision-making within Victorian schools: 'Few would doubt the sincerity of the Minister's efforts to engage parents in school decision-making, however it may have been difficult to anticipate some of the complexities that would obstruct the realization of this ideal' (1984: 62).

Joan Reidy (1988), who is very active in the Victorian Parent Advocacy Collective, an organization which closely addresses the issue of parent empowerment in integration through advocacy, has gathered an extensive list of 'red alerts' which parents and their advocates may encounter when attempting to ensure the successful integration of a child into a regular school. Many of these relate to ways teachers, principals and consultants confound the collaborative process during Integration Support Group meetings. Reidy observes, for example, that the membership of meetings is frequently 'stacked' with additional experts. Such a situation was observed in the school studied in this research. It was rare for the membership of the group to *conform* to ministerial directives. However, some principals have even refused to set up Integration Support Group meetings at all, or have called on the school council to refuse a child permission to attend the school, although the council has no mandate to do so. In schools where an Integration Support Group has been set up for a particular child, it is not uncommon for issues to be decided by vote, rather than on the consensus model; for the agenda to be decided without parental consultation; for the principal to deny the parent the right to have an advocate; for no minutes to be kept; for the meetings to be arranged at times when the parent cannot attend, and so on. The list is extremely lengthy. Such a dossier does not even touch on the way language may be used within the meeting further to disempower the parent.

The roles within bureaucracies are hierarchical, a system that has changed little within the current Victorian educational climate of collaboration and participation, despite the rhetoric of the Ministerial Papers (1983, 1985). The role of principal is still clearly defined and carries with it explicit responsibilities. For individuals, such as principals, who work within bureaucratic systems such as schools, 'a consequence of the hierarchical arrangement of roles is that, whatever substantive work a person may be required to do, his or her position is always qualified by its status in the hierarchy' (Rizvi and Kemmis, 1987: 297). For what other reasons would it be the principal who is required to run the Integration Support Group meetings, arrange the collection of agenda items, and keep and distribute minutes? To whom will angry or disappointed parents go within the school if integration does not appear to be working satisfactorily for their child?

And again, if a teacher is suffering from stress because of lack of support within the classroom or school for integration, it will be the principal who will be approached first. As in all bureaucracies the centralization of power is at the apex of the hierarchy. 'Authority is vested in positions rather than persons, with more senior positions having greater responsibilities for the co-ordination of tasks and for administrative decision making' (Rizvi and Kemmis, 1987: 297).

Principals are not alone in having difficulty allowing parents credibility within the decision-making processes of integration. Teachers too have been ascribed a role within the educational hierarchy, a role that is clearly marked by a vertical credentialling push. This was made very clear when the Senior Education Officer joined Dane's meeting, and the nature of the teacher's discourse changed. Although not directly relevant to Dane's educational program and needs, he immediately made a point of illustrating the numerous extracurricular activities in which his grade was involved. At the same time he took considerable care to stress his awareness of his legal responsibilities. This was noticeably absent in the earlier part of his discourse. The teacher in Simon's meeting, however, chose to play the role of expert, by generating an unmanageably large list of goals for the child. By its very magnitude, the list was difficult to challenge, and it was presented in such a way that the parent in the meeting had little chance to contribute. Even the psychologist in the group was unable to hide her admiration of such a masterly exhibition of expertise! This tactic had a tremendously disempowering effect on the parent, who normally contributes at great length in meetings, and is herself an advocate for parents at other local schools. Prunty (1984: 61) observes:

> Teachers as a whole have built up a barrier by giving parents the impression that they (teachers) are the 'experts' and that the parents have their place in such activities as 'working bees'. Parents see themselves as 'outsiders' and they see themselves as people that have little to contribute and feel threatened in the school situation. And teachers feel threatened by parents too.

Interestingly, Sallis (1988: 47), who is very active in the parents' movement in England, also showed some sympathy for the position of the teacher who may be having difficulty assimilating the idea of parental participation in education. She quips:

> Teachers ... feel that they are more at the mercy of enthusiastic amateurs than anyone else except the paper-hanger, and that every know-all on the bus has something to say about what it has taken them years to learn. It is not therefore easy to get them switched on to the idea of that organized interference we call participation!

What is patently clear from a study of Integration Support Group meetings within this one *supportive* school is the paramount importance of parent advocacy. In the case of Simon's meeting, where the parent attending was a mother well known for her assertiveness and her willingness to speak openly about her son and his disability, the distribution of power was very clearly asymmetrical, although Simon's mother made frequent attempts to redress the balance. Certainly, in the shared information phases of the meeting she contributed at length. Her contribution was considerably less, however, when actions were decided on, decisions made or responsibility allocated. In these phases those group members traditionally empowered to comment on these issues 'took the floor'. In Dane's meeting, the need for an advocate was urgent. Dane's father attends the meetings because Dane's mother finds them too intimidating. However, Dane's father is under considerable stress throughout *all* meetings. In the one under discussion he rarely spoke unless questioned. On the one occasion he really wished to object to what was said, his contribution was so couched in modality to be almost indecipherable. There is absolutely nothing to suggest that Dane's father has been in any way empowered by the introduction of collaborative decision-making into the integration process in Victorian schools. That one meeting started without him and that the 'shared' information phases were completed before his arrival confirm this conclusion. Empowerment and collaborative decision-making are misnomers for the involvement of this parent. His participation at a working bee building the new school playground would have just as much chance of altering his son's educational program as his involvement at Integration Support Group meetings.

It is possible that Dane's father's timidity during Integration Support Group meetings would have been less great had the meetings not been so 'hung' with experts. School personnel would do well to ensure that 'experts', whether school-based or outsiders, are not automatically present at Integration Support Group meetings unless co-opted. Principals and parents alike also need to be alerted to the fact that integration aides and integration teachers do *not* have automatic membership rights but must also be co-opted, and that only *two* additional members may be requested to attend meetings. As well, the decision to co-opt additional members must be made for *each* individual meeting.

It must be concluded from the research described in this report that emancipatory change, which is designed to empower, may frequently be fraught with considerable difficulty and conflict. The Ministry of Education, since the election to office of the Victorian Labor Government, has gone to considerable efforts to ensure a smooth transition into parental empowerment and the incorporation of collaborative approaches into decision-making in schools. However, as Kemmis and Rizvi (1987: 199–200) suggest, and this research goes some way to confirm:

> While this approach understands itself as a form of representative democracy, its democratic aspirations may mask a more bureaucratic reality. The actual workings of the structure may in fact be elaborations of existing bureaucratic forms of organization, in which the democratic decision making over policy questions and the processes of consultation between representatives and their constituencies are increasingly attenuated.

The new decision-making practices prescribed by the Ministry of Education will only be truly effective when school principals use their authority to ensure that the guidelines are conformed to and not just honoured in the breach. This research has shown that a number of forces of control and resistance, both unconscious and overt, operate within the use of language to maintain traditional patterns of disempowerment. To fail to observe the ministerial guidelines for collaborative decision-making within Integration Support Group meetings is further to disempower the very people whom the ministerial review aimed to empower. It is to make a mockery of emancipatory change.

References

DAHL, R.A. (1970) *After the Revolution?* New Haven, Conn., Yale University Press.
DE JOIA, A. and STENTON, A. (1980) *Terms in Systemic Linguistics: A Guide to Halliday*, London, Batsford Academic and Educational.
EXECUTIVE MEMORANDUM NO. 34 (1986) *Enrolment and Support Group Guidelines for Regular Schools*, Ministry of Education, Victoria, 13 March.
EXECUTIVE MEMORANDUM NO. 144 (1987) *Integration Support Group Procedures for Regular Schools*, Ministry of Education, Victoria, 17 August.
FISHER, M.C. (1987) *The Victorian System of Integration: A Model*, Geelong, Vic., Deakin University.
FISHER, M.C. (1989) 'Integration in Victoria: A Model', in MARKS, G. (Ed.), *Each an Individual*, Geelong, Vic., Deakin University Press.
FREIRE, P. (1973) *Education for Critical Consciousness*, New York, Seabury Press.
FRIED, R. (1980) *Empowerment vs Delivery of Services*, Concord, N.H., New Hampshire State Department of Education, pp. 1–16.
FULCHER, G. (1986) 'Australian Policies on Special Education: Towards a Sociological Account', *Disability, Handicap and Society*, 1, 1, pp. 19–52.
FULCHER, G. (1987) 'Bureaucracy Takes Round Seven: Round Eight to Common Sense?', *The Age*, Tuesday, 14 April, p. 22.
FULCHER, G. (1989) 'Integrate and Mainstream? Comparative Issues in the Politics of These Policies', in BARTON, L. (Ed.), *Integration: Myth or Reality?*, Lewes, Falmer Press.
HALLIDAY, M.A.K. (1985) *An Introduction to Functional Grammar*, London, Edward Arnold.
HALLIDAY, M.A.K. and HASAN, R. (1985) *Language, Context, and Text: Aspects of Language in a Social-semiotic Perspective*, Geelong, Vic., Deakin University.
KEMMIS, S. (1989) 'Curriculum in Australia: Contemporary Issues', Working Paper in LANGFORD, P. and D'CRUZ, V. (in press), *Issues in Australian Education*, London, Longman, Cheshire.
KING, R.J.R. and YOUNG, R.E. (1986) *A Systematic Sociology of Australian Education*, Sydney, George Allen and Unwin.
KIRNER, SALLY (1987) Recording of Integration Support Group meeting, Melbourne.
KRESS, G. (1985) *Linguistic Process in Sociocultural Practice*, Geelong, Vic., Deakin University.
KRESS, G. and FOWLER, R. (1979) Interviews, in FOWLER, R., KRESS, G. and TREW, T. (1979) *Language and Control*, London, Routledge and Kegan Paul, pp. 63–80.
KRESS, G. and HODGE, B. (1979) *Language as Ideology*, London, Routledge and Kegan Paul.
LEWIS, J. (1989) 'A Reflection on Five Years of Victorian Integration Policy', in MARKS, G. (Ed.), *Each an Individual*, Geelong, Vic., Deakin University Press.
MEHAN, H. (1983) 'The Role of Language and the Language of Role in Institutional Decision Making', *Language and Society*, pp. 187–211.
MEHAN, H. (1984) 'Institutional Decision Making', in ROGOFF, B. and LAVE, J. (Eds), *Everyday Cognition: Its Development in Social Context*, Cambridge, Mass., Harvard University Press, pp. 41–66.
MINISTERIAL PAPER NUMBER ONE (1983) *Decision-Making in Victorian Education*, Ministry of Education, Victoria.
MINISTERIAL PAPER NUMBER SIX (1985) *Curriculum Development and Planning in Victoria*, Ministry of Education, Victoria.

Genée Marks

Ministerial Structures Project Team (1986) *Taking Schools into the 1990s*, Ministry of Education, Victoria.
Ministry of Education-Victoria (1984) *Integration in Victorian Education: Report of the Ministerial Review of Educational Services for the Disabled*, Melbourne, Victorian Government Printer.
Newman, G.R. (1972) 'Educational Segregation in Victoria 1900–1968: A View from the Sociology of Deviance', *Australian Journal of Education*, 18, 1, pp. 50–67.
Potts, P. (1985) 'What Difference Would Integration Make to the Professionals?' in Booth, T. and Potts, P. (Eds), *Integrating Special Education*, Oxford, Basil and Blackwell.
Prunty, J. (1984) 'An Analysis of Citizen Participation and Regional Consultant Support Services', in Angus, L., Prunty, J. and Bates, R., *Restructuring Victorian Education: Regional Issues*, Working Papers in Educational Change Number 1, Geelong, Vic., Deakin University, School of Education, Social and Administrative Studies Research Group.
Reidy, J. (1988) 'Parent Advocacy as Parent Empowerment', in Marks, G. (Ed.), *Each an Individual*, Geelong, Vic., Geelong University Press.
Rizvi, F. and Kemmis, S. (1987) *Dilemmas of Reform: The Participation and Equity Program in Victorian Schools*, Geelong, Vic., Deakin University, Deakin Institute for Studies in Education.
Sallis, J. (1988) *Schools, Parents and Governors: A New Approach to Accountability*, London, Routledge and Kegan Paul.
State Board of Education-Victoria (1987) *Legislative Changes to Implement the Integration of Students with Impairments, Disabilities or Problems in Schooling*, Melbourne, February.
Stone, K. (1987) *The Integration Action Manual!*, Melbourne, Vic., Western Suburbs Community Integration Group: Schools.
Talbot, R. (1987) Recording of Integration Support Group meeting, rural Victoria.
Thompson, D.F. (1982) 'Bureaucracy and Democracy', in Duncan, G. (Ed.), *Democratic Theory and Practice*, London, Cambridge University Press, pp. 235–250.
Tomlinson, S. (1982) *A Sociology of Special Education*, London, Routledge and Kegan Paul.
White, D. (1987) *Education and the State: Federal Involvement in Educational Policy Practice*, Geelong, Vic., Deakin University Press.

Chapter 12

Inclusive Learning Initiatives: Educational Policy Lessons from the Field

Roger Slee

Meaning and Language in Integration Policy

Pressed to delineate the essential difference between a novel and a play, one Australian writer, Robert Drewe, seized upon the interpretive relationship between the text and the reader. Distances between intended meaning and eventual understanding become greater as the play moves from the page to the performance. 'Unlike a finished, published book, a play metamorphoses constantly as the players interact with director, stage and (if he is lucky) writer: You give up all thought of control' (Drewe, 1991: 52). While I do not wish to make too much of Drewe's statement as an exercise in linguistic or literary analysis, he inadvertently touches upon a central issue for educational policy-makers. Between the formulation and implementation of policy we encounter numerous 'intruders' who also want to leave their mark.

Certainly the possibilities for reinterpretation, distortion and misrepresentation are expanded as the cast, production crew and director sit down to workshop and rehearse the author's written text and its silences. A process of artistic 'negotiation', otherwise known as squabbling, will be embarked upon in order to bring form and meaning to the production which satisfies all those engaged by the theatre company for this performance.

We know that this is not accurate. The cast needs to eat. Players may perhaps acquiesce in others' interpretations. Employment is preferable to having to audition elsewhere were they to enunciate their own reading of the play. This is still not a guarantee that one of the troupe won't be given to capricious artistic temperament on the night and attempt to hijack the performance to imprint their own rendition indelibly in the critics' notes.

We are also aware that the voice, appearance or temperament of one particular player may reshape characters as the director and cast read together. Continually new meanings are being forged. This is happening at all levels of the production process. For myself, sitting in the audience, this rendition is altogether different from the last performance of the same play I went to. Moreover it is further away from my own reading of the text. They have not understood the author's silences or the nuances of her words, if only these had been made more explicit. If only I had been the director. If only I were in the cast. Perhaps it should have been a novel!

Educational policy-making and politics provide a matrix of similar complexity. Like a play, policy is not written and delivered in static contexts. Nor do we have control over all of the players. Ball (1987, 1990a) depicts something of this chaos in his analysis of the lateral struggles endemic within the micropolitics of schools and the often internecine conflicts within large and small bureaucracies.

> The field of policy analysis is dominated by commentary and critique rather than by research. Abstract accounts tend towards tidy generalities and often fail to capture the messy realities of influence, pressure, dogma, expediency, conflict, compromise, intransigence, resistance, error, and pragmatism in the policy process. (1990a: 9)

As Fulcher (1989) and Rizvi *et al.* (1987) have observed, policy is made at all levels. Consequently, policy enacted may lurch in directions opposite to the intentions of original policy statements. Integration policy in Victorian Ministry of Education schools provides a wealth of data to support this trend (Fulcher, 1989; Slee, 1991). Theorized in terms of a rights model based upon a systems perspective (Ministry of Education-Victoria, 1984: Ch. 2), it is paradoxical to see the way in which resourcing integration in Victoria is contingent upon the ascertainment and labelling of individuals. This conceptual fragmentation is reflected in an address by a Senior Integration Officer from the Victorian Ministry of Education to an Integration Conference in Queensland. He cites 2950 active cases of integration in 1037 regular schools in Victoria (Tarr, 1988: 65). The point here is that this continues to typify the individual gaze where the 'dysfunctional' individual is the focus rather than a model of educational delivery that takes all comers, a model of authentic inclusion.

A further complication that clouds policy is the role of discursive practice. The application of integration policy reveals divergence between the stated and the actual function of integration. Integration generates what Barthes (1972: 143) contends is a discourse of concealment. While all employ an integration discourse, practices reveal contradictions between extensions of the control of difference and the movement towards an authentic place for all in the regular classroom. While the language employed may be modified, traditional practices, and more particularly their effects, prevail. Failure to recognize such contradictions depoliticizes language, thereby satisfying the functionalist imperative of fixing kids to minimize disruption to the schooling process. Special educators frequently dispense the discourse of integration devoid of the corresponding paradigmatic shift (Skrtic, 1986). Old alchemies and practices are packaged in 'integration' wrapping.

These distortions in part stem from the silences in policy that allow for divergent agendas to be inserted and pursued at various levels of the policy process. That *Integration in Victorian Education* (Ministry of Education-Victoria, 1984) neglected issues of pedagogy and curriculum as essential factors in the inclusive schooling equation is significant. As a result, the ensuing debates revolved around technical issues of resource deployment to cater for the needs of children identified as being in need of integration. This process inexorably leads to what Branson and Miller point to as the inherent contradiction of integration, another step in the pursuit of the effective administration of difference (1989: 144). Rather than addressing issues of changing school culture through a reconceptualization of curriculum and pedagogy toward more inclusive schooling, the imperative, for many, remained the regulation and control of disability and hence the minimization of disruption to establish patterns of regular and special educational delivery. This is not to dismiss the resource debate as unimportant. How that debate is pursued is critical in determining whether schools become inclusive or managers of individuals.

After briefly reconsidering some of the problems within integration discourses and their implications for policy development and implementation, this chapter describes an 'inclusive learning initiatives project' to suggest some findings from the field. The intention is not prescriptive, it is suggestive. I will return to this point when considering the effective schools research.

The Displacement and Regulation of Disability

The marginalization of those who fail 'to satisfy the culturally specific, historically specific standards of physical or behavioural *normality*' (Branson and Miller, 1989) has drawn much historical and sociological interest and analysis (Foucault, 1987; Kanner, 1964; Searle, 1979; De Swann, 1990; Gilman, 1988; Henriques *et al.*, 1984; Kamin, 1974). The processes of marginalization and segregation in educational provision are attracting increasing levels of research interest (McCallum, 1990; Lewis, 1989; Ford *et al.*, 1982; Barton, 1987, 1989; Tomlinson, 1981, 1982; Skrtic, 1991; Fulcher, 1989). Despite the growth in such studies, of which the above list is indicative rather than exhaustive, the individual gaze on educating those with perceived 'special educational needs' predominates, even when the language would seem to suggest otherwise.

Warnock's concession to the conceptual ambiguity of the notion of 'special educational needs', the term she used as the title for the influential report on special educational provision in the United Kingdom (see Chapter 3, this volume) is telling.

> Perhaps the main reason for the newly apparent poverty of special needs is in its definition ... or rather its lack of definition ... the concept of 'special need' carries a fake objectivity. For one of the main, indeed almost overwhelming, difficulties is to decide whose needs are special, or what 'special' means. (Warnock, 1982: 372)

Gartner and Lipsky's (1987) research in the United States supports the earlier British findings by researchers, including Ford *et al.* (1982), Tomlinson (1982) and Galloway (1985), that the incidence of disability in schools corresponds with the level of service provision. To reflect the elasticity, as opposed to scientific basis, of 'special educational needs', Gartner and Lipsky have challenged the dubious technology of ascertaining needs. This is documented in the report of their interviews with educational psychologists in the United States.

> ...when test results do not produce the desired outcome, evaluators
> often change the yardstick: 'If the test scores indicate the child is ineli-
> gible, but the teacher really feels the child needs help, we try to select
> other tests that might make the child eligible. . . .' The tests then become
> 'a means of corroborating referral decisions. Testing, therefore, does not
> drive decisions but is driven by decisions'. (Gartner and Lipsky, 1987: 372)

A euphemism for school failure, Barton (1988) links the application of 'special educational needs' to broader political and economic agendas. Those students traditionally at risk of failure in regular schools have become increasingly
so under Conservative British government education reforms. The expansion of
special education outside the regular system, accompanied by the identification of
increasing numbers of students within for special attention, generates greater
capacity for the containment of youth.

The press for national measurement, comparison and competition under the
populist guise of choice places even greater numbers of children at risk of being
labelled as 'special needs' or 'statemented students' as schools narrow their curriculum to project traditional academic profiles (Ball, 1990b; Chapter 4, this
volume). In this way schools become decidedly schizophrenic about 'special needs'.
The identification of students with 'special needs' provides opportunity for additional funding. It also may be publicly perceived as contributing to a diminution
of standards, delimiting the school's capacity to attract able students in sufficient
numbers to maintain funding for the school. This is not simply a criticism of
education politics in the UK; Victorian schools were able to use the delayed
admission clause to deter parents. Some Victorian schools pursued integration
funding following requests from parents to enrol their disabled child. Some other
schools went about the ascertainment of students already enrolled to attract integration funding. Other schools simply did not want to know.

Rather than the expansion of opportunity, progress towards more inclusive
schooling, integration written as a rights policy became a rather cynical vehicle
for containment and regulation as more players walked onto the policy stage
(Cook, Lewis and Slee, in press). This should not have been a source of surprise.
Pastoral care and student welfare programs had been mobilized in much the
same way to control the behaviour of difficult or different students (Lang and
Hyde, 1987; Slee, 1992).

The vulnerability of students experiencing difficulty with curriculum and
teaching at times of crisis in the youth labour market (Sweet, 1988) is intensified.
Rather than providing the vehicle to transport previously segregated students to
the centre of school academic and social life, integration was convenient for the
identification and containment of failing students who stayed on at school since
the dole had been abolished at the margins of school life. Corbett (Chapter 5, this
volume) also notes the expansion of special educational provision in times of
labour market shrinkage. Those traditionally disadvantaged in schools are placed
at even greater risk of failure when the opportunities for labelling are expanded
(Tomlinson, 1978; Galloway and Barrett, 1984; Kenway, 1990).

Another important aspect of integration policy as enunciated in Victorian
government documents and memoranda is the commitment to the 'practice rather
than the rhetoric of devolution' (Ministry of Education-Victoria, 1983). Decision-making was to be collaborative. Decisions were to reflect consensus arrived

at through the due process of representative forums. Experts would not make decisions for parents and their children; rather, the community of parents, teachers and support personnel would arrive at mutually agreeable outcomes.

As Marks (Chapter 11, this volume) concludes on the basis of close analysis of the operation of the Integration Support Groups, education remains very much a contested arena (Kemmis, 1990). Research elsewhere reflects the institutional disadvantage of parents in school forums in general (Beattie, 1985; Sallis, 1988), and in 'special needs' bodies in particular (Galloway, 1985; Biklen, 1974).

Amidst official commitment to integration policy and practice in Victoria, a curious development has been noted. Segregated provision continues to expand (Fulcher, 1989; Chapter 1, this volume). Segregated educational provision was attracting increasing levels of funding, while special educators and psychologists discovered new clients in the mainstream, who are now paradoxically known as 'integration students'. Tomlinson has previously registered her concern about this kind of expansion of special education (1985).

Shifting the Focus to Schools

Following the publication of *Integration in Victorian Education* (Ministry of Education-Victoria, 1984), concern was expressed over a range of implementation issues. Fulcher (1987) drew attention to increasing bureaucratization, while Slee (1986) focused on the application of integration procedures to deal with disruptive behaviour in schools. The press to create more off-site centres for disruptive students, who are subject to ascertainment as integration students under the official category of 'students with problems in schooling', continues. A group of Ministry of Education personnel, teachers and academics met during 1986 to highlight the contradiction between the Ministry of Education's integration rhetoric and the segregation of disruptive students under the auspices of 'social-emotional disturbance'.

In 1987 an unpublished Ministry of Education discussion paper drew together all the significant Ministry of Education and State Board of Education documents pertaining to school curriculum, organization and policy. This paper was used as the point of embarkation for the Learning Initiatives to Include All Students in the Regular Classroom Project. Commencing as an initiative of the Ministerial Standing Committee to Advise on the Education of Pupils with Impairments and Disabilities (SCAEPID), the project sought to identify the critical issues of implementing integration policy and successful learning initiatives which enabled more students to be successful in regular classrooms.

An early challenge for the group was establishing the project's focus. An attempt was made to shift the glare of scrutiny and conflict away from those who were 'impaired', 'disabled' or having 'problems in schooling' to all students, and to document how schools were including or enabling students. Put simply, the project wanted to push integration forward through exemplifying practices and programs that schools felt were successful, rather than further inflaming immobilizing debates. We were attempting to effect a shift from disability as an individual issue to a systems issue. The Learning Initiatives Project sought to establish a framework for considering the implications of pedagogy, curriculum and school organization for the success or failure of inclusive education.

The Project Design

Two key aspects of the project design are worth noting from the outset. First, considerable time was devoted by the project committee, which included representatives from teachers' and principals' organizations as well as parent and student groups, to designing a process that would allow a representative cross-section of Victorian state schools to nominate programs or initiatives they believed to have been successful in including all students in the regular classroom. Second, the project committee was careful not to constrain the schools to a centrally imposed definition of integration or inclusion.

Each of the Regional Education Offices in Victoria was then requested to identify three schools that they believed had developed successful inclusive learning initiatives. It was stipulated that one school must be a primary school and one a secondary school; the third could be either primary or secondary. Although some time was spent discussing the aims of the project with regional office personnel, differing interpretations of successful learning initiatives arose. Regional priorities, predispositions and cultures generate diverse perceptions about the aims of integration. This, with hindsight, remains a strength of the project as it led us immediately into the fragmented nature of policy implementation. What counts as good practice in urban centres in construed quite differently in remote rural centres. Policy needs to incorporate and celebrate diversity.

Following an invitation to join the project, nominated schools were all sent a survey instrument. The proforma was very open, requesting the school to describe the school, its context and the successful learning initiatives put in place to include all students. Schools were then advised to send representatives to a workshop/ seminar in the Ministry's central office where they could discuss integration implementation issues, their learning initiatives and the next phase of the project.

This workshop was more significant than the project committee had envisaged. For many, it was the first integration professional development exercise that they had participated in. Following the workshop there was much correspondence suggesting that the opportunity to talk with teachers from all over the state about their experience of developing inclusive educational initiatives was mutually beneficial. Unfortunately, such testimonies speak more loudly about the lack in professional development than they do about the virtues of this particular project. The sessions at the workshop were positive in tone, as participants felt that they had been recognized for achievement and were eager to share their success and learn from others — a refreshing change of atmosphere given the acrimony of many integration forums at that time. It is also important to note that the responses were not restricted to initiatives or programs concerned with access or resources for disabled students. Some of the respondents documented broader initiatives aimed at access and success for all students. Gender and schooling, community languages, student governance and participation, community involvement in school decision-making, and the reconceptualization and/or reorganization of curriculum to address all students' needs rather than the needs of tertiary entrance or school administration are indicative.

Seven schools were selected from within the original cohort. These schools were chosen to represent diversity and were subject to more intensive observation and research. Diversity was necessary so that, upon completion of the report, more readers would be able to identify with the documented experiences of the schools. The completed proforma from all the schools formed a continuing bank of data to be used in the final report.

Members of the project steering committee visited each of the seven schools with me. Time was spent with school council representatives, administrators, integration teachers and aides, classroom teachers, students, parents and support personnel. School programs were observed, and supplementary interviews were conducted.

The seven schools exhibited a variety of approaches to including all students, but they were consistent in a number of features. These schools, to varying extents, perceived integration as extending beyond opening their doors to students with conspicuous disabilities. Their understanding embraced considerations of how they were supporting all students to continue successfully within the school.

One of the schools within the cohort was a large secondary school in a low socio-economic metropolitan area. A technical school, it was seen as a suitable destination for students considered less capable in the academic curriculum. Changes in the labour market had had an impact upon technical schools so that through the 1970s and 1980s they were offering a more comprehensive curriculum. Still many traditional academic high schools referred their difficult and failing students to technical schools as they thought that they would keep these students busy with their manual subject offerings. This particular technical school was compelled by the failure of schools around it to function as a repository for a range of students with special needs. Students were referred to it when they failed at, or refused to attend, other local schools.

This places such schools in a perplexing dilemma. Do they maintain curricula to which they have been historically and culturally wed? Or do they consider change consistent with the needs of their student population? The principal put it thus:

> When it came time to consider integration submissions, I thought that I could legitimately name eighty five per cent of the students here. Many of them turn up here after being sent from elsewhere, others do have special needs or are having 'problems with schooling'. So, do I label them all, or do I change the school. We've taken the second option at this school. (Principal, Metropolitan Secondary School, 1988)

Faced with drafting integration funding submissions, their choice seemed to be: do we label an expanding group of students who in other schools may well be categorized as integration students, or do we develop a school culture and curriculum that enable all students to work toward more successful educational outcomes?

We also spoke to a number of students at Metropolitan Secondary. One of the students arrived at the school, not voluntarily, having been diagnosed 'school phobic' following numerous referrals to Student Services by a number of other local schools. Indeed, he had a long history of truancy. The extensive dossiers compiled on him chronicled a string of disturbing incidents that had caused trouble in schools.

When we met and spoke with him, the preceding story seemed implausible. He was now succeeding in year 11 and seemed intent on completing secondary school. Whereas his previous reports screamed failure and prematurely leaving school, he was now a regular attender. Perhaps the chronic truancy and school phobia were in remission. Previously, psychologists' reports diagnosed his lack of social skills; now he was at the centre of a number of school committees and extracurricular activities.

When asked why he now attended school, his understated explanation provided an indictment of his previous educational experience: 'I can't stay away from here because I've got too much responsibility to stay away.' Chairperson of the Student Council, a member of the school debating team, performing a central role in the school production and a comprehensive year 11 program, he certainly did have his share of responsibility. A range of curriculum options and teaching strategies, together with direct participation in school governance, contributed to the enabling of this student to pursue a more successful school life — social *and* academic. As Knight (1991) argues, some schools place their students at greater risk than others.

Metropolitan Secondary provides an interesting history of change. Curriculum has become more flexible, responding to a range of student interests and needs. Assessment underwent radical revision so that students and teachers negotiated contracts for goals and work to be covered. Timetabling, the administrative heart of school physiology, was transformed to a unitized system where electives augmented the core, allowing students to repeat skill areas without having to endure the boredom of repeating a content area. More importantly, progressing at appropriate levels did not incur the stigma of getting out of chronological groupings which characterizes most schools.

This was achieved without a diminution in standards; quite the reverse. The school delivered according to a range of traditional indicators. More students progressed and stayed in higher education via Metropolitan Secondary than they did from the so-called academic schools that surrounded it. The request that the school made to involve tertiary providers in the construction of the revised curriculum and assessment programs was strategic. First, it engendered independent learning; and second, it promoted links between the school and higher education. More students entered further education or the training sector, and the articulation between school and the workforce was more bountiful. Many of these students would definitely have been assigned to integration status in their previous schools. Many more would have exhibited the disturbances attributed to integration students had Metropolitan Secondary not changed its culture, organization, curriculum and pedagogy. This remains a powerful lesson from the field about enabling students.

Skrtic provides a rigorous examination of the administrative and political imperatives of special education.

> Thus, the institutional practice of special education (and the very notion of student disability) is an artifact of the functionalist quest for rationality, order, and certainty in the field of education, a quest that is both intensified and legitimized by the institutional practice of educational administration. As such, special education distorts the problem of school failure and, ultimately, prevents the field of education from entering into a productive confrontation with uncertainty ... the problem is that this distortion of school failure prevents public education from seeing that it is not living up to its democratic ideals. (Skrtic, 1991: 153)

This returns us to our earlier point that how language is used matters. Technical discourse about the resource driven dialogue about meeting students' special needs deflects focus from schools' selectivity in determining whose needs they will address and whose cannot be addressed, deflects from the failure of schools.

Integration and the Effective Schooling Debate

Biklen, searching for the 'complete school', establishes integration and learning as correlated goals (1985: 61). The goal is not the appeasement of our collective conscience through social interaction; it is more a commitment to improving life chances through improved learning programs. The project steering committee thus considered the effective schooling research as it seemed to address questions relating to school improvement for all students.

It is worth stressing that this was not done without some reservation. Stephen Ball (1988: 132) has earlier registered his misgivings about the way in which the findings of the effective schools research can be mobilized within conservative discourse against schools and teachers. Lists are constructed against which schools can be measured and manipulated. Such applications are evident also in the United States (Pink, 1988).

Reynolds registers similar anxiety about the abuses of such research, arguing that schools would do better to examine school culture and the social relations of school life rather than consider only the structural features of schooling in their quest for reform (1982: 234). Together with his colleagues, Reynolds later calls for a shift away from the 'simplistic five, seven or nine factor theories derived from school effectiveness research that is itself now over a decade in age' (Creemers *et al.*, 1989: 382). Recognition of the problems within such research underpins Ramasut and Reynolds' chapter in this collection (Chapter 14). What applies in some schools is clearly untenable in others. Process, it would seem, is one of the most significant contributions of this research paradigm.

The unpublished report of the project, *Successful Schooling* (Fulcher, Semmens and Slee), maintains that while the effective schooling literature is normative and has the capacity to be redirected by those seeking to instil corporate practice and values in schools, effective schools have as their central concern the achievement of broader educational objectives: developing talent, tolerance and participation (Ball, 1988: 150), critical literacy and civic courage (Giroux, 1984). Effective schools are so because they aim to produce a culture to reduce inequalities among students and improve the credentials of all students. These objectives are not inconsistent with the educational and political aims of integration or inclusive schooling.

Correspondence between the characteristics of 'successful schools' identified by Ramsay *et al.* (1983) in New Zealand schools and the schools within our cohort seemed significant to us at the time of the research. Schools claiming to be successful shared a number of common characteristics:

1 a clearly articulated philosophy or statement of goals;
2 clear patterns of formal and informal communication;
3 democratic decision-making processes;
4 systematic attention to student records (to enhance performance rather than as a form of surveillance);

5   parents involved as helpers, teachers and in decision-making, and stu-
    dents working in projects outside school;
6   school resources were available and used;
7   students and teachers worked together to improve the school environment;
    and
8   senior staff took responsibility for maintaining the high morale of junior
    staff.

Subsequent studies, including Reynolds (1985), Pink (1988) and Mortimore *et al.*
(1988), extend this list. The common characteristics of 'successful schools' cited
by Corcoran and Wilson (1989) include:

   positive teacher and principal attitudes to students;
   strong and effective leadership;
   high expectations and standards;
   high levels of commitment among teaching staff;
   concentration on achievement in academic subjects;
   provision of support for 'at-risk' students;
   close relationship between school and its catchment area to provide support
      for policy development.

Having warned against simplistic recipe approaches to school improvement,
the State Board of Education in Victoria prioritized the following items as fundamental to school evaluation and improvement:

   educationally effective administration;
   positive school climate;
   goal-focused curriculum;
   participatory structures;
   school evaluation based on problem-solving practices.

Building on the work of Mortimore *et al.* (1988), Stoll (1991) suggests that effective
schooling is more than the sum total of its constituent parts. Ramasut (1989)
proposes a whole school approach to the effective inclusion of 'special needs' in
the school program, and with Reynolds (Chapter 14, this volume) warns of the
difficulties in the application of the research findings.

   Effective inclusion, as opposed to add-on provision for 'special needs', through
whole school approaches refers to the acknowledgment that whole school means
all aspects of schooling: curriculum, pedagogy and organization. However, changing whole schools is no simple matter that can be achieved by working through
a checklist of effective schooling research. Context is critical; identification of
achievable initiatives as steps toward school improvement is fundamental (Ramasut
and Reynolds, Chapter 14, this volume).

   The acknowledgment of the diversity of schools and their communities, and
the necessity of manageable projects as a basis for school development and change,
formed the basis of the Learning Initiatives Project. Moving schools from segregative to inclusive curriculum, pedagogy and organization requires more than
legislation and policy redrafting. It has to reach all levels and engage all actors.

Consequently, the project reported on modest but significant projects in schools in the belief that the examples cited would be seen to be plausible and adaptable at school and classroom levels. Schools were not expected to respond by grafting the initiative onto their own program in the hope that such cosmetic surgery would prove effective. Rather, the intention was that teachers, parents and education administrators reading the report would recognize, in the brief accounts, the thinking which informed schools' attempts to include all their students, and engage in similar processes of negotiation and planning to generate more inclusive education on their own schools.

Major Findings from the Project

Dealing comprehensively with the findings of the Learning Initiatives Project is difficult; here I summarize some of the central issues and comment on how the project relates to policy development and evaluation.

1. Rethinking the resources debate. Numerous schools have developed a cargo cult approach to integration. Many of the disputes over unmet resources submissions have resulted in students being denied access to the classroom. The intercession of the Minister of Education, by placing a delayed admission clause in the enrolment process to defuse debate, reinforces the widespread belief that integration is principally about the allocation of resources. Our earlier discussion of the role of schools in regulating the flow of students into special needs categories indicates that resources are only one element in the 'access and success' equation. Resources underpin successful schooling, but further consideration must be given to how they are deployed within the context of the range of variables that contribute to inclusive schooling.

There remains the paradox of the expansion of resources within segregated centres (Chapter 1, this volume), while searching for additional resources to facilitate integration in times of shrinking education budgets. This is complicated when trying to determine what resources are indispensable to integration. Complexity arises from the divergent agendas of those writing the resources submissions. The abuse of resource requests to delay admission indefinitely is one example. It is further complicated by evidence to suggest that in some cases the deployment of an integration aide actually impedes student inclusion and progress. While some students felt isolated by being in the constant company of an adult and would have preferred seeking assistance from their peers when they required it, others fell victim to learned helplessness because of the well intentioned but sometimes inappropriate assistance of the aide.

Where resources were not plentiful, some schools pursued provision for all students by collaboratively considering their actual needs and deploying all available resources, rearranging teaching organization and calling upon community assistance. One teacher aide told us that her aim was to make herself redundant as quickly as possible. To this end she would consult with the various support personnel in the district to learn how to administer support for children in the regular classroom and meet their various exercise needs, and then immediately commence teaching those skills to all teachers in the school. Where appropriate, the other students in the class broadened their knowledge and skills so that they

195

too could help their 'disabled', rather so that they could enable, their peers. In this way students were not forced to be absent for extended consultations with therapists in the regional centre. The expert's role became that of evaluating progress and advising on enhancing performance.

At the centre of the resources conundrum rests the question of how we allocate resources so that they move with children as they require assistance. This is made more difficult by the present reluctance to challenge the separation of resources into specialist centres to which children are allocated.

2. Curriculum as a central focus. Participants in the Learning Initiatives project approached the task of including all students by addressing curriculum in its broader definition of formal and informal learnings as a result of the teaching program, rituals, organization and ethos. The focus for these schools was placed on systematically sponsoring change. This contrasts with the traditional special educational gaze upon the perceived pathology and deficits of the individual in need of help (Ainscow, 1989).

To this end, vertical modular grouping, where students were able to plot, together with their teachers, their academic pathways with an emphasis on success, provides an example of how schools may become flexible to meet the needs of all students. In this way students could take additional elective units in specific areas to consolidate or extend skills without being stigmatized in any way. Failure becomes redundant when the emphasis is placed on facilitating successful outcomes (see Chapter 10, this volume).

Peer tutoring, cross-age tutoring and cooperative learning programs provided the variety in teaching that enabled more students to grasp requisite knowledge and skills. Problem-solving approaches were encouraged, negotiated decision-making preferred.

The practice of streaming students was avoided. High and reasonable expectations were extended to all students. Where students felt valued by the organization, curriculum and pedagogy of the school, resistance was diminished. Remediation in separate centres or classrooms was anathema.

3. Reducing bureaucratic procedures, increasing communication. Members of the project committee observed the continuing struggle of parents as they deal with teachers, school administrators, medics, psychologists and the host of other professionals who move in and out of the lives of their disabled children. The procedures designed to regulate communication between the school and the parents of these children present difficulties to parents and teachers alike (Chapter 11, this volume). Parents assuming the proper role of advocates for their children are considered hostile. Parents lacking confidence or who are less articulate described their manipulation by experts who removed their children from their own control, symbolically or physically. Displaying little regard for the deterministic power of their behaviour, teachers and others confidently make prognoses which are speculative rather than authoritative (Slee, 1991).

Teachers reflected upon their lack of knowledge about the implications of students' impairments for teaching and learning. The vulnerability of the class-room teacher in the area of special needs is intensified by bureaucratic processes which maintain expert control in the hands of special educational consultants. Their language, like that of other professionals, deskills the classroom teacher and nurtures perceptions of professional inadequacy, heightening the reluctance to work with 'their clients'.

Where schools had moved away from the formal integration procedures in order to develop more continuous links with their community, communication seemed more effective. Parents and teachers welcomed formal and informal access to each other so that progress could be monitored and extended. Local initiatives that were locally effective were chronicled. Some schools keep journals that travel from home to school with the student. Parents and teachers use this as a continuous point of dialogue. Concerns are noted, successes celebrated and setbacks considered. Other schools established coffee and tea rooms where parents can meet with each other and invite teachers in to reflect on issues relating to their children's educational progress.

Teachers often expressed their concern that some of their 'integrated' children did not seem to be progressing. Conversation with the parents led one to wonder whether it was the same child in question. What seemed of little significance to the teacher represented a milestone to the parents. When this was communicated to the teacher, it provided the basis for continued planning and progress with teachers and parents as the educational partners.

4. Expertise versus experts. A group of parents told us that the town's paediatrician was given to bold prognostication. One mother's story was particulary salutary. Not long after the birth of her daughter she was told that the child was profoundly impaired and would be unable to communicate with others. Her best interest would be served by referral to the special developmental school, which is reserved for those not able to attend a special school. The parents resisted and their persistence meant a place in one of the regular primary schools. The child copied her new found peers' words. One of the other children in the class suggested a 'five word party' when she said five words in a logical sentence. By all accounts it was a particularly joyous party for everyone.

One wonders about her progress had she only been able to learn language as directed through the expert guidance of a therapist, one monosyllable at a time. The expertise of parents is too frequently ignored when it does not concur with the opinion of the 'expert' professional. Expertise is important, wherever it comes from, and should be locally applied so that as many participants in the education program as possible can derive benefit. Expertise is most effective when it is empowering rather than when it reinforces the professional hierarchy and dependence. Perhaps it is apposite to ask whose 'special needs' are being met, the child's or the professionals'?

5. Teaching the teachers' teachers. Fundamental to resistance to inclusive education is a widespread belief among teachers that until they have received special educational training, they will not be able to teach disabled students. Consequently, if they must have these disabled children in their classrooms, then they must also have an integration teacher and integration aide in the room. Special educators have done little to dispel this thinking.

Teacher education, undergraduate and postgraduate, should be organized around a curriculum that confronts issues of inclusive teaching rather than management of individual problems through exclusive individual and special educational paradigms (see Chapter 13, this volume). Resistance to this is robust, as

Semmens illustrates (Chapter 8, this volume) and has a long tradition (Lewis, 1989; and Chapter 1, this volume). Integration continues to stumble into contests and struggles at all levels of the educational organization.

Conclusion

Rather than being conclusive and prescriptive, the Learning Initiatives project was suggestive. It speaks to issues of how schools deal with policy reception and implementation at local levels. Identification of contests and struggles was not used as policy directives. The aim was to illustrate how ordinary schools experiencing pressures, like those which beset all other schools, confront challenges and facilitate school improvement conducive to including all students.

A number of lessons emerge from the project for policy-makers. Consideration needs to be given to enlisting players at all levels in the production and implementation of policy. This is consistent with research which warns against the imposition of top-down administrative directives (Ball, 1987, 1990a; Bates, 1988; Fullan, 1991). It also addresses the issue of the manipulation of language. Silences and distances between the dialects of localities or professional interest groups should be recognized and accounted for. Clarity in the statement of aims, preferred outcomes, and definition of conceptual underpinnings of policy are essential. Moreover, inclusive initiatives should be encouraged and celebrated to enhance teachers' sense of professional achievement and parents' and students' hopes. Acknowledgment of progress is essential to sustain local effort and provide encouragement for adaptation elsewhere. The fundamental and most forgotten lesson from the project was the affirmation of the need to listen to those in the field. Some have been denied a voice, particularly the disabled and their families. Inclusive policy is recognized by the resonance of these voices at every level.

References

AINSCOW, M. (Ed.) (1989) *Special Education in Change*, London, David Fulton Publishers.

BALL, S.J. (1987) *The Micro-Politics of the School*. London, Methuen.

BALL, S.J. (1988) 'Comprehensive Schooling, Effectiveness and Control: An Analysis of Educational Discourses', in SLEE, R. (Ed.), *Discipline and Schools: A Curriculum Perspective*, Melbourne, Macmillan.

BALL, S.J. (1990a) *Politics and Policy Making in Education*, London, Routledge.

BALL, S.J. (1990b) 'Education, Inequality and School Reform: Values in Crisis!', Inaugural Professorial Lecture, University of London, King's College, Centre for Educational Studies.

BARTHES, R. (1972) *Mythologies*, New York, Hill and Wang.

BARTON, L. (1987) *The Politics of Special Educational Needs*, Lewes, Falmer Press.

BARTON, L. (1989) *Integration: Myth or Reality*, Lewes, Falmer Press.

BATES, R. (1988) *Evaluating Schools: A Critical Approach*, Geelong, Deakin University Press.

BEATTIE, N. (1985) *Professional Parents*, Lewes, Falmer Press.

BIKLEN, D. (1974) *Let Our Children Go: An Organising Manual for Advocates and Parents*, New York, Human Policy Press.

BIKLEN, D. (1985) *Achieving the Complete School*, New York, Teachers College Press.

BRANSON, J. and MILLER, D. (1989) 'Beyond Integration Policy: The Deconstruction of Disability', in BARTON, L., *Integration: Myth or Reality*, Lewes, Falmer Press.

COOK, S., LEWIS, J. and SLEE, R. (in press) *Special Education, Inclusive Education?* Hawthorn, Australian Council for Educational Research.

CORCORAN, T. and WILSON, B. (1989) *Successful Secondary Schools*, Lewes, Falmer Press.

CREEMERS, B., PETERS, T. and REYNOLDS, D. (1989) *School Effectiveness and School Improvement*, Amsterdam, Swets and Zeitlinger.

DE SWANN, A. (1990) *The Management of Normality*, London, Routledge.

DREWE, R. (1991) From an interview in *The Bulletin*, Sydney, 10 September.

FORD, J., MONGON, D. and WHELAN, M. (1982) *Invisible Disasters: Special Education and Social Control*, London, Routledge and Kegan Paul.

FOUCAULT, M. (1987) *Madness and Civilization*, London, Tavistock.

FULCHER, G. (1987) 'Bureaucracy Takes Round Seven: Round Eight to Commonsense?', *The Age*, 14 April.

FULCHER, G. (1989) *Disabling Policies? A Comparative Approach to Education Policy and Disability*, Lewes, Falmer Press.

FULCHER, G., SEMMENS, R. and SLEE, R. (unpublished) *Successful Schooling*, Melbourne, Victorian Ministry of Education.

FULLAN, M. (1991) *The New Meaning of Educational Change*, London, Cassell.

GALLOWAY, D. (1985) *Schools, Pupils and Special Educational Needs*, London, Croom Helm.

GALLOWAY, D. and BARRETT, C. (1984) 'Factors Associated with Suspension from New Zealand Secondary Schools', *Educational Review*, 36, 3, pp. 277–285.

GARTNER, A. and LIPSKY, D.K. (1987) 'Beyond Special Education: Toward a Quality System for All Students', *Harvard Educational Review*, 57, 43, pp. 367–395.

GILMAN, S.L. (1988) *Disease and Representation: Images of Illness from Madness to Aids*, Ithaca, N.Y., Cornell University Press.

GIROUX, H. (1984) 'Public Philosophy and the Crisis in Education', *Harvard Educational Review*, 54, 2, pp. 186–194.

HENRIQUES, J., HOLLOWAY, W., URWIN, C., VENN, C. and WALKERDINE, V. (1984) *Changing the Subject: Psychology, Social Regulation and Subjectivity*, London, Methuen.

KAMIN, L.J. (1974) *The Science and Politics of IQ*, Harmondsworth, Penguin.

KANNER, L. (1964) *A History of the Care and Study of the Mentally Retarded*, Springfield, Ill., Charles C. Thomas.

KEMMIS, S. (1990) 'Curriculum in Australia: Contemporary Issues', in LANGFORD, P. and D'CRUZ, V. (Eds), *Issues in Australian Education*, Melbourne, Longman Cheshire.

KENWAY, J. (1990) *Gender and Education Policy: A Call For New Directions*, Geelong, Deakin University Press.

KNIGHT, T. (1991) 'At-risk Schools: A Problem for Some Students', *Principal Matters*, 2, 4, pp. 15–17.

LANG, P. and HYDE, N. (1987) 'Pastoral Care: Not Making the Same Mistakes Twice', *Curriculum Perspectives*, 7, 2, pp. 1–10.

LEWIS, J. (1989) Removing the Grit: The Development of Special Education in Victoria 1887–1947, Unpublished PhD thesis, Bundoora, Vic., LaTrobe University.

MCCALLUM, D. (1990) *The Social Production of Merit*, Lewes, Falmer Press.

MINISTRY OF EDUCATION-VICTORIA (1983) *Decision Making in Victorian Education*, Ministerial Paper Number One, Melbourne, Victorian Government Printer.

MINISTRY OF EDUCATION-VICTORIA (1984) *Integration in Victorian Education*: Report of the Ministerial Review of Educational Services for the Disabled, Melbourne, Victorian Government Printer.

MORTIMORE, P., SAMMONS, P., STOLL, L., LEWIS, D. and ECOB, R. (1988) *School Matters: The Junior Years*, Wells, Open Books.

PINK, W.T. (1988) 'School Climate and Effective School Programmes in America', in SLEE, R. (Ed.), *Discipline and Schools: A Curriculum Perspective*, Melbourne, Macmillan.

RAMASUT, A. (1989) *Whole School Approaches to Special Needs*, Lewes, Falmer Press.

RAMSAY, P., SNEDDON, D., GRENFELL, J. and FORD, I. (1983) 'Successful and Unsuccessful Schools: A Study in Southern Auckland', *Australian and New Zealand Journal of Sociology*, 19, 2, pp. 272–303.

REYNOLDS, D. (1982) 'The Search for Effective Schools', *School Organisation*, 2, 3, pp. 214–237.

REYNOLDS, D. (Ed.) (1985) *Studying School Effectiveness*, Lewes, Falmer Press.

RIZVI, F., KEMMIS, S., WALKER, R., FISHER, J. and PARKER, Y. (1987) *Dilemmas of Reform*, Geelong, Deakin University Press.

SALLIS, J. (1988) *Schools, Parents and Governors: A New Approach to Accountability*, London, Routledge.

SEARLE, G.R. (1979) 'Eugenics and Politics in Britain in the 1930s', *Annals of Science*, 36, pp. 159–169.

SKRTIC, T. (1986) 'The Crisis in Special Education Knowledge: A Perspective on Perspective', *Focus on Exceptional Children*, 18, 7, pp. 1–16.

SKRTIC, T. (1991) 'The Special Education Paradox: Equity as the Way to Excellence', *Harvard Educational Review*, 61, 2, pp. 148–206.

SLEE, R. (1986) 'Integration, the Disruptive Student and Suspension', *The Urban Review*, 18, 2, pp. 87–103.

SLEE, R. (1991) 'Learning Initiatives to Include All Students in Regular Schools', in AINSCOW, M. (Ed.), *Effective Schools for All*, London, David Fulton Publishers.

SLEE, R. (Ed.) (1992) *Discipline in Australian Public Education: Changing Policy and Practice*, Hawthorn, Vic., Australian Council for Educational Research.

STOLL, L. (1991) 'School Effectiveness in Action: Supporting Growth in Schools and Classrooms', in AINSCOW, M. (Ed.), *Effective Schools for All*, London, David Fulton Publishers.

SWEET, R. (1988) 'What Do Developments in the Labour Market Imply for Post-compulsory Education in Australia?', *Australian Journal of Education*, 32, 3, pp. 331–356.

TARR, P. (1988) 'Integration Policy and Practice in Victoria: An Examination of the Victorian Government's Educational Provision for Students with Impairments, Disabilities and Problems in Schooling since 1984', in ASHMAN, A. (1988) *Integration 25 Years On*, The Exceptional Child Monograph Number 1, Brisbane, Fred and Eleanor Schonell Special Education Research Centre.

TOMLINSON, S. (1978) 'West Indian Children and ESN-M Schooling', *New Community*, 6, 3.

TOMLINSON, S. (1981) *Educational Subnormality: A Study in Decision Making*, London, Routledge and Kegan Paul.

TOMLINSON, S. (1982) *A Sociology of Special Education*, London, Routledge and Kegan Paul.

TOMLINSON, S. (1985) 'The Expansion of Special Education', *Oxford Review of Education*, 11, 2, pp. 157–165.

WARNOCK, M. (1978) *Special Educational Needs*, London, Her Majesty's Stationery Office.

WARNOCK, M. (1982) 'Children with Special Needs in Ordinary Schools: Integration Revisited', *Education Today*, 32, 3, pp. 56–61.

Chapter 13

Teacher Education as a Strategy for Developing Inclusive Schools

Mel Ainscow

Introduction

Throughout the world there is evidence of countries seeking to formulate national policies for special education (Unesco, 1988). There are also indications that many countries see plans for the integration of children with special needs as an essential element of these policies. Despite this well intentioned rhetoric, however, the situation on the ground gives considerable cause for concern.

As a result of an analysis of the international scene, Hegarty (1990) argues that 'those with disabilities, who ironically have the greatest need of education, are the least likely to receive it.' This is true, he suggests, of both developed and developing countries alike. In developed countries many pupils with disabilities, and lots more who fail to achieve satisfactory progress, are formally excluded from the mainstream education system or receive less favourable treatment within it than other children. On the other hand, in many developing countries the continuing struggle to achieve compulsory education for a majority of children takes precedence over finding ways of educating those with disabilities.

A further cause for concern is the growing body of evidence suggesting that despite the introduction of policies that are intended to encourage integration, the proportion of pupils being excluded from mainstream education in some Western countries is increasing. For example, as a result of her analysis of policies in different parts of the world, Fulcher (1989) suggests that the increased bureaucracy that is often associated with these policies, and the inevitable struggles that go on for additional resources, have the effect of escalating the numbers of school children who come to be tagged as disabled. As an example of this process, Fulcher describes how in Victoria, Australia, some pupils in regular schools come to be described as 'integration children'. Thus their actual right to be educated in ordinary schools is challenged, since their new identity presumes that extra resources are, at least potentially, required. She notes that at the time of writing 3000 pupils in regular schools in Victoria were labelled as 'integration children', a category of disability that had not even existed in 1984.

Similar trends are apparent in other countries. In England, for example, the 1981 Education Act led to a general acceptance that up to 20 per cent of the school population are likely to have special educational needs at some stage in their school lives. Evidence from the United States points to even greater moves to create new categories of exclusion as a means of dealing with an increasing proportion of students seen as presenting difficulties (e.g. Skrtic, 1991a; Wang, 1991). As an example, Anderson and Pellicer (1990) note that in South Carolina at least a quarter of the children enrolled in public schools are in state-funded compensatory and remedial programs. Furthermore, Ysseldyke *et al.* (1983) suggest that approximately 80 per cent of all American school children could be classified as learning disabled by one or more of the procedures used currently in the USA.

From one angle, of course, these developments look to be positive steps. They appear to be significant moves to provide positive discrimination towards children and young people perceived as being at risk. This being the case, we may be encouraged to see approaches of this type developed in the West having an influence in many Third World countries as they seek to achieve educational opportunities for all their children. However, there is increasing concern in many Western countries that there are grave disadvantages to this orientation. Indeed, it has been argued that such approaches to defining and attempting to respond to pupils said to have special needs may well have the effect of limiting opportunities for the very pupils they set out to serve (Ainscow, 1991a).

Specifically, there is concern that the process of segregation, in whatever form, and the inevitable labelling with which it is associated, have negative effects upon the attitudes and expectations of pupils, teachers and parents. Also the presence of designated special needs specialists may encourage teachers to pass on responsibility for children they regard as being in some way exceptional. At the same time resources that might otherwise be used to provide flexible and responsive forms of schooling are channelled into separate provision. Finally, perhaps the greatest concern of all, the nature of the educational experiences provided to children regarded as having special needs is too often characterized by narrowness of opportunity and low levels of achievement (Anderson and Pellicer, 1990; Bennett, 1991; Wang, 1991).

Therefore, any initiatives that set out to help schools and teachers to respond to pupils with disabilities and others experiencing difficulties need to be aware of these arguments. It would be foolish, not to say unethical, to work in ways that seem certain to replicate previous mistakes.

This chapter describes the work of an international project that is seeking to avoid these errors. It explains the project's guiding principles, gives a brief analysis of the work that has been undertaken so far, and draws out some of the implications of these developments.

Special Needs in the Classroom

The Special Needs in the Classroom project was initiated by Unesco just over three years ago.[1] The aim is to develop and disseminate ideas and materials that can be used by teacher educators to support teachers in mainstream schools as they seek to accommodate pupil diversity. Accounts of the evolution of the project are provided in Ainscow (1990, 1991b). This section provides a brief summary of what has occurred so far.

The initiative for the project grew out of Unesco's continuing work in encouraging member states to develop strategies for responding to children's special needs in ordinary schools. A survey of fourteen countries, commissioned by Unesco and carried out by a research team from the University of London (Bowman, 1986), identified three major priorities for policy development:

1   the provision of compulsory education for all children in the population;
2   the integration of pupils with disabilities into ordinary schools; and
3   the upgrading of teacher training as a means of achieving the first two priorities.

The findings of this survey were used as the basis of a series of regional workshops. An outcome of these events was that Unesco was urged to assist in the dissemination of teacher training materials that could be used to facilitate improvements with respect to meeting special needs in ordinary schools. The regional workshops also generated more specific recommendations as to the content and emphasis to be placed within any materials that might be produced. Consequently, in 1988 I was invited by Unesco to direct a project that would aim to develop and disseminate a resource pack of teacher education materials. A pilot version of the pack was field tested in eight countries (Canada, Chile, India, Jordan, Kenya, Malta, Spain and Zimbabwe) during 1990–91.

The design of suitable teacher education materials represents an enormous challenge. In particular there is the central issue of how to produce a pack that can be relevant to and take account of such a wide range of national contexts, especially those in developing countries. Measures were taken during the formulation of materials to achieve a level of flexibility that could take account of diverse settings as follows:

— a pilot workshop for teachers and teacher educators from various African countries was held in Nairobi, Kenya in April 1989; this allowed various materials and approaches to be evaluated;
— further trials were carried out in Turkey during September 1989;
— a number of advisory teams consisting of teacher educators and teachers were created in different parts of the world; these teams provided comment on draft materials and contributed materials and ideas of their own for inclusion in the pack;
— a number of special educators and others involved in teacher development around the world read and commented upon draft materials;
— an international resource team was created to field test and evaluate pilot materials; this team is also involved in the further development of the materials.

Extensive use was also made of evaluative and research evidence from other similar initiatives and a wider theoretical literature to critique the developing rationale of the pack. This has led to a rejection of the functionalist assumptions that have dominated thinking and practice in special education and guided much of the work that has gone into teacher development (Skrtic, 1991a). Rather, the work of the project has been influenced by an alternative perspective which offers a very different way of considering human behaviour. This perspective, sometimes referred to as a constructivist or constructionist view, assumes that our perceptions, appreciations and beliefs are rooted in worlds of our own making that we come to regard as reality (Goodman, 1978). Consequently, initiatives that operate on the basis of this perspective, described by some as a 'new paradigm' (e.g., Heshusius, 1989; Iano, 1986; Lincoln and Guba, 1985; Reason, 1988), emphasize the following assumptions:

1 human behaviour can only be understood with respect to particular contexts;
2 this understanding can only be achieved by a consideration of these contexts as 'wholes'; and
3 events that occur within a given context are assumed to be constructed in the minds of participants and can, therefore, only be understood by taking account of these multiple realities.

The constructivist perspective, and its associated assumptions, have been influential in the development of the project, including its approach to special needs, teacher development, dissemination and evaluation (Ainscow, 1991b). It has become the guiding theory that has been used with some success to construct an initiative that can be relevant across diverse contexts and cultures. However, as we will see, it is a perspective that challenges many existing practices in schools and in teacher education. Consequently, it must be adopted with care.

Rejecting the Dominant Perspective

In seeking to avoid earlier mistakes associated with policies for facilitating the integration of pupils said to have special needs, we have taken particular note of a relatively new set of voices that have emerged, in some cases from within the ranks of special education, to argue for reform.[2] Interestingly, and significantly from the point of view of this project, these voices reflect developments in different parts of the world. While they are not in full agreement with respect to their analysis and recommendations, they all adopt critical perspectives, seeking to facilitate improvement by questioning the field's guiding theoretical assumptions. Examples of writers who may be included in this category include: in Australia, Fulcher (1989) and Slee (1991); in England, Barton (1988), Booth (1988) and Tomlinson (1982); in New Zealand, Ballard (1990); in Papua New Guinea, Carrier (1983); and in North America, Biklen (1989); Heshusius (1989) and Skrtic (1991a). A significant feature of the work of all these writers is the extent to which they draw on ideas from outside the traditional boundaries of special education knowledge, including perspectives taken from sociology, political theory, philosophy and organizational analysis. Their work, and that of others adopting similar stances (including many of the authors in this book), offers a more radical analysis of the policy and practice of special education. It also points to some significant pathways for improvement.

One of the concerns that these writers share is with the ways in which pupils within schools come to be designated as being *special*. They see these as social and political processes. Consequently, they need to be continually scrutinized and challenged. More specifically, they argue that the dominant approach of explaining educational difficulties in terms of child-centred characteristics promotes injustice and prevents progress in the field.

Following these radical perspectives has led us, within the project, to reconstruct the special needs task. This reconceptualization suggests that significant progress towards schooling that accommodates pupil diversity is dependent upon a realization that difficulties experienced by pupils come about as a result of the way we choose to organize schools and the forms of teaching that are provided (Slee, 1991). In other words, as Skrtic (1991c) puts it, pupils with special needs are artifacts of the traditional curriculum. Consequently, the way forward must be to improve and, if necessary, reform schools and, in so doing, develop forms of teaching that respond positively to pupil diversity, seeing individuality as something to be nurtured and celebrated. Within such a conceptualization, a consideration of difficulties experienced by pupils (and by teachers) can provide an agenda for improvement and, indeed, insights as to how progress might be achieved.

There is growing recognition that this kind of approach is only likely to occur in contexts where there exists a respect for individuality (Eisner, 1990), and, critically, within a culture of collaboration that encourages and supports problem-solving (Fullan, 1991; Joyce *et al.*, 1991; Thousand and Villa, 1991; Skrtic, 1991a). A striking and relevant example of the importance of collaboration is provided by Rosenholtz (1989). Her study of seventy-eight schools indicates that in those where there is a shared consensus, teachers are much more likely to incorporate new ways of responding to their pupils. In such schools teachers seem more willing to persevere, to define 'problem pupils' as a challenge and actually to foster pupil progress. This research leads Rosenholtz to conclude that: '. . . . teachers' optimism and enthusiasm are tractable virtues by which students grow, and schools can either strengthen or weaken them through the contextual design of teachers' work' (1989: 138). While our concern here is primarily with children perceived as having special needs, it is important to recognize that organizational cultures that encourage collaboration as a basis for problem-solving are likely to facilitate the learning of *all* pupils and, alongside them, the professional learning of all teachers (Fullan, 1991; Louis and Miles, 1990). Ultimately, therefore, the logic of this argument makes a case for increased equity in schools as a means of achieving educational excellence (Skrtic, 1991b; Slee, 1991).

At this point in my argument it is important to recognize that reconstructing the special needs task in terms of school improvement and teacher development is likely to lead to a challenge to the status quo of schooling and teacher education. At a political level it addresses questions to those who create and administer policy; and at the professional level it presents challenges to individual teachers and those involved in their education. Specifically, it requires many to suspend their existing beliefs and assumptions about the origins and nature of educational difficulties in order to consider alternative perspectives. Instead of the traditional search for specialist techniques that can be used to ameliorate the learning difficulties of individual pupils, the focus must be on finding ways of creating the conditions that will facilitate and support the learning of *all* children.

These changes of perspectives are not easy to achieve. Teaching is a demanding and intensive activity leaving little time for reflection. Furthermore, the perspectives of teachers are often deeply rooted, having been established through the process of professionalization that occurs during initial training and, perhaps even more significantly, within the workplace (Rosenholtz, 1989). This is why the Unesco project materials seek to influence teacher educators and others involved in the training and further professional development of teachers.

A critical aspect of the change in perspective required relates to the way teachers and others in education conceptualize educational difficulty — in other words, as Schon (1987) suggests, the ways in which problems are 'named and framed'. He notes: 'Through complementary acts of naming and framing, the practitioner selects things for attention and organizes them, guided by an appreciation of the situation that gives it coherence and sets a direction for action' (1987: 4). This is, in effect, the constructivist notion of 'world making', as defined by Nelson Goodman (1978).

Our aim is to help teachers and teacher educators to break out of what Fulcher (1989) refers to as the 'individualistic gaze'. This is an approach to naming and framing the problems experienced by pupils and teachers which takes little or no notice of the wider environmental, social and political contexts in which they occur. By focusing attention on particular pupils in this individualized way, it leads the school population to be divided into 'types' of children to be taught in different ways or even by different types of teachers. This has the effect of deflecting attention away from the central issue of how schooling can accommodate pupil diversity. It does this by characterizing special needs as a technical task requiring the provision of special techniques, personnel and physical resources. Within this individualistic gaze, the teacher education task with respect to special needs is seen as being concerned with introducing teachers to approaches that can be used to ameliorate the problems of individual pupils. Furthermore, the responses that result are often very limiting in that they underestimate the importance of social interaction as a means of facilitating learning (Ainscow and Tweddle, 1988).

Reframing the Special Needs Task

Within the project, therefore, the underlying aim is to help teachers and teacher educators to consider alternatives to the individualized gaze. Beyond this we also try to encourage them to see pupils experiencing difficulties in their learning as a source of understanding how teaching and classroom conditions can be improved. These improvements, it should be recalled, are seen as being to the advantage of all pupils.

In developing the rationale for the materials and approaches recommended in the resource pack, the work of Donald Schon (1983, 1987) concerning professional development has been particularly important and helpful. Schon stresses the importance of what he calls professional artistry as a basis for the improvement of practice. His analysis leads him to be highly critical of existing approaches to professional development in a number of fields, including that of teacher education. The central problem, he argues, lies in the doctrine of technical rationality that dominates thinking within the professions. Embedded in technical rationality is the assumption that a profession is an occupational group whose practice is grounded in knowledge derived from scientific research. As a result, professional competence is seen as the skilful application of theoretical knowledge to the instrumental problems of practice. Within such a view of practice, artistry has little place.

Schon argues that such a view of professional knowledge and practice is inadequate in a number of ways. In terms of our concern here specifically, he suggests that although technical rationality portrays professional competence as a technical problem-solving competence, the problems of the real world do not present themselves as givens. Rather, they are messy, indeterminate and problematic situations that arise often because of conflicting values. Such problems cannot be resolved by the use of techniques derived from theoretical research, but call for what Schon calls 'artful competence'. This is a process of clarification of a problematic situation that enables practitioners to redefine their problems in terms of both the ends to be achieved and the means for their achievement. As a result of his analysis, Schon argues that the technical rational model should be replaced by an emphasis on what he calls reflective enquiry. This leads him to seek approaches to professional development that encourage practitioners to reflect upon taken for granted knowledge that is implicit in their actions.

Within the Unesco project we have been exploring approaches that are informed by Schon's arguments. The traditional, individualistic perspective in special needs work can be seen as an example of the technical rational model with all its limitations and disadvantages (Iano, 1986). In seeking ways of working that are based upon reflective enquiry, therefore, we are attempting to overcome the domination of this perspective. Our hope is that by helping teachers to become confident in their own abilities to learn from their experience, we can help them to break out of the individualized gaze.

In addition to reflective enquiry, our other area of emphasis is with social processes as a means of facilitating professional development and learning. As we have already seen, effective schools seem to be characterized by a culture of collaboration leading to a shared consensus. While our project does not always operate at the whole school level, it does emphasize the importance of collaboration at all levels of the school system as a means of facilitating problem-solving and learning. In this respect we have accepted the argument of Handy and Aitkin (1986), who state: 'Groups allow individuals to reach beyond themselves, to be part of something that none of them would have attained on their own and to discover ways of working with others to mutual benefit.'

In summary, the Special Needs in the Classroom project is attempting to help teacher educators and teachers to become more confident and skilful in developing their own practice. It does this by encouraging them to use the resources of others around them (including their pupils) to stimulate their reflections upon difficulties that arise in their classrooms. It is anticipated that where this approach is successful, it will lead teachers to become more confident about their ability to cater for pupil diversity. In this way the special needs task is reframed as school improvement and teacher development.

The Project Materials

There is considerable evidence to indicate that programs of teacher education and staff development can help to facilitate improvements in professional practice provided they are well planned and based on sound principles (e.g., Ainscow and Muncey, 1989; Browdler, 1983; Joyce and Showers, 1988; Loucks-Horsley *et al.*, 1987; Powers, 1983; Stevenson, 1987). In this context I am using the term 'staff development' to include a variety of processes and activities by which teachers can be helped and can help one another to develop their practice.

In relation to the arguments presented earlier in this chapter, the materials in the resource pack developed for use in the Special Needs in the Classroom project emphasize the following five strategies:

1 *Active learning.* Active approaches to problem solving, with a particular emphasis on cooperative group learning are used, as opposed to the didactic learning style so often found in teacher education. These approaches are intended to encourage participation, stimulate individuals to consider alternative perspectives and help overcome fear of change. They also model the benefits that can occur as a result of collaborative ways of working.
2 *Negotiation of objectives.* The involvement of participants in the negotiation of their own learning objectives within the overall framework of a course, or series of workshop sessions, is intended to provide a means of taking account of their varied interests and needs. It also encourages them to take responsibility for their own learning and to have a commitment to the implementation of ideas and approaches that are developed.
3 *Demonstration, practice and feedback.* Implementation of new ideas or ways of working seems to be more likely when these three elements are used together. Demonstration allows participants to see what is possible; practice with the support of colleagues encourages 'risk taking'; and feedback, preferably from a trusted colleague, provides further encouragement and advice. This approach, involving pairs of teachers working in partnership, is sometimes referred to as 'peer coaching' (Joyce and Showers, 1988).
4 *Continuous evaluation.* The active involvement of participants in monitoring their own learning is intended to enhance motivation. The aim here is to encourage reflection and, once again, to emphasize the idea of participants taking responsibility for their own learning. Various techniques are used here, including learning journals in which individuals write about the development of their own thinking and practice. Continuous evaluation is also important as a means of influencing the planning of course activities and priorities in response to the interests of individual participants.
5 *Support.* Finally, the importance of providing support for learners is modelled through the course sessions. Efforts are also made to encourage teachers to establish partnerships with colleagues as a means of providing longer-term support as they attempt to develop aspects of their classroom practice. This support is seen as being an essential way of promoting the risk-taking that is necessary when attempting to develop new ways of teaching.

The main elements of the resource pack are as follows:

1 *Study materials.* These include an extensive range of readings, stimulus sheets and classroom activities.
2 *Course leaders' guide.* This provides detailed guidance as to how to organize courses and facilitate sessions based on the study materials. A

series of case studies describing projects that have been carried out in a number of countries is also included.

3   *Training videos.* These include examples of the various recommended approaches in use during courses and film of follow-up activities in schools.

It is important to understand that the materials and activities in the pack encourage course leaders to model, at the adult level, strategies for teaching that take account of student diversity. In this way the features of the pack that are seen as facilitating adult learning within course sessions are intended to be used as a basis for working with classes of children in school.

Dissemination and Evaluation

The limited dissemination that has taken place so far has been carried out in order to field test a pilot version of the resource pack and, in so doing, to develop an international resource team that can be used to support the widening of the work of the project. In April 1990 two coordinators from each of the eight countries referred to earlier took part in a two-week workshop/seminar at the University of Zimbabwe. The group included university lecturers, educational administrators, teachers and one headteacher. The first week took the form of a demonstration workshop during which I used materials from the resource pack to conduct a series of course sessions for the coordinators and a further group of local teachers and student teachers. In the second week the demonstration workshop was evaluated as the basis of a seminar in which the international coordinators planned together the ways in which they would field test the resource pack in their own countries.

This field testing was completed by March 1991 and each team of coordinators prepared an evaluation report about their work. The main aim of the field testing was to gather information that could be used to inform the further development of the resource pack and to plan its future dissemination. In this way it has been possible to develop the sixteen coordinators into an international resource team who are now collaborating in the design and promotion of the overall project.

In terms of evaluation, our central question was, 'How can the resource pack be developed and disseminated in a way that will be appropriate for teachers in different countries?' With this in mind the evaluation was based upon a multisite case study approach (Miles and Huberman, 1984) in which individual reports attempted to explain what happened as the resource materials were used in a particular context. To be consistent with the constructivist perspective, reports included interpretations of these events from the points of view of *all* participants. A particular interest was the ways in which the materials and ideas related to the social, cultural and educational tradition of each participating country (Miles, 1989).

While the emphasis was on providing accounts that made sense of what happened in each national context, there was also a need to make comparisons between the experience in different countries. Consequently, a common framework was agreed among the team of coordinators in order that evaluation reports would have a common pattern. This framework consisted of a series of evaluation questions addressed to course leaders and participants related to the following aspects of the field testing:

Implementation — the use of materials from the resource pack within teacher education contexts;
Process — interactions based upon the materials associated with the resource pack;
Content — ideas and approaches presented in the materials;
Design — the format of the resource pack, including the various written materials;
Outcomes — changes of attitude, thinking or practice thought to have occurred as a result of the use of the resource pack.

Data that could be used to address the evaluation questions were collected using a range of procedures, including learning journals, group reports, question-naires, interviews, video recordings and observations. These data were collected both during and after the courses. Care was taken in establishing the trustworthi-ness of findings. In particular, coordinators were asked to collaborate with their colleagues, including participants, in order to verify their interpretations. Throughout the emphasis was placed on recording and taking account of multiple perspectives. Interpretations of the data were also subject to triangulation, a pro-cess of using two or more sets of information to study and validate an account of one event (Lincoln and Guba, 1985).

The Findings

Some details of the contexts within which the field testing took place are pro-vided in Figure 1. In total the sixteen coordinators worked with 235 participants. As can be seen the sites involved represented a diversity of national, cultural, linguistic and teacher education contexts. All involved the use of materials from each of the four modules in the resource pack in courses or workshops consisting of at least thirty hours of instructional contact. Some of these were intensive in style (e.g., one week workshops), whereas others involved sessions spread over months. Most included opportunities for participants to carry out follow-up activ-ities with pupils in schools.

The great mass of data that has been collected through processes of collabo-rative enquiry in each of the eight countries is still subject to scrutiny. This process of analysis will, in due course, inform the production of the final version of the resource pack and the organization of its wider dissemination by Unesco. How-ever, interesting findings have emerged that are relevant to the discussions in this chapter about using teacher education as a strategy for developing inclusive schools.

The evaluation data indicate that in all of the field testing sites the materials were used as intended and the course leaders worked in ways that were largely consistent with the five strategies outlined earlier in this chapter. Difficulties did arise as coordinators attempted to utilize these approaches, and an analysis of these problems will be very useful in rewriting the materials.

Some coordinators found difficulty in moving away from their previous ways of working, based, as they were, on a technical rational perspective. Many

Figure 1. Summary of Field Testing Sites

Canada	Site 1 — used as part of a school-wide staff development project in a large community school serving a remote community in the north (seventeen participants, plus awareness sessions with forty-five members of staff). Site 2 — part of an award-bearing university summer school for experienced teachers (twenty-three participants).
Chile	A course conducted in Spanish for eighteen teachers from regular schools, including fourteen headteachers.
India	Site 1 — an in-service course, in English, for sixteen primary and secondary teachers, including seven special education teachers. Site 2 — a workshop for twenty-six student teachers in a college, conducted in Hindi.
Jordan	A course for eleven teachers representing one private school and ten teachers from five government schools; medium of communication, Arabic.
Kenya	Used with sixteen second year students in a teachers' college in preparation for and during a period of school practice.
Malta	A workshop for twenty-eight learning support teachers working with underachieving pupils in primary schools.
Spain	A course carried out in Spanish for twenty teachers from ten schools involved in the government's integration program, plus seven advisers.
Zimbabwe	A program for fifteen teacher educators from different colleges and representing different subject areas.

reported experiencing considerable strain as a result of the intellectual demands that teaching approaches based upon active learning and reflective enquiry create. In particular, the need to organize and monitor group processes, debrief activities and summarize outcomes was very demanding. Many also referred to problems associated with use of time during course sessions, particularly when these were part of intensive programs that did not allow sufficient opportunities for course leaders and participants to reflect upon activities that had taken place. However, all the evaluation reports reflect a sense of acceptance and optimism about the approaches that were used. This was apparent even when coordinators were working in very difficult and stressful conditions, not least in Jordan where the field testing took place during the period just prior to the outbreak of war.

Particular contextual factors created difficulties in certain places. For example, a number of coordinators reported hostility from certain of their colleagues who, it seems, were unhappy with the emphasis on active learning approaches. Some of the student teachers experienced negative reactions from experienced teachers when they attempted to reorganize classrooms in order to move away from more traditional organizational formats. Difficulties sometimes arose when the materials were used as part of school-based staff development programs. Once again negative reactions seemed to occur when approaches were introduced that appeared to challenge existing patterns of working.

The data indicate that the five strategies emphasized in the project were well received and had a significant impact in all the sites. The use of cooperative group work and the idea of negotiating learning objectives were particularly well regarded. However, there is also a clear indication in many of the reports that the introduction of these ways of working tended to create some negative reactions during early course sessions. For example, a number of the reports note that the participating teachers were not used to taking responsibility for their own learning and showed discomfort when this idea was introduced. This can be very stressful for course leaders, leading them to be tempted into reverting to more didactic styles of working.

Some of the coordinators also felt a need to offer more practical strategies to their participants, perhaps feeling that the emphasis on reflective enquiry lacked 'hard content'. This tendency needs to be considered further, particularly if we are to take seriously the view of Donald Schon when he states: '. . . the more we integrate in a curriculum the knowledge and skills that students, in our judgement, need to learn, the more we make it difficult for them to function as reflective designers of their own education' (1987: 341).

Overall, there is a strong feeling from the data that the subject content of the materials in the resource pack is seen as relevant to teachers in all these national contexts. By and large the materials seem to be concerned with topics and issues that are perceived to be real and relevant. One coordinator reported that towards the end of the course a participant had been most surprised to hear that the materials had not been written especially for teachers in her own country. Clearly, the constructivist approach of using stimulus materials as a means of encouraging participants to draw out ideas from their own experience is an effective strategy for taking account of diversity. In this way, to a large extent participants are constructing their own content. The opportunity to negotiate individual learning objectives and programs of activity is also a significant way of catering for individual interests.

Thus it would seem that the resource pack has appropriate stimulus materials, focusing on issues that are meaningful and relevant to teachers in different countries, and using activities and processes that enable participants to construct their own agendas for discussion through enquiry, reflection and collaboration. Indeed, a participant in Chile remarked: 'The course has no content and so enables us to learn how to reflect.' Similarly, a teacher in Spain noted: 'I have learned that if we want to look for and find solutions to our pupils' problems we have to reflect — because the solution is in ourselves.' One pattern that needs to be considered, however, concerns reactions of those teachers who had previously been exposed to specialized training with respect to special education. There is some evidence in the data that members of this group experienced greater difficulty in accepting the value of the approaches used in the resource pack. Their previous experience of techniques reflecting the 'individualized gaze' may act as a barrier when they are asked to consider unusual ways of working. It may also be that they see these alternative approaches as threatening their status as experts in teaching special children, a status that has been given credibility by the widespread acceptance of the doctrine of technical rationality.

Outcomes

It is very difficult to measure the outcomes of a project of this sort. Our aspirations are ambitious, and evidence of their achievement would require prolonged engagement within the contexts of the various participants, including those of the teachers and the teacher educators. Nevertheless, the indications with respect to both course participants and coordinators are, to say the least, very encouraging. In all the reports there is extensive evidence that the activities made a significant impact on people's ideas. As one participant noted, 'I go to bed with the course in mind.'

The data include many interesting anecdotal accounts that provide insights into the ways in which participants reacted to their experiences during courses and workshops. One example gives a flavour of these accounts. A teacher in Canada wrote about the way in which her participation in a course based upon the resource pack had transformed her thinking. She writes about her unease about being asked to take responsibility for her own learning and how she felt uncharacteristically tongue-tied when asked to participate in group activities. Noting the insecurity that can arise when traditional teaching approaches are absent, she writes:

> I began to nostalgically think back to courses past where I could succeed by staying in safe boundaries. I had learned to feel secure when I was told how to think and at peace in a learning environment where I was only required to passively absorb what information I could and repro- duce it at well-scheduled intervals.

She refers to the fact that the Chinese character for change is a combination of the characters 'fear' and 'opportunity' (an idea presented in the resource pack). She recalls experiencing the fear, but was helped through the course activities to take the opportunities for learning. All of this led her to reflect on the issue of pupils with special needs. At the outset of the course there had been little doubt in her mind that the problem was the child's and so it was the child that needed attention. She writes: 'The classroom was the mountain, and the child, Moham- med. Of course it made sense that Mohammed was the one to move.' Through the experience of the course, however, she sensed her assumptions being challenged and her point of view changing. She concludes:

> Although individual learning styles influence the rate of a child's de- velopment, the learning environment can adapt to the individual if tasks are presented differently, resources teachers provide are varied, and the ways in which the teacher organizes the classroom and its priorities are modified. The mountain can move to Mohammed.

Many of the participants describe their intention to change their practice in the light of their experiences. Examples of changes are also reported in some detail. This may lead to difficulties since, as we have already noted, such devel- opments may be perceived as challenging existing policies with respect to organ- ization, curriculum and assessment. Attempting to teach in ways that respond to pupil diversity may be seen as a subversive activity. This indicates the need to use the resource pack in contexts where extensive negotiations have been undertaken prior to any initiative in order to clarify expectations and ensure positive support.

Probably the most significant impact of the field testing has been upon the thinking and practice of the members of the international resource team. Through their journals and evaluation reports there is ample evidence that all the coordinators have experienced significant rethinking of the theoretical basis of their work. For example, a very experienced teacher educator in Spain describes how the project has altered his perspectives on special needs and the role of teacher education. He refers to 'discovering that both the learning modalities and the learning situations we foster in the children are equally applicable in the training of adults' and 'Verifying that the best learning source is the analysis of our own experience in a context of support and collaboration among colleagues.' He concludes: '. . . in future I will not be able to work with the traditional approach.'

The coordinators' reactions to their experiences and the changes these fostered in their thinking and practice seemed to be entirely positive. The statement made by the members of the resource team in Chile was typical: 'Professionally speaking, as concerns the training activities we have been involved in, we think that the work carried out has been the most gratifying and positive experience we have encountered.' Continued contact with the resource team following completion of the field testing suggests that these changes in thinking and practice have been sustained and, indeed, generalized throughout their work. In this respect there is strong evidence from this project, confirming findings from elsewhere (e.g., Joyce and Showers, 1988), that approaches to the professional development of teacher educators that involve demonstrations of method followed by peer collaboration at the stage of implementation of new ways of working are very powerful.

Conclusion

At the time of writing, plans are being made by Unesco for the further development of the project described in this chapter. We are extremely encouraged by the success of the field testing of the pilot version of the resource pack. We also feel that the establishment of the international resource team provides a strong basis for wider dissemination. Consequently, the main strategy during the next few years is to strengthen existing national projects as a basis for gradual regional development. As part of this strategy, we believe that the resource team members must be encouraged to develop their expertise and, at the same time, establish new teaching partnerships within their own communities. In this way we hope to increase the number of resource people that will be available to demonstrate the use of the resource pack in different parts of the world.

Already projects based upon the resource pack are underway in India, South America, the Middle East and South East Asia. In addition, planning is taking place to facilitate initiatives in Africa, the Caribbean and Europe. Beyond the Unesco project it is possible to begin drawing out implications for others who wish to help teachers to respond positively to pupil diversity. Specifically, we can draw attention to the importance of conceptual clarity when planning such initiatives.

My colleague at Unesco, Ture Jonsson, makes a distinction between efficiency and effectiveness.[3] Efficiency, he suggests, is to do with 'doing things right'. Effectiveness, on the other hand, is about 'doing the right things'. This distinction helps us to understand some of the mistakes that have occurred in the special needs field. So much of the time and effort that have been used in attempts to develop policies for integration have been concerned with matters of efficiency.

Regrettably, much less attention has been paid to conceptualizing what it is we should be trying to achieve. As a consequence we have witnessed the development in a number of countries of policies and practice that, despite good intentions, seem to work to the disadvantage of the very children they set out to serve. Furthermore, we see the continued expansion of separate provision of various forms, despite the stated aim of achieving integrated schooling.

The central message that has emerged from the work of this project is that those engaged in attempting to foster forms of schooling that are inclusive must pay careful attention to the ways in which they 'name and frame' their activities. Specifically, they would be wise to conceptualize their special needs tasks in terms of school improvement (and, quite possibly, school reform) and teacher development. Such a perspective will enable them to recognize the importance of contextual influences on the learning of children and teachers, thus avoiding the limitations of the individualized gaze.

Having said that, it is vital to keep in mind some of the difficulties experienced by course leaders and participants as they attempted to engage with the ideas and perspectives presented through the materials in the resource pack. In particular, we should note the difficulties experienced by those who had previously been exposed to special education training courses. These difficulties can be explained, at least in part, as arising when individuals attempt to break out of the technical rational perspective that still dominates so much thinking and practice in education, particularly in the special needs field. This doctrine assumes a belief in science-based professional action; it also ignores conflict by assuming consensus about ends and by attending exclusively to means. In this way it encourages a concern with efficiency rather than effectiveness.

Olson (1989) analyzes why, despite mounting criticism, the technical rational orientation persists in education. He comes to the conclusion that this is because of the way it appears to meet the needs of administrators and teachers. Central to his argument is the notion of hazards, a concept he borrows from Goffman. Hazards are occasions when reputations are at risk. The great appeal of technical rationality is that it makes decision-making and problem-solving less hazardous, since failures can be blamed on science itself. Olson sums up the argument as follows: '.... Being able to involve science in support of one's decision offsets some of the risks of failure since science has to carry some of the blame if things do not go well' (Olson, 1989: 105). A project of the sort described in this chapter increases the risk of hazard in that it requires those involved to look to themselves and their colleagues in order to find solutions to the problems they face. It adds further pressure by encouraging participants to work in ways that are very different from existing practice and, in so doing, raise questions that may be perceived as being threatening or even subversive by those around them. It is hardly surprising, therefore, that despite attempts to encourage a supportive environment, there will be times when some will prefer to stay within safer boundaries.

Notes

1 I acknowledge the contribution of my colleague at Unesco, Lena Saleh, who inspired and encouraged this project. Those interested in using the project materials should contact her at Unesco, 7, Place de Fontenoy, 75700 Paris, France.

2 Among the many significant influences upon the development of this project, of
   course, was my own previous experience. In wanting others to be reflective about
   their practice, it was essential that I adopted a similar stance in my own work. An
   account of my attempt to analyze my own practice is provided in Ainscow (1991c).
   This explains how my involvement in previous projects has influenced my perspectives on educational difficulties and teacher development. This explanation gives
   further insights regarding the approaches used in the Unesco project.
3 This distinction between efficiency and effectiveness is sometimes used in educational management (see, for example, West and Ainscow, 1991).

References

AINSCOW, M. (1990) 'Special Needs in the Classroom: The Development of a Teacher
   Eduction Resource Pack', *International Journal of Special Education*, 5, 1, pp. 13–
   20.
AINSCOW, M. (Ed.) (1991a) *Effective Schools for All*, London, Fulton; Baltimore, Paul
   H. Brookes.
AINSCOW, M. (1991b) 'Towards Effective Schools for All: An Account of the Ration-
   ale of the Unesco Teacher Education Project, "Special Needs in the Classroom"',
   in UPTON, G. (Ed.), *Staff Training and Special Educational Needs*, London, Fulton.
AINSCOW, M. (1991c) 'Becoming a Reflective Teacher', in BOOTH, T., *et al.* (Eds),
   Learning for All, Vol. 1, Milton Keynes, Open University.
AINSCOW, M. and MUNCEY, J. (1989) *Meeting Individual Needs in the Primary School*,
   London, Fulton.
AINSCOW, M. and TWEDDLE, D.A. (1988) *Encouraging Classroom Success*, London,
   Fulton.
ANDERSON, L.W. and PELLICER, L.O. (1990) 'Synthesis of Research on Compensatory
   and Remedial Education', *Educational Leadership*, 48, 1, pp. 10–16.
BALLARD, K.D. (1990) 'Special Education in New Zealand: Disability, Politics and
   Empowerment', *International Journal of Disability, Development and Education*,
   37, 2, pp. 109–124.
BARTON, L. (1988) 'The Politics Of Special Educational Needs: An Introduction', in
   BARTON, L. (Ed.), *The Politics of Special Educational Needs*, Lewes, Falmer Press.
BENNETT, N. (1991) 'The Quality of Classroom Learning Experiences for Children
   with Special Educational Needs', in AINSCOW, M. (Ed.), *Effective Schools for All*,
   London, Fulton.
BIKLEN, D.P. (1989) 'Redefining Schools', in BIKLEN, D., FERGUSON, D. and FORD, A.
   (Eds), *Schooling and Disability: Eighty-eighth Yearbook of the National Society
   for the Study of Education Part II*, Chicago, Ill., University of Chicago Press.
BOOTH, T. (1988)'Challenging Conceptions of Integration', in BARTON, L. (Ed.), *The
   Politics of Special Educational Needs*, Lewes, Falmer Press.
BOWMAN, I. (1986) 'Teacher Training and the Integration of Handicapped Pupils: Some
   Findings from a Fourteen Nation Unesco Study', *European Journal of Special
   Needs Education 1*, pp. 29–38.
BROWDLER, D. (1983) 'Guidelines for Inservice Planning', *Exceptional Children*, 49, 3,
   pp. 300–306.
CARRIER, J.G. (1983) 'Masking the Social in Educational Knowledge: The Case of
   Learning Disability Theory', *American Journal of Sociology*, 88, pp. 948–974.
EISNER, E.W. (1990) 'The Meaning of Alternative Paradigms for Practice', in GUBA,
   E.G. (Ed.), *The Paradigm Dialogue*, London, Sage.
FULCHER, G. (1989) *Disabling Policies? A Comparative Approach to Education Policy
   and Disability*, Lewes, Falmer Press.

FULLAN, M.G. (1991) *The New Meaning of Educational Change*, London, Cassell.

GOODMAN, N. (1978) *Ways of World Making*, Indianapolis, Ind., Hackett.

HANDY, C. and AITKEN, R. (1986) *Understanding Schools as Organisations*, London, Penguin.

HEGARTY, S. (1990) *The Education of Children and Young People with Disabilities: Principles and Practice*, Paris, Unesco.

HESHUSIUS, L. (1989) 'The Newtonian Mechanistic Paradigm, Special Education, and Contours of Alternatives: An Overview', *Journal of Learning Disabilities*, 22, 7, pp. 403–421.

IANO, R.P. (1986) 'The Study and Development of Teaching: With Implications for the Advancement of Special Education', *Remedial and Special Education*, 7, 5, pp. 50–61.

JOYCE, B. and SHOWERS, B. (1988) *Student Achievement through Staff Development*, London, Longman.

JOYCE, B., MURPHY, C., SHOWERS, B. and MURPHY, J. (1991) 'School Renewal as Cultural Change', in AINSCOW, M. (Ed.), *Effective Schools for All*, London, Fulton.

LINCOLN, Y.S. and GUBA, E.G. (1985) *Naturalistic Inquiry*, Beverley Hills, Calif., Sage.

LOUCKS-HORSLEY, S., *et al.* (1987) *Continuing to Learn: A Guidebook for Teacher Development*, Andover, Mass., Regional Laboratory for Education Improvement of the Northeast and Islands.

LOUIS, K. and MILES, M.B. (1990) *Improving the Urban High School: What Works and Why*, New York, Teachers College Press.

MILES, M. (1989) 'The Role of Special Education in Information Based Rehabilitation', *International Journal of Special Education*, 4, 2, pp. 111–118.

MILES, M.B. and HUBERMAN, A.M. (1984) *Qualitative Data Analysis*, Beverley Hills, Calif., Sage.

OLSON, J. (1989) 'The Persistence of Technical Rationality', in MILBURN, G., GOODSON, I.F. and CLARK, R.J. (1989) *Reinterpreting Curriculum Research*, Lewes, Falmer Press.

POWERS, D.A. (1983) 'Mainstreaming and the Inservice Education of Teachers', *Exceptional Children*, 49, pp. 432–439.

REASON, P. (Ed.) (1988) *Human Inquiry in Action*, Beverley Hills, Calif., Sage.

ROSENHOLTZ, S. (1989) *Teachers' Workplace: The Social Organisation of Schools*, New York, Longman.

SCHON, D.A. (1983) *The Reflective Practitioner*, New York, Basic Books.

SCHON, D.A. (1987) *Educating the Reflective Practitioner*, San Francisco, Calif., Jossey Bass.

SKRTIC, T.M. (1991a) *Behind Special Education: A Critical Analysis of Professional Culture and School Organisation*, Denver, Colo., Love.

SKRTIC, T.M. (1991b) 'The Special Education Paradox: Equity as the Way to Excellence', *Harvard Educational Review*, 61, 2, pp. 148–206.

SKRTIC, T.M. (1991c) 'Students with Special Educational Needs: Artifacts of the Traditional Curriculum', in AINSCOW, M. (Ed.), *Effective Schools for All*, London, Fulton.

SLEE, R. (1991) 'Learning Initiatives to Include All Students in Regular Schools', in AINSCOW, M. (Ed.), *Effective Schools for All*, London, Fulton.

STEVENSON, R.B. (1987) 'Staff Development for Effective Secondary Schools: A Synthesis of Research', *Teaching and Teacher Education*, 3, 3, pp. 233–248.

THOUSAND, J.S. and VILLA, R.A. (1991) 'Accommodating for Greater Student Variance', in AINSCOW, M. (Ed.), *Effective Schools for All*, London, Fulton.

TOMLINSON, S. (1982) *The Sociology of Special Education*, London, Routledge.

UNESCO (1988) *Review of the Present Situation in Special Education*, Paris, Unesco.

WANG, M.C. (1991) 'Adaptive Instruction: An Alternative Approach to Providing for Student Diversity', in AINSCOW, M. (Ed.), *Effective Schools for All*, London, Fulton.

WEST, M. and AINSCOW, M. (1991) *Managing School Development: A Practical Guide,* London, Fulton.
YSSELDYKE, J.E., THURLOW, M., GRADEN, J., WESSON, C., DENO, S. and ALGONZZINE, B. (1983) 'Generalisations from Five Years of Research on Assessment and Decision Making', *Exceptional Educational Quarterly*, 4, 1, pp. 75–93.

Chapter 14

Developing Effective Whole School Approaches to Special Educational Needs: From School Effectiveness Theory to School Development Practice

Arlene Ramasut and David Reynolds

The movement to integrate children with special educational needs into mainstream or 'ordinary' classes and schools is now so firmly established in many societies that it can be called a world-wide movement in educational reorganization. Linked with this trend has been the associated movement to relocate helping initiatives for pupils to the ordinary school, rather than at the level of separate specialist provision. At the same time as the new ideological paradigms and associated methods of education and support have grown in popularity within the special education community, the school effectiveness and school improvement 'movements' (as they have been labelled by friends and foes alike) have also generated a growing international reputation for offering helpful blueprints of 'good practice' that may, if implemented, improve the education of all pupils within schools, both those with special needs and those without.

Within the community of special education practitioners and policy-makers, there is no doubt that the stress within all school effectiveness research upon the school as the unit of analysis linked well with the integration movement's stress on 'whole school' policies, since the latter involved the organizational change of *all* educational arrangements within schools, rather than merely those educational arrangements within schools that related to the experience of those children with special educational needs. Similarly, the emphasis within the school improvement movement on *whole school* change to benefit children with problems, rather than on the use of additional *outside school* specialist institutions and personnel to combat learning and behavioural difficulties, was appealing to those within the special educational needs community who were consistently arguing for the inclusion of these services within normal school provision.

The interrelationship between the two fields of school effectiveness/improvement and special education is only in its early stages at present and has some considerable way to go. The aim of this chapter is to facilitate the linking of the two fields further by outlining the knowledge base of school effectiveness research, and by further considering the problems that may face those within the special education community who wish to implement change in mainstream educational provision based on this knowledge base. Descriptions are given of the ways in which programs of school development planning may provide the ideal vehicle for the implementation of whole school change, based upon the insights derived from school effectiveness knowledge and on the perceptions and knowledge base of the special education community.

The School Effectiveness Knowledge Base

The last decade has seen a veritable explosion in the quantity and the quality of the knowledge available concerning the role of the school in generating positive, or for that matter negative, pupil social and academic outcomes from schools. In Britain early work by Power *et al.* (1967) into substantial variations between schools in their delinquency rates was followed by research from Gath (1977) into the reasons for the large variation between schools in their rates of reference for child guidance. Subsequent research has included work by one of us on Welsh schools (Reynolds, 1976, 1982; Reynolds *et al.*, 1987), that by Gray *et al.* (1990), and the important recent studies into primary school effectiveness by Mortimore *et al.* (1988) and by Smith and Tomlinson (1989) into secondary school effectiveness. Reviews are available in Reynolds (1991b).

In the United States the early research contributions came out of both educational practice and the educational research community, with Ron Edmonds, a black school board superintendent, responsible for the former (Edmonds, 1979) and Brookover *et al.* (1979) for the latter. Recently, the 'cutting edge' research has been generated by the Louisiana School Effectiveness Study, a multiphase, mixed methodology study which has produced substantial increments in knowledge (Stringfield and Teddlie, 1990; Wimpelburg *et al.* (1989). Reviews of these and other studies are available in Levine and Lezotte (1990). Other countries productive in generating school effectiveness research include the Netherlands (see chapters in Creemers *et al.*, 1989; Reynolds, Creemers and Peters, 1989), together with recent policy initiatives that involve further data collection about 'effective practices' as in the Effective Schools Project of the Australian Council for Educational Research. Slee (1991) explores linkages between school effect and special needs in the Australian context.

This British and international knowledge base relates generally to four key questions.

1 How much do individual schools affect their pupils' academic and social development? The early work by Reynolds and Rutter in Britain above argued for schools having substantial effects, as did the early work of Gray (1981), who argued that the 'competitive edge' possessed by the most effective tenth of state secondary schools amounted to approximately one to one-and-a-half of the old British O-level passes, or their equivalent. This work was followed by a series of studies which showed smaller sized school effects, such as the subsequent studies of Gray, Jesson and Jones (1986), who concluded that the difference between their most effective and least effective schools was only of the order of an old low grade British CSE examination pass in size.

More recently, substantial effects of pupils' schools have again been argued for Cuttance's (1992) Scottish data, suggesting that 8–10 per cent of the differences between individual pupils' examination results are due to the effects on them of their schools, and also that the difference between the most effective and the least effective groups of schools is in size approximately two of old O-level examination passes per pupil. Smith and Tomlinson's (1989) study also shows large differences in the effects of schools, with, for example, a child of above average ability who managed to obtain an old CSE grade 3 in English at one school obtaining an old O-level grade B in the same examination at another school. For certain groups of pupils, in fact, the variation in examination results between individuals in different schools was as much as one-quarter of the total variation in their examination results.

Whatever the precise size of school effects, and contemporary research is suggesting they are of large size, it is important to note that the school environment is a modifiable or alterable influence on young people, unlike their community, family background or the wider systems of inequality and social stratification that affect them. Schools can do little to change these wider influences on young people but it is clear that they can have substantial direct, positive effects upon young people's development.

2 Are effective schools consistently effective upon all areas of pupils' academic and social development?   Early suggestions had been that effective schools were consistently effective across a wide range of types of pupil 'outcomes', such as academic attainment, levels of attendance, rates of delinquency, and levels of behavioural problems (Reynolds, 1976; Rutter *et al.*, 1979). However, more recent work has suggested that schools may be differentially effective on different areas of pupil development, as shown for example by the Reynolds *et al.* (1987) study comparing the comprehensive and selective systems of education, in which comprehensive schools performed well academically but underperformed on their social outcomes by comparison with the selective system. In Galloway's (1983) study of four effective schools in New Zealand with very low levels of behavioural problems, one of the schools had unexpectedly low levels of academic attainments also, no doubt the result of a policy of imposing minimal demands on pupils to reduce the behavioural problems! Mortimore *et al.*'s (1988) study also shows a substantial independence in the academic and the social outcomes of primary schools.

Even if we take only one area on which to assess school effectiveness, namely schools' academic attainments, it is clear from recent work (Smith and Tomlinson, 1989) that there are large variations in the departmental effectiveness levels even within one school. Of eighteen schools, the school that came first in mathematics examination attainments came fifteenth in English, and the school that came second in mathematics attainments came tenth in English!

3 Are 'effective' schools so for all pupils?   Recent findings suggest that schools can have somewhat different effects upon pupils of different backgrounds or abilities. Cuttance (1992) argues that pupils from disadvantaged home environments are more affected by their schools than more socially advantaged pupils. Similarly, McPherson and Willms (1987) provide interesting evidence that comprehensivization in Scotland varied considerably in its effects upon pupils according to their backgrounds, with pupils from working-class homes consistently benefitting more than others.

Using the new statistical techniques of multilevel modelling, which enable the differences within the pupil group in different schools to be explored, Nuttall *et al.* (1989) show large differences, for different types of pupils, in the relative effectiveness of schools in London. If we look at the experience of able pupils (labelled VR Band 1 in London) and the experience of less able pupils (labelled VR Band 3 in London), in some schools the difference in the groups' performance as they leave school is as small as eleven VRQ points and in others is as large as twenty-eight points, even after adjusting for differences in the pupils' abilities at the time of joining their schools. In this study the performance of schools also varies in the way they have an impact on boys and girls, and in their effects upon pupils who come from different ethnic groups, with some schools narrowing the gaps between these different groups over time and some widening the gaps in both instances.

4 What factors exist in schools which are effective? It is important to note that we know at present far more about which factors are associated with academic effectiveness than about those factors which are associated with social outcomes. Rutter *et al.* (1979) identified over twenty factors associated with academic effectiveness but only seven associated with social effectiveness as measured by a school's possession of a low delinquency rate. The recent London-based study of Mortimore *et al.* (1988) found only six school factors associated with behavioural effectiveness (such as low rates of misbehaviour) and thirteen school factors associated with academic effectiveness judged in terms of good reading scores, even though the schools' overall effect sizes were the same on the two different outcomes. Our relative ignorance of the factors making for social effectiveness is also unlikely to be remedied by other international research, since virtually all the North American studies (with the notable exception of Brookover *et al.*, 1979) look only at academic effectiveness (see reviews in Anderson, 1982; Purkey and Smith, 1983, Levine and Lezotte, 1990).

If we look in detail at British research, the Rutter *et al.* (1979) study found that certain factors were not associated with overall effectiveness, among them class size, formal academic or pastoral care organization, school size, school administrative arrangements (i.e., whether a school was split site or not), and the age and size of school buildings.

The important within school factors determining high levels of effectiveness were argued by Rutter (1980) to be:

1 the balance of intellectually able and less able children in the school — when a preponderance of pupils in a school were unlikely to meet the expectations of scholastic success, peer group cultures and an anti-academic or anti-authority emphasis may have formed;

2 the system of rewards and punishments — ample use of rewards, praise and appreciation being associated with favorable outcomes;

3 school environment — good working conditions, responsiveness to pupil needs and good care and decoration of buildings were associated with better outcomes;

4 ample opportunities for children to take responsibility and to participate in the running of their school lives appeared conducive to favourable outcomes;

5 successful schools tended to make good use of homework, to set clear academic goals and to have an atmosphere of confidence as to their pupils' capacities;

6 outcomes were better where teachers provided good models of behaviour by means of good time-keeping and willingness to deal with pupil problems;

7 findings upon group management in the classroom suggested the importance of preparing lessons in advance, of keeping the attention of the whole class, of unobtrusive discipline, of a focus on rewarding good behaviour and of swift action to deal with disruption;

8 outcomes were more favourable when there was a combination of firm leadership together with a decision-making process in which all teachers felt that their views were represented.

Work in South Wales, although undertaken in a group of secondary modern schools and in a relatively homogeneous former mining valley that was very different in its community patterns from the communities of inner London, has produced findings that in certain ways are parallel to those of Rutter. We studied the school processes of eight secondary modern schools, each of which was taking the bottom two-thirds of the ability range from clearly delineated catchment areas (see references above for full details of methods and findings). We found substantial differences in the quality of the school outputs from the eight schools, with a variation in the delinquency rate of from 3.8 per cent of pupils delinquent per annum to 10.5 per cent, in the attendance rate of from 77.2 per cent average attendance to 89.1 per cent proceeding to the local technical college, to 52.7 per cent proceeding to further education. These differences were not explicable by any variation in the intakes into the schools.

Detailed observation of the schools and the collection of a large range of material upon pupils' attitudes to school teachers' perceptions of pupils, within school organizational factors and school resource levels revealed a number of factors within the school that were associated with more 'effective' regimes. These included a high proportion of pupils in authority positions (as in the Rutter study), low levels of institutional control, positive academic expectations, low levels of coercive punishment, high levels of pupil involvement, small overall school size, more favourable teacher pupil ratios and more tolerant attitudes to the enforcing of certain rules regarding 'dress, manners and morals'.

Crucially, our observation revealed differences between the schools in the ways that they attempted to mobilize pupils towards the acceptance of their goals, differences that were associated with their effectiveness. Such differences seemed to fall within the parameters of one or other of two major strategies, 'coercion' or 'incorporation'. Five more effective schools that took part in the research appeared to be utilizing the incorporative strategy to a greater (three schools) or lesser (two schools) extent. The major components of this strategy were twofold: the incorporation of pupils into the organization of the school; and the incorporation of their parents into support of the school. Pupils were incorporated within the classroom by encouraging them to take an active and participative role in lessons and by letting them intervene verbally without the teacher's explicit directions. Pupils in schools which utilized this strategy were also far more likely to be allowed and encouraged to work in groups than their counterparts in schools utilizing the coercive strategy. Outside formal lesson time, attempts were made to incorporate pupils into the life of the school by utilizing other strategies. One of these was the use of numbers of pupil prefects and monitors, from all parts of the school ability range, whose role was largely one of supervision of other pupils in the absence of staff members. Such a practice appeared to have the effect of inhibiting the growth of anti-school pupil cultures because of its effects in creating senior pupils who were generally supportive of the school. It also had the latent and symbolic function of providing pupils with a sense of having some control over their within school lives; the removal of these symbols also gave the school a further sanction it could utilize against its deviants. Attempts to incorporate pupils were paralleled by attempts to enlist the support of their parents, by the establishment of close, informal or semi-formal relations between teachers and parents, by the encouraging of informal visits by parents to the school and the frequent and full provision of information to parents that concerned pupil progress and governor and staff decisions.

Another means of incorporation into the values and norms of the school was the development of interpersonal rather than impersonal relationships between teachers and pupils. Basically, teachers in these incorporative schools attempted to 'tie' pupils into the value systems of the school and of the adult society by means of developing 'good' personal relationships with them. In effect, the judgment was made in these schools that internalization of teacher values was more likely to occur if pupils saw teachers as 'significant others' deserving of respect. Good relationships were consequent upon minimal use of overt institutional control (so that pupil behaviour was relatively unconstrained), low rates of physical punishment, a tolerance of a limited amount of 'acting out' (by smoking or gum chewing, for example), a pragmatic hesitancy to enforce rules which may have provoked rebellion and an attempt to reward good behaviour rather than punish bad behaviour. Within this school ethos instances of pupil 'deviance' evoked therapeutic rather than coercive responses from within the school.

In contrast, schools which utilized the 'coercive' strategy to a greater or lesser extent (three ineffective schools) made no attempt to incorporate pupils into the authority structure of the school. Furthermore, these schools made no attempt to incorporate the support of parents, because the teachers believed that no support would be forthcoming, and they exhibited high levels of institutional control, strict rule enforcement, high rates of physical punishment and very little tolerance of any 'acting out'. The idea, as in the incorporative schools, of establishing some kind of 'truce' with pupils in these schools was anathema, since the teachers perceived that the pupils would necessarily abuse such an arrangement. Pupil deviance was expeditiously punished, which, within the overall social context of these schools, was entirely understandable; therapeutic concern would have had little effect because pupils would have had little or no respect for the teacher-therapist.

The most likely explanation of the choice of different strategies was to be found in the differences (in the two groups of schools) in the teacher perceptions of their intakes. In schools which adopted a 'coercive' strategy there was a consistent tendency to overestimate the proportion of pupils whose background can be said to be 'socially deprived' — in one such school teachers thought such children accounted for 70 per cent of their intake, while in one of the incorporative schools teachers put the proportion only at 10 per cent — and a consistent tendency to underestimate their pupils' ability. In these coercive schools teachers regarded pupils as being in need of 'character training' and 'control' which stemmed from a deficiency in primary socialization, a deficiency which the school attempted to make good by a form of custodialism. Such perceptions were germane seeds for the creation of a school ethos of coercion.

In addition to research on secondary school processes, characteristics of effective *primary* school organizations have been identified that are associated with high performance in cognitive areas such as reading and writing and in non-cognitive areas such as low truancy levels (Mortimore *et al.*, 1988). Mortimore's research identified a number of schools which were effective in both academic and social areas, which possessed the following characteristics:

1 *Purposeful leadership of the staff by the head.* This occurred where the head understood the school's needs, was actively involved in it but good at sharing power with the staff. He or she did not exert total control over teachers but consulted them, especially in decision-making such as spending plans and curriculum guidelines.

2 *Involvement of the deputy head.* Where the deputy was usually involved in policy decisions, pupil progress increased.

3 *Involvement of teachers.* In successful schools the teachers were involved in curriculum planning and played a major role in developing their own curriculum guidelines. As with the deputy head, teacher involvement in decisions concerning which classes they were to teach was important. Similarly, consultation with teachers about decisions on spending was important.

4 *Consistency among teachers.* Continuity of staffing had positive effects, but pupils also performed better when the approach to teaching was consistent.

5 *A structured day.* Children performed better when their school day was structured in some way. In effective schools pupils' work was organized by the teacher, who ensured there was plenty for them to do yet allowed them some freedom within the structure. Negative effects were noted when children were given unlimited responsibility for a long list of tasks.

6 *Intellectually challenging teaching.* Not surprisingly, pupil progress was greater where teachers were stimulating and enthusiastic. The incidence of 'higher order' questions and statements was seen to be vital — that is, where teachers frequently made children use powers of problem-solving.

7 *A work-centred environment.* This was characterized by a high level of pupil industry, with children enjoying their work and being eager to start new tasks. The noise level was low, and movement around the class was usually work-related and not excessive.

8 *A limited focus within sessions.* Children progressed when teachers devoted their energies to one particular subject area and sometimes two. Pupil progress was marred when three or more subjects were running concurrently in the classroom.

9 *Maximum communication between teachers and pupils.* Children performed better when there was more communication with their teacher about the content of their work. Most teachers devoted most of their

time to individuals, so each child could expect only a small number of contacts a day. Teachers who used opportunities to talk to the whole class by, for example, reading a story or asking a question were more effective.

10 *Thorough record-keeping.* The value of monitoring pupil progress was important in the head's role, but it was also an important aspect of teachers' planning and assessment.

11 *Parental involvement.* Schools with an informal open-door policy which encouraged parents to get involved in reading at home, helping in the classroom and on educational visits tended to be more effective.

12 *A positive climate.* An effective school has a positive ethos. Overall, the atmosphere was more pleasant in the effective schools for a variety of reasons.

While there are some clear differences among the three British studies in their respective findings, the degree of commonality on the factors associated with organizational effectiveness is quite impressive. However, it is important not to overemphasize the extent of the agreement among the various British studies and between these British studies and the international literature. Rutter *et al.* (1979), for example, find that high levels of staff turnover are associated with secondary school *effectiveness*, a completely counter-intuitive finding that is not in agreement with the Reynolds' (1976, 1982) findings of an association between high levels of staff turnover and *ineffectiveness*. Similarly, the consistent American findings on the link between frequent monitoring of pupil progress and academic *effectiveness* are not in agreement with the findings of Mortimore *et al.* (1988) that pupil monitoring which involves frequent testing of children is a characteristic of *ineffective* schools.

In addition to the three studies outlined above, which all possess data on a comprehensive range of school (and to a lesser extent classroom) processes, there are further British studies which have data on a more limited range of school data. A clutch of studies on difficult or deviant pupils has appeared in the last few years, with Maxwell (1987) suggesting that high levels of suspension arise from schools where staff groups do not believe in their capacity to affect this problem. McManus (1987) related school suspension rates and school organizational policies on 'pastoral care', showing that an incorporative, relationship-based approach minimized pupil problems. McLean (1987) also suggested that a preventive, child-centred approach minimized pupil disruption, and Gray and Nichol (1982) generally replicated the findings of Rutter, and the Reynolds' findings on effective schools' rule enforcement policy, in their study of two differentially effective secondary schools in disadvantaged communities.

Many of the British findings about the characteristics of effective secondary schools are also paralleled by the large volume of international studies into school effectiveness, although the great majority of work in all other countries has been undertaken in samples of elementary rather than secondary schools. In the United States Lezotte (1989) and others have popularized the 'five factor' theory of school effectiveness which sees schools which are academically highly performing as possessing the following characteristics:

1 strong principal leadership and attention to the quality of instruction;
2 a pervasive and broadly understood instructional focus;

3   an orderly, safe climate conducive to teaching and learning;
4   teacher behaviours that convey the expectation that all students are expected to obtain at least a basic mastery of simple skills;
5   the use of measures of pupil achievement as the basis for program evaluation.

Although the original development of the five factor theory was from research in the elementary school sector, very similar theories have been utilized to describe and explain the highly effective high school (or secondary school) in North America; and such research as there has been into the secondary sector confirms the general applicability of the theory above (for a comprehensive summary of research see Levine and Lezotte, 1990). Corcoran and Wilson's (1989) study of exceptionally successful secondary schools generated a list of common elements in their effective schools which has distinct similarities with the findings noted above from the British secondary school studies. Their common elements were:

a positive attitude towards the students by teachers and the principal;
strong and competent leadership;
highly committed teaching staff;
high expectations and standards;
an emphasis upon high achievement in academic subjects;
intensive and personal support services for 'at-risk' students;
stable leadership and public support in the catchment area of the school for
    a period of years sufficient to implement new policies.

From School Effectiveness to School Development: The Principles

While it is clear that we now have a quite robust knowledge base concerning effective schools and their characteristics, the problem remains of how to ensure that the knowledge reaches practitioners within schools to benefit all students. The experience of those who have tried to ensure the passage of knowledge into practice has not been particularly reassuring. Consultancy-based methods whereby outside school 'school process' advisers give schools the knowledge base in a non-directive fashion do not seem to be effective (see Reynolds, 1987, for an example), and the Rutter team's attempts to change school practice directly, based on a transplant of their research findings, produced disappointing results (Maughan *et al.*, 1990).

It is much more likely that the adoption of school effectiveness knowledge will take place when schools are engaged on major, whole school programs of review and improvement, unlike the fragmented approaches noted above. Indeed, there is now abundant evidence of the effectiveness knowledge being used for school improvement programs (e.g., Fullan, 1991; Hopkins, 1990) in general, and to resource whole school approaches for special educational needs in particular (e.g., Ramasut, 1989; Reynolds, 1991a).

To look at the principles that need to underlie whole school improvement programs before we turn to descriptions of practical examples, our experience would suggest the following:

1 It is clear that improvement programs should be school-based, school-focused and be 'whole school' in orientation. Improvement aimed only at fractions of the school will run the risk of failure because of the continuing effects of the non-improved, unchanged portions of the school.

2 School change needs outside support to resource it, whether this be consultative assistance (Murgatroyd and Reynolds, 1984, 1985), or more direct provision of advice and assistance as in the case of the Inner London Education Authority's IBIS (Inspectors Based In Schools) approach (Hargreaves, 1984).

3 Change must involve both the organization and structure of schools *and* the informal cultural world of staff relationships, expectations, feelings and so on, that may be partially independent of the formal structure of a school. To change the formal world without also the informal world would lower the prospects of increased effectiveness.

4 Change in a school comes much more satisfactorily if it is based upon school-based review or school appraisal, since the remediation of any within school problems is then related directly to their identification, and also because the dissatisfaction with certain aspects of school organization revealed by the review process will be a motivator for the change process.

5 School change at an organizational level comes much more satisfactorily if it is tied in some ways to curriculum change and to change in teaching methods also, since the latter are aspects of their job that teachers are most involved in and committed to. Organizational change must be tied to teachers' focal concerns.

6 Change should be behaviourally oriented. Changes in the behaviours of staff are more likely to generate the attitude changes among pupils and other teachers on which successful long-term reinforcement of change depends. Change that is oriented only towards changes of attitude is likely to 'wash out' quicker because of the resulting lack of reinforcement.

7 The change process should be long-term, involving a review/improvement/evaluation/further improvement cycle of at least three and probably five years.

8 Change is not necessarily a simple linear process of school movement from point A (unimproved) to point B (improved). There will be times of rapid improvements and of plateaus when little of note seems to be happening in a school; and there may even be other occasions when school processes may in the short term become more ineffective as the school adjusts to the demands being made on it.

9 The change process needs effective management. This should not be in a 'top-down' manner, since it is important that teachers themselves should 'own' the change process. However, it is not likely that change attempts can be completely group or teacher owned, since there may not be enough momentum in the dynamics of the group to ensure that there is continuing and genuine movement within the school. Change attempts must, therefore, have both internal ownership and a degree of extra-group direction at the same time.

10 Change must be evaluated in its impact upon the organization of the school and in its effects upon the 'outcomes' of the schools involved,

since these data are essential to feed back to the participants in the change program, both to generate reinforcement of the change program if it is effective and/or to show areas where new or revised change attempts are needed.

11 The precise change program for the school should be tied partially to the nature of the school, its catchment area, its historical traditions and its personnel. No attempt should be made to impose a blueprint that is completely independent of these contextual factors. Early school effectiveness research showed that *how* schools attempted to improve themselves could be very different in differing circumstances, with the different policies being equally effective in the differing circumstances of the schools (Brookover *et al.*, 1979).

12 The change process will need very careful handling at the levels of interpersonal relations and group dynamics if it is to be successful in changing school practices. Ineffective institutions are often characterized by defective relationships and may need group work, psychodynamic analysis or other forms of group therapy to generate the relationships that are necessary between colleagues who wish to change their practice and their organizations. Any change process must repair damaged psyches and probably poor inter-group levels of communication, as well as being concerned with the organization of the school.

From School Effectiveness to School Development: The Practice of Development Planning

The devolution of authority to individual schools in Britain in the late 1980s through the 1988 Education Reform Act and more specifically through Local Management of Schools (LMS) has seen a restructuring of institution-based management and a growth in development planning. Schools are now required to make public their aims and policies on a wide range of issues, which include special educational needs. The annual governors' report to parents gives account of the developments and achievements of the school, but does not necessarily indicate to what extent outcomes were linked to planning! While the report may give the track record for the year, it can only be regarded as providing a full audit if it is read in conjunction with the school development plan for the same period. Given that schools have been forced into the business mode by central government, it is now incumbent on them to provide more than a summary sheet at the end of each academic year. Devolved resourcing through LMS means that parents and governors can realistically expect to know *in advance* how a school intends to manage its budget and more specifically how it intends to plan special educational needs.

The School Development Plan (SDP) therefore serves as the 'business plan' in the allocation of resources. It should not, however, be regarded only as a financial and administrative tool. The literature on school improvement cites the SDP as one of the two most effective strategies for bringing about organizational innovation, the other being school-based review with which it is inextricably linked (Hopkins, 1987; Hargreaves and Hopkins, 1991). It is through the systematic review of all of the component parts of the institution that strengths and weaknesses will be identified and plans for improvement will stem. Bollen and Hopkins (1987) regard school-based review as providing the tools for evaluation, a mode of implementing improvement and, through the process itself, a strategy for achieving improvement.

We regard the SDP as fundamental in ensuring that schools become fully comprehensive in meeting the needs of the full ability range of pupils and in achieving the status described by Thousand and Villa (1991) of 'heterogeneous' schools. Such schools display the characteristics of inclusion (in that they welcome all pupils and accommodate all differences), of incorporative decision-making which extends to pupils, parents and the community, and of true comprehensiveness in the value they place on each individual and his or her contribution to school life.

To achieve such goals, the whole school approach to meeting special educational needs has been widely supported in the British literature (Dessent, 1987; Bines, 1988; Ramasut, 1989; Ainscow and Florek, 1989). This has been variously defined by Ainscow and Muncey (1989: 3) as a 'whole school approach'. A whole school approach is where attempts are made to utilize all the resources of a school to foster the development of all the children; more specifically, Ramasut (1990: 10) sees it as 'the commitment of the headteacher, teaching staff and governors of a school to ensure that all pupils, whatever their attainment, are given fair and equal access to the resources of that school in order to achieve academic progress and personal development.'

It is axiomatic that a whole school approach, by its very philosophy, can only be achieved if it is part of a school development plan and if it benefits from whole school improvement strategies. The questions which may be asked at the outset of a school-based evaluation of provision for pupils of all abilities will include:

Where are we now?
Where do we want to be by next year; at the end of five years?
What changes do we have to make?
How will we make these changes?
Who will take responsibility for them?
How will we monitor and evaluate the change? (NARE, 1990)

Whole School Curriculum Planning

While the above questions may serve to spur consideration of the present organizational situation and formalize aspirations for future organizational provision, they will need to be closely associated with *curriculum development plans* if they are to be realized. Changes in the structure of provision for the lower attaining and less able pupils in a school are unlikely to succeed unless they embrace the main principles of entitlement and access to a broad, balanced, relevant and differentiated curriculum.

The 1988 Education Reform Act in Britain makes explicit this right of all children to a broad and balanced curriculum which includes the National Curriculum. Every registered pupil of compulsory school age, irrespective of whether the child has a statement of special educational needs, is therefore entitled to access to the National Curriculum. While Wedell (1990) has expressed concern that the subject-based specification of the National Curriculum is the only entitlement on offer, and that the entitlement may only be applied in a partial and uncertain way for pupils with special educational needs, the DES (1989a) has urged the need to envisage the 'setting of the National Curriculum in the context of the whole school curriculum'. The Curriculum Council for Wales (CCW, 1991) has further documented a framework for planning which encompasses 'aspects of learning' and 'themes, competences and dimensions' to assist schools in incorporating the principles of the whole curriculum in their own curricular plans.

It is noticeable that, with curriculum defined as part of the SDP process, the National Curriculum is being delivered to pupils with severe learning difficulties through innovative programs which serve to raise the expectations of teachers and parents alike, while also providing pupils with a wider and more demanding curriculum. A degree of innovation can be seen in many primary and secondary schools, indeed one secondary school, in an area of high unemployment with many social problems, has produced exemplary work in differentiating the GCSE geography syllabus for National Curriculum Key Stage 3. This had been achieved by close collaboration between the subject specialist and the special educational needs coordinator and has resulted in each topic being broken down into five levels of potential response. All Level 1 work was taped, and instructions were listened to by individual pupils who responded in a variety of modes. However, in disseminating this program, the staff involved have been pressured by colleagues to reduce it from five to three levels. While not as finely tuned to individual needs, the three level differentiation will enable a range of successful learning to take place.

While good practice is in evidence, our experience indicates that many teachers are struggling to apply the National Curriculum in differentiated format to full mixed ability groups. In a small survey undertaken in four junior and four infants schools in an urban social priority area, Olivier (1992), found high levels of agreement with regard to functional integration in theory but less consensus with regard to the flexibility of the National Curriculum in meeting the needs of pupils with learning difficulties. While differentiation of the National Curriculum is being urged on teachers (Department of Education and Science, 1991), central government is issuing seemingly contradictory directives which, in our opinion, could, result in a reversion to streaming. In July 1991 Kenneth Clarke made clear that 'Attainments and Levels 1–3 would not lead to the award of a GCSE certificate' (cited in *WJEC Newsletter*, February 1992). The Special Education Advisory Council (SEAC) responded to this by advising the DES that it had identified the Welsh Joint Education Committee (WJEC) Certificate of Education as an appropriate lower level examination which satisfied the National Curriculum requirement for these three levels (WJEC, 1992). Thus separate certification for lower attaining pupils is highly likely to be perpetuated in Wales, if not in England, and separate certification with separate syllabi almost always leads to separate teaching groups. What then is the future of the common differentiated curriculum?!

Whole School Organizational Planning

The 1990s are a time of great uncertainty for educators in the field of special needs, especially with the changes in funding heralded by Circular 7/91 (see Bowers,

1991, for a detailed account of the implications of LMS). What we can be sure of, however, is that pupils with special educational needs are increasingly in mainstream schools. Warnock's figure of 20 per cent of pupils in schools having special needs was reiterated in the findings of Gipps *et al.* (1987), while Croll and Moses (1985) found that three-quarters of the teachers they surveyed had taught pupils with special needs. In Olivier's (1992) small-scale survey the figure was 25 per cent. The likelihood that mainstream teachers will have to cater for special needs pupils, whether they are statemented or not, is confirmed by figures released by the CSIE (1991), which revealed that despite the non-resourcing of the integrationist 1981 Act, trends among LEAs between 1982 and 1990 were strongly in that direction.

The whole school approach to organizing schools to meet special educational needs is a concept which has evolved as a result of general and widespread dissatisfaction with more traditional forms of provision for pupils with learning difficulties, the majority of whom are in mainstream schools (Warnock, 1978). Surveys of such provision have consistently drawn attention to inadequate re- sources, a lack of specially qualified teachers, inappropriate or limited curricula, a diversity of aims and objectives, the low status accorded to many remedial pupils and teachers, their isolation from the rest of the school, and the low level of priority and policy attention given to remedial work (Sampson and Pumfrey, 1970; DES, 1971, 1979, 1984, 1989a, 1990; McCall, 1978; Brennan, 1979). As early as 1975 the Bullock Report suggested that 'remedial help in learning to read should, wherever possible, be related to the rest of the child's learning' (18.12). However, an HMI survey of support services for special educational needs published in 1989 reported that, 'In fewer than 5 per cent of sessions were chil- dren given help in following up or preparing for a classroom lesson. In too many instances withdrawal work was self-contained and the relevance and value to the child's overall curricular needs were questionable' (DES, 1989b, para. 32).

Withdrawal groups, remedial or special classes which function separately from the rest of the year groups, whether they are at primary level or secondary level and whether the help is given by permanent staff of peripatetic staff, cannot be said to be offering equal educational opportunity to their pupils.

The formulation of a whole school organizational policy based on rigorous self-evaluation can aid this translation of policy to practice and provide the focus to enable staff to realize their management and curriculum goals in a collabora- tive and collegial manner. Kloska (1989) suggests that a whole school approach does not imply the total 'overthrow' of organization and management structure of schools, his basic premise being that the majority of schools already contain good practice which can be built upon. However, he does conclude that schools will need to be self-analyzing across the school organization, with particular re- ference to how teachers work, how pupils cope, how transitions occur, how choices are made, as well as also examining attitudes, ethos, motivation and teacher expectations. Kloska admits that such close inspection may be perceived as a challenge to authority and independence and that whole school policies require the communication of vast amounts of information and the cooperation of all concerned. Dessent (1987), however, states that 'it is in this area, the develop- ment of whole school approaches, that we can glimpse the potential which special education has to improve, and indeed, "revolutionise" our schools and our sys- tems of education.'

Let us consider two of the main issues involved in establishing a whole school approach.

1 Defining policy.   Underpinning all school-based programs for meeting special educational needs should be the published policy statement of the local education authority. While this will be non-specific with regard to school structure, it will set out the authority's recommendations for provision based on the 1981 and 1988 Acts. It is the bottom line guide for the headteacher and governors with respect to their responsibilities. If schools in an authority consider the policy statement to be inadequate or ineffective, then they may work through their special needs advisory service to advise the LEA to update or improve it. One of us was involved in such an exercise with the secondary headteachers of one Welsh LEA in 1988, which resulted in the adoption of a policy statement as follows:

> Two strands of current thinking in meeting special educational needs have developed; they are: —
> i)   the requirement that schools should develop whole school policies towards children with special needs
> ii) the appreciation that all teachers are teachers of children with special needs.

A headteacher or staff may use LEA policy as a springboard for change in the school. At school level the policy provides a statement of intent which demonstrates the 'will' of a school. While strong and clear leadership is essential in drawing up such a policy, it is our experience that the more a staff is consulted in the formulation of the policy, the more they will 'own' it and the greater the effort they will make to carry it out. This is also true of policy statements with regard to anti-racist and anti-sexist education. The 'top-down' imposition of a policy is likely to increase resentment and decrease the probability of success.

One school's experience in moving towards a whole school policy shows the negative reactions encountered when the staff were not consulted at the policy-making stage (Ramasut and Owen, 1990). Closely linked to the process of consultation is, of course, the need for in-service training.

2 The whole school review.   Before translating policy to practice as part of the SDP, schools will need to undertake a detailed analysis of current organization and practice, and schools will need to examine all aspects of the institution which impinge on the educational experience of pupils. The National Curriculum Council (NCC, 1989b) suggests four elements which need to be considered in merging past and future practice:

A   the school's curriculum development plan
B   its schemes of work
C   the learning environment
D   the teaching needs of pupils with learning difficulties and disabilities.

Specifically with regard to these needs:

1   The curriculum development plan in all schools is expected to review the existing curriculum, the availability and allocation of resources, staffing, in-service training needs and arrangements, and to identify shortfalls in existing provision. The statutory requirements of the Education Reform Act on reporting and record keeping are also anticipated to require modifications to current practice in areas such as management of time and resources in the context of LMS, deployment of staff, and monitoring and evaluation procedures.

2   In relation to schemes of work, it is made explicit (NCC, 1989b) that schemes of work should 'reflect whole-school approaches to teaching and learning' and be 'a practical guide to teaching within the school's curricular programme' for pupils age 5 to 16. Planning for progression and differentiated teaching strategies are highlighted for attention, and schools are urged to consider special educational needs as integrated within all schemes of work. A variety of response modes is encouraged so that pupils with learning difficulties will be enabled to demonstrate learning in ways other than through writing, and a range of communication methods is advocated for pupils with language problems.

3   The learning environment has been identified elsewhere (Upton, 1989) as crucial to the successful education of pupils with learning difficulties, while Rutter *et al*. (1979), and others in the school effectiveness literature mentioned earlier, demonstrated that the 'ethos' of a school had a clear influence on pupils' educational attainment. These views have since been reiterated by the National Curriculum Council:

> The environment of the classroom and the school as a whole will influence the extent to which schemes of work can be successfully brought together with the National Curriculum to meet each pupil's needs. The quality of the environment will depend not only on the classroom teacher. It will reflect the policies and provisions of the headteacher, other members of school staff, the governing body and the local education authority. (NCC, 1989a)

The characteristics of a good learning environment are noted by the NCC and are described in very similar terms to those of the effective school above:

> the atmosphere of encouragement, acceptance, respect for achievement and sensitivity to individual needs, in which all pupils can thrive;
> a classroom layout and appearance which will stimulate pupil-teacher interaction and adjustment to changing curricular needs;
> easy access to resources including information technology;
> flexible grouping of pupils;
> management of pupil behaviour through a whole-school approach to discipline;
> cooperative learning among pupils;
> communication and cooperation among staff and with governors;

effective management of support from SEN support staff, classroom
assistants, parents and volunteers;

access to specialist advice through SEN advisory and support services, school psychological services, speech therapy, health and social
services and other sources;

cooperation between special and ordinary schools in providing the
National Curriculum;

in-service training, both school and centre-based;

continuous communication with parents and mutual parent-teacher
support.

The learning environment most conducive to facilitating progress for all
children is considered by the NCC to be best achieved through a whole
school approach (NCC, 1989a).

4 In relation to the teaching needs of pupils, as one of us has said elsewhere (Ramasut, 1989), children with special educational needs are no
different from other children; in general they have the same need to
achieve, though their difficulties will be more pronounced than those of
their peers. They make demands on a system which must be able to
respond with a caring ethos and structured opportunity for success. Phillips
(1989) reminds us of the many studies which have demonstrated the
influence of teacher attitudes, expressed by their expectations, on the
academic achievements of their pupils, while Reynolds (1982: 234) noted:
'It is likely that the key to the successful modification of school practice
lies in the mutual perceptions that govern teacher and pupil relations.'

The NCC (1989a) also recognizes that pupils with special educational
needs are likely to have greater needs than the majority of their peers
and suggests that the effective school will provide:

positive attitudes from school staff who are determined to ensure
the full participation of pupils with SEN in the National Curriculum;

partnerships with teachers which encourage them to become active
learners, helping to plan, build and evaluate their own learning
programs wherever possible;

a climate of warmth and support in which self-confidence and self-
esteem can grow and in which all pupils feel valued;

emphasis on profiles of achievement which encourage self-assessment;

home-school partnerships which enable families to support the
teaching program for the child with SEN;

special teaching and classroom arrangements;

access to specialist staff;

aids and equipment for physical, sensory or communication difficulties.

Managing the Institutional Change

The role of the headteacher in facilitating whole school organizational development is crucial. School effectiveness studies noted above have indicated that
autocratic styles of leadership were associated with ineffective schools (Reynolds,

1976, 1982). The evidence also suggests that 'top-down' innovation is difficult to implement (Georgiades and Phillimore, 1975). However, with so many initiatives being introduced into schools from external agencies, principally central government, the headteacher needs to employ human resource management skills which facilitate good communication and which encourage an exchange of ideas and opinions. The 'human touch' cannot be overstated in bringing about change in schools. Where staff are won over by reasoned argument and, wherever possible, by good example, and where they are convinced that change will be for the benefit of the pupils, then the change agent has a greater chance of success.

Reynolds (1992) puts forward the view that the importance of the staff sub-culture and the network of interpersonal relations which 'control' so much of the daily happenings in a school have been far too long ignored in the effective school research agenda. We welcome a move towards an appreciation of the power of attitudes, with particular reference to special needs pupils. Phillips (1989) emphasizes the importance of teacher attitudes towards pupils with learning difficulties and especially in relation to expectation. He refers to much research work in putting the evidence for high teacher expectations leading to improved pupil performance, and this, of course, is one of the main planks of the integration argument. Pauline Howell (1985), in a small school-based research project, found that where teachers had direct contact with special needs children, their attitudes towards functional integration became more positive. This was also the finding of Hegarty, Pocklington and Lucas (1981) in their larger research study. Evidence and common sense combine to tell us that teachers are humans who have their fears, foibles and weaknesses as well as their professional skills and strengths; they need a knowledge base from which to proceed, an opportunity to think through and voice uncertainties and the time and place to learn new skills and develop new attitudes.

Conclusions

In this chapter we have attempted to link together the body of knowledge concerning school effectiveness and the concerns of the special educational needs community. We know that there are certain factors within the control of schools themselves that are associated with the generation of positive student outcomes. Introducing these factors into schools is likely to improve the performance of children with special educational needs.

However, historically the take up of this knowledge has not been necessarily very great, a problem which is intensified as the devolution of power to schools maximizes their variation in quality. The school development planning process was outlined whereby school planning and whole school approaches to the generation of effective mainstream educational environments are used to develop the capacities within schools for curricular and organizational modification. These enhanced capacities are then utilized to ensure increased knowledge transfer of those 'effective' educational processes, in ways that will be more useful than other approaches utilized to date.

The benefit of these links between school effectiveness knowledge and school development/whole school approaches is easy to comprehend. For the knowledge base, the programs of school reform and change provide the perfect test of whether the relationships between school processes and outcomes are causal. For practitioners in the schools, the knowledge can act as a valuable complement to their own practitioner 'folk lore' or 'craft knowledge' of teaching and learning. For children with special educational needs, the result of the interaction between theory and practice, and between effectiveness knowledge and development practice, may well be a better level of academic and societal skills.

References

AINSCOW, M. and FLOREK, A. (1989) *Special Educational Needs: Towards a Whole School Approach*, London, David Fulton.

AINSCOW, M. and MUNCEY, J. (1989) *Meeting Individual Needs in the Primary School*, London, David Fulton.

ANDERSON, C.A. (1982) 'The Search for School Climate: A Review of the Research', *Review of Educational Research*, 52, 3, pp. 368–420.

BINES, H. (1988) 'Developing a Whole School Policy for Primary Schools', *British Journal of Special Education*, 16, 2.

BOLLEN, R. and HOPKINS, D. (1987) *School Based Review: Towards a Praxis*, Leuven, Belgium, ACCO.

BOWERS, T. (1991) *Management Issues in the Wake of LMS*, Cambridge, Perspective Press.

BRENNAN, W. (1979) *Curricular Needs of Slow Learners*, London, Evans/Macmillan Education.

BROOKOVER, W.B., BEADY, C., FLOOD, P., SCHWEITZER, J. and WISENBAKER, J. (1979) *School Social Systems and Student Achievement*, New York, Praeger.

BULLOCK REPORT (1975) *A Language for Life*, London, Her Majesty's Stationery Office.

CENTRE FOR STUDIES ON INTEGRATION IN EDUCATION (CSIE) (1991) Press Release, 22 February.

CHAPMAN, J. and STEVENS, S. (1989) 'Australia', in REYNOLDS, D., CREAMERS, B.P.M. and PETERS, T. (Eds), *School Effectiveness and Improvement*, Gröningen, RION.

CORCORAN, T. and WILSON, B. (1989) *Successful Secondary Schools*, Lewes, Falmer Press.

CREEMERS, B., PETERS, T. and REYNOLDS, D. (1989) '*School Effectiveness and School Improvement: Proceedings of the Second International Congress, Rotterdam, 1989*, Lisse, Swets and Zeitlinger.

CROLL, P. and MOSES, D. (1985) *One in Five*, London, Routledge and Kegan Paul.

CENTRE FOR STUDIES IN INTEGRATION IN EDUCATION (CSIE) (1991) Press release, 22 February.

CURRICULUM COUNCIL FOR WALES (CCW) (1989) *Bulletin No. 3, The National Curriculum and Special Educational Needs*, Cardiff, Welsh Office.

CURRICULUM COUNCIL FOR WALES (CCW) (1991) *National Curriculum: A Basic Entitlement*, Cardiff, CCW.

CUTTANCE, P. (1992) 'Assessing the Effectiveness of Schools', in REYNOLDS, D. and CUTTANCE, P. (Eds), *School Effectiveness*, London, Cassell.

DES (1970) *The Education (Handicapped Pupils) Act*, London, Her Majesty's Stationery Office.

DES (1971) *Slow Learners in Secondary Schools*, London, Her Majesty's Stationery Office.

DES (1975) *A Language for Life (Bullock Report)*, London, Her Majesty's Stationery Office.

DES (1978) *Special Educational Needs (Warnock Report)*, London, Her Majesty's Stationery Office.

DES (1979) *Aspects of Secondary Education in England*, London, Her Majesty's Stationery Office.

DES (1981) *The Education Act*, London, Her Majesty's Stationery Office.

DES (1984) *Slow Learning and Less Successful Pupils and Secondary Schools*, HMI Report, London, Her Majesty's Stationery Office.

DES (1988) *The Education Reform Act*, London, Her Majesty's Stationery Office.

DES (1989a) *From Policy to Practice*, London, Her Majesty's Stationery Office.

DES (1989b) *A Survey of Support Services for Special Education*, London, Her Majesty's Stationery Office.

DES (1990) *Provision for Primary Aged Pupils with SEN Statements in Mainstream Schools*, London, Her Majesty's Stationery Office.

DES (1991) *National Curriculum and Special Needs: A Report by HMI*, London, Her Majesty's Stationery Office.

DESSENT, T. (1987) *Making Ordinary Schools Special*, Lewes, Falmer Press.

EDMONDS, R.R. (1979) 'Effective Schools for the Urban Poor', *Educational Leadership*, 37, 15–18, pp. 20–24.

FULLAN, M. (1982) *The Meaning of Educational Change*, New York, Teachers College Press.

FULLAN, M. (1991) *The New Meaning of Educational Change*, London, Cassell.

GALLOWAY, D. (1983) 'Discipline, Pupils and Effective Pastoral Care', *School Organization*, 13, pp. 245–254.

GALLOWAY, D. (1985) *Schools and Persistent Absentees*, Oxford, Pergamon Press.

GATH, D. (1977) *Child Guidance and Delinquency in a London Borough*, London, Oxford University Press.

GEORGIADES, N.J. and PHILIMORE, L. (1975) 'The Myth of the Hero Innovator and Alternative Strategies for Organisational Change', in KIERNAN, C.C. and WOODFORD, F.P. (Eds), *Behaviour Modification with the Severely Retarded*, Amsterdam, Associated Scientific Pubs.

GIPPS, C., GROSS, H. and GOLDSTEIN, H. (1987) *Warnock's Eighteen Per Cent: Children with Special Education Needs in Primary Schools*, Lewes, Falmer Press.

GRAY, J. (1981) 'A Competitive Edge: Examination Results and the Probable Limits of Secondary School Effectiveness', *Educational Review*, 33, 1, pp. 25–35.

GRAY, J. and NICHOLL, P. (1982) 'Comparing Examination Results in Two Social Priority Comprehensives: Four Plausible Hypotheses', *School Organization*, 3, pp. 255–272.

GRAY, J., JESSON, D. and JONES, B. (1986) 'The Search for a Fairer Way of Comparing Schools' Examination Results', *Research Papers in Education*, 1, 2, pp. 91–122.

GRAY, J., JESSON, D. and SIME, N. (1990) 'Estimating Differences in the Examination Performances of Secondary Schools in Six LEAs: A Multi Level Approach to School Effectiveness', *Oxford Review of Education*, 2, pp. 132–158.

HARGREAVES, D. (1984) *Improving Secondary Schools*, Report of the Committee on the Curriculum and Organization of Secondary Schools, London, ILEA.

HARGREAVES, D. and HOPKINS, D. (1991) *The Empowered School*, London, Cassell.

HEGARTY, S., POCKLINGTON, K. and LUCAS, D. (1981) *Educating Pupils with Special Needs in the Ordinary School*, Windsor, NFER-Nelson.

HOLLY, P. (1986) 'Soaring Like Turkeys: The Impossible Dream', *School Organization*, 6, 3, pp. 346–364.

HOPKINS, D. (Ed.) (1987) *Improving the Quality of Schooling*, Lewes, Falmer Press.

HOPKINS, D. (1990) 'The International School Improvement Project (ISIP) and Effective Schooling: Towards a Synthesis', *School Organization*, 10, 3, pp. 179–194.

HOWELL, P. (1985) The Attitudes of Teachers towards Children with Special Educational Needs in an Urban Development Area, Unpublished BEd dissertation, Cardiff, UCC.

KLOSKA, T. (1989) 'Institutional Change: A Whole School Approach', in RAMASUT, A. (Ed.), *Whole School Approaches to Special Needs*, Lewes, Falmer Press.

LEZOTTE, L. (1989) 'School Improvement Based on the Effective Schools Research', *International Journal of Educational Research*, 13, 7, pp. 815–825.

LEVINE, D. and LEZOTTE, L. (1990) *Universally Effective Schools: A Review and Analysis of Research and Practice*, Madison, Wisc., NCESRD Publications.

McCALL, C. (1978) 'Ways of Providing for the Low Achiever in Secondary School', *Educational Review*, University of Birmingham, Occasional Publications No. 7, pp. 59–67.

McLEAN, A. (1987) 'After the Belt: School Processes in Low Exclusion Schools', *School Organization*, 7, 3, pp. 303–310.

McMANUS, M. (1987) 'Suspension and Exclusion from High School: the Association with Catchment and School Variables', *School Organization*, 7, 3, pp. 261–271.

McPHERSON, A. and WILLMS, D. (1987) 'Equalisation and Improvement: Some Effects of Comprehensive Re-organization in Scotland', *Sociology*, 21, 4, pp. 509–540.

MAXWELL, W.S. (1987) 'Teachers' Attitudes towards Disruptive Behaviour in Secondary Schools', *Educational Review*, 39, 3, pp. 203–216.

MAUGHAN, B., OUSTON, H., PICKLES, A. and RUTTER, M. (1990) 'Can Schools Change 1: Outcomes at Six London Secondary Schools', *School Effectiveness and Improvement*, 1, 3, pp. 188–210.

MORTIMORE, P., SAMMONS, P., ECOB, R. and STOLL, L. (1988) *School Matters: The Junior Years*, Salisbury, Open Books.

MURGATROYD, S.J. and REYNOLDS, D. (1984) 'Leadership and the Teacher', in HARLING, P. (Ed.), *New Directions in Educational Leadership*, Lewes, Falmer Press.

MURGATROYD, S.J. and REYNOLDS, D. (1985) 'The Creative Consultant', *School Organization*, 4, 3, pp. 321–335.

NATIONAL ASSOCIATION FOR REMEDIAL EDUCATION (NARE) (1990) *Curriculum Access for All: An INSET Training Pack for Staff Development*, Stafford, NARE.

NATIONAL CURRICULUM COUNCIL (NCC) (1989a) *Curriculum for All: Special Needs and the National Curriculum*, York, NCC.

NATIONAL CURRICULUM COUNCIL (NCC) (1989b) Circular No. 5, *Implementing the National Curriculum: Participation by Pupils with SEN*, York, NCC.

NUTTALL, D., GOLDSTEIN, K., PROSSER, R. and RASBASH, J. (1989) 'Differential School Effectiveness', *International Journal of Educational Research*, 13, 7, pp. 769–776.

OLIVIER, R. (1992) Classteachers' Perception of Role with Regard to Children with Special Educational Needs in Mainstream Primary Classrooms, Unpublished BEd dissertation, Cardiff, UWCC.

PHILLIPS, D. (1989) 'Teachers' Attitudes to Pupils with Learning Difficulties', in RAMASUT, A. (Ed.), *Whole School Approaches to Special Needs*, Lewes, Falmer Press.

POWER, M.J., *et al.* (1967) 'Delinquent Schools?', *New Society*, 10, pp. 542–543.

PURKEY, S. and SMITH, M. (1983) 'Effective Schools: A Review', *Elementary School Journal*, 83, pp. 427–452.

RAMASUT, A. (1989) *Whole School Approaches to Special Needs*, Lewes, Falmer Press.

RAMASUT, A. (1990) 'Meeting Special Educational Needs through a Whole School Approach', *The Welsh Journal of Education*, 2, 1 and 2, pp. 9–17.

RAMASUT, A. and OWEN, L. (1990) 'Meeting Special Educational Needs through a Whole School Approach 2: Practice', *The Welsh Journal of Education*, 2, 1 and 2, pp. 18–28.

RAYMOND, J. (1990) 'The National Curriculum and Special Educational Needs', *The Welsh Journal of Education*, 2, 1 and 2, pp. 29–36.

REYNOLDS, D. (1976) 'The Delinquent School', in WOODS, P. (Ed.), *The Process of Schooling*, London, Routledge and Kegan Paul.

Arlene Ramasut and David Reynolds

REYNOLDS, D. (1982) 'The Search for Effective Schools', *School Organization*, 2, 3, pp. 215–237.

REYNOLDS, D. (1987) 'The Consultant Sociologist: A Method for Linking Sociology of Education and Teachers', in WOODS, P. and POLLARD, A. (Eds), *Sociology and Teaching*, London, Croom Helm.

REYNOLDS, D. (1991a) 'Changing Ineffective Schools', in AINSCOW, M. (Ed.), *Effective Schools for All*, London, David Fulton.

REYNOLDS, D. (1991b) 'School Effectiveness in Secondary Schools: Research and Its Policy Implications', in RIDDELL, S. and BROWN, S. (Eds), *School Effectiveness Research*, Edinburgh, Her Majesty's Stationery Office.

REYNOLDS, D. (1992) 'School Effectiveness and School Improvement in the 1990s', in REYNOLDS, D. and CUTTANCE, P. (Eds), *School Effectiveness*, London, Cassells.

REYNOLDS, D., CREEMERS, B. and PETERS, T. (1989) *School Effectiveness and Improvement: Proceedings of the First International Congress, London 1988*, Gröningen, University of Gröningen, RION.

REYNOLDS, D., SULLIVAN, M. and MURGATROYD, S.J. (1987) *The Comprehensive Experiment*, Lewes, Falmer Press.

RUTTER, M. (1980) *Changing Youth in a Changing Society*, Oxford, Nuffield Provincial Hospitals Trust.

RUTTER, M., MAUGHAN, B., MORTIMORE, P. and OUSTON, J. (1979) *Fifteen Thousand Hours: Secondary Schools and Their Effects on Children*, London, Open Books.

SAMPSON, O. and PUMFREY, P. (1970) 'A Study of Remedial Education in the Secondary Stage of Schooling', *Remedial Education*, 5, pp. 102–111.

SLEE, R. (1991) 'Learning Initiatives to Include All Students in Regular Schools', in AINSCOW, M. (Ed.), *Effective Schools for All*, London, David Fulton.

SMITH, D. and TOMLINSON, S. (1989) *The School Effect: A Study of Multi Racial Comprehensives*, London, Policy Studies Institute.

STRINGFIELD, S. and TEDDLIE, C. (1990) 'School Improvement Effects: Qualitative and Quantitative Data from Four Naturally Occurring Experiments in Phases 3 and 4 of the Louisiana School Effectiveness Studies', *School Effectiveness and School Improvement*, 1, 2, pp. 139–161.

THOUSAND, J. and VILLA, R. (1991) 'Accommodating for Greater Student Variance', in AINSCOW, M. (Ed.), *Effective Schools for All*, London, David Fulton.

TREML, G. (1991) 'Non-statutory Special Educational Needs and Local Management in Schools', BOWERS, T. (Ed.), *Management Issues in the Wake of LMS*, Cambridge, Perspective Press.

UPTON, G. (1989) 'Overcoming Learning Difficulties', in RAMASUT, A. (Ed.), *Whole School Approaches to Special Needs*, Lewes, Falmer Press.

WARNOCK, M. (1978) *Special Education Needs*, London, Her Majesty's Stationery Office.

WEDELL, K. (1990) in DANIELS, H. and WARE, J. (Eds) (1990) *Special Educational Needs and the National Curriculum*, London, Kogan Page.

WELSH OFFICE (1989) *National Curriculum: A Teacher's Guide*, Cardiff, Welsh Office.

WIMPELBERG, R., TEDDLIE, C. and STRINGFIELD, S. (1989) 'Sensitivity to Context: The Past and Future of Effective Schools Research', *Educational Administration Quarterly*, 25, pp. 82–107.

WJEC (1992) *Newsletter No. 13: Certificate of Education and the National Curriculum*, Cardiff, WJEC.

Part 4

Compelled to Speak:
Parents, Students and Integration

Chapter 15

How Disabling Any Handicap Is Depends on the Attitudes and Actions of Others: A Student's Perspective

Becky Walsh

Like many people of my age, I'm currently enrolled in my third year at university. Unlike most of them, how I got here is marked by a number of differences.

If you have a significant sight deficiency, you're also considered to be 'impaired', 'disabled' and/or 'handicapped'. That's how most people seem to see it.

In the latter stages of 1983 I was in Grade 6 and diagnosed as having an incurable eye disease called 'macular degeneration'. It's a condition that most people won't suffer until much later in their lives — if at all. I had 'survived' my years at primary school rather well, despite not seeing the blackboard and being 'dropped' from most of the inter-school sports teams.

Many special forms of assistance and facilities are available to provide those with a sight deficiency with an equal chance in schools, sports, areas of employment and the like. In 1984 Mum contacted Narbethong, a school for the visually impaired. She wanted to see if there was any way to help me in my schooling.

At the Narbethong Clinic eye tests were carried out and I was given new glasses, a monocular device which enabled me to read the blackboard for the first time in four years, and an observer/adviser came to visit me at six to eight weekly intervals. During these visits I was taken from the classroom, asked where I needed help and given new magnifying devices and resources such as large print dictionaries. I then rejoined my classmates and the adviser explained the newest piece of equipment, allowed them to use it, and warned them not to use it again! Such openly special treatment always embarrassed me, and still does. I've never approved of being thought of as *different and needing exceptional handling.*

I believe I was fortunate that I wasn't diagnosed with such bad eyesight until later in my school life, even though the assistance didn't go astray and opened up many doors. The attitudes of my peers and teachers didn't change towards me through the last year. I was able to 'fit in'. They had all known me and what I could do *before* all the special treatment began. This, I think, is the best way to gain an understanding of the person behind the handicap.

My family never allowed me to assume that I was unique. They were responsible, in the main, for keeping my feet on the ground. Just because my vision wasn't '20/20' didn't mean that I couldn't wash dishes or do my homework. Nor did it mean that they couldn't teach me to cook, water ski or play and enjoy sport.

Given such treatment within the family, I always hoped to go on to study at my local high school, just as my brothers and sisters had, after graduating from primary school. Other plans were being made for me. Mum had spoken to the teachers, optometrists and guidance officers at Narbethong. They were all convinced that I should go to Cavendish Road State High School because of the facilities and special teacher assistance available there. I was horrified! Why couldn't I go on coping the way I had always done? I didn't want to lose my friends and go to a place that was a thirty-minute drive away from home just so that people could cater for my *special needs*! But I had no option, the matter was settled for me 'in my best interests'.

I was not required to complete the TOLA (Test of Learning Ability) tests at the end of year 7 because my lack of vision could not be accounted for in the test results. Instead, I visited the guidance officer at Narbethong and was given an IQ test of my own. These tests, I was told, were designed to assess my aptitude and gauge how well I would cope (if at all) in an integrated high school system. Ironical, when I had already been in an integrated situation for the previous seven years!

The few tests that I can remember doing at Narbethong still strike me as unusual. Let me explain this by describing some of the tests. Each test I remember was timed. A series of cards, each with a drawing of related events such as women going to the supermarket to do some shopping, was placed in front of me in random order. The object of the test was to sort the cards into their correct sequence in the shortest time I could. Another test included a set of blocks with varied red and white shapes on them being placed in front of me. I had to create, with those blocks, the shape shown on a picture card, once again as quickly as possible. It had always seemed a little 'inaccurate', not to mention bewildering and unfair, to be testing someone who couldn't see properly using 'visual' tests. Yet this was the criterion which determined my fitness for integration.

Although there were rumours at the time that if you didn't perform to the guidance officer's satisfaction, you would be kept at Narbethong, I was sent to Cavendish Road. Nowadays the IQ testing of visually disabled students has supposedly diminished. Guidance officers, I've been told, take on the job of counselling rather than testing and classification.

I was to attend a high school specifically designed to handle people with my 'problem'. Mum, my doctors and even I believed that school life from then on would be so different, that there would be numerous opportunities at this new school, and that I would benefit from it. Well . . . I did, and I didn't. We certainly didn't expect some of the obstacles that confronted me.

The Secondary Special Education Unit is a section of classrooms set amidst the rest of the high school on Cavendish Road, where we 'special ed kids', as we were known, would attend every day for at least one period. Here we got the teacher help and technological aids and equipment we were told we needed in order to reach our full academic potential.

Let me explain a few of the barriers I had to overcome, and those I couldn't, within the workings of this new system of so-called integration. To enable us 'special ed kids' to use the equipment and teachers set aside for us in the unit, in our first year at high school we weren't allowed to take geography. Perhaps it was felt that we, as visually impaired students, couldn't cope with the requirements of the subject, for example mapping (although I still had to study and construct maps in history); or perhaps that we couldn't derive any benefits from the particular subject; or perhaps there wasn't any other subject that the special education teachers believed we could drop. We simply had no choice in the matter. It was decided for us, without consultation.

You will have observed earlier that those of us who attended the unit were known as, and called, 'special ed kids'. This label was in itself a barrier to integration. Being a 'special ed kid' meant 'getting out of' doing at least one 'proper' lesson every day; being tutored in all the subjects we studied; not having to do a compulsory Grade 8 subject: geography; being exempt from playing sport; having extensions of time to finish assignments; and receiving extra time during examination sessions. These are just some of the privileges we received that the rest of the students in the mainstream didn't. Most of the adjustments made to our timetables and study arrangements were done to bring the students who had a decided disadvantage in the mainstream classroom, because of their lack of sight, up to a level considered equal to the others. Ignorant students and teachers didn't see it this way. Through their unfriendliness, lack of understanding and sometimes their wrath, we were set back into our inferior and disadvantaged positions. We were segregated by invisible barriers of human unkindness and immaturity. Some people even saw the assistance I had as the sole reason for my success in school. They placed the credit for the hours of hard work that I had done, both at school and at home, somewhere where it didn't entirely belong.

I could sometimes understand ill feelings generated by the help I got. The feelings of desperation, anger and hurt I felt when confronted by these people were often subdued by my pity for them. I always liked to employ the 'explanation strategy' so that I might help them understand my situation and the system within which we, the 'special ed kids', had to operate. Sometimes, when my pity was pushed aside, I was less than diplomatic.

I have often considered the question of who was helping the other kids, not just the ones who couldn't see, when they needed it? The answer to that, as far as I thought, was *nobody*. There's an old saying in my family, especially when children are concerned: 'What you give to one, you should give to the other.' This is a principle difficult to enforce in the classroom, but not impossible, even if pursued in small steps. One example may be that in a practical cooking lesson, if there is an adult helping the blind student to cook, they should also be encouraged to help the rest of the class just as the teacher does.

Every Wednesday afternoon the entire school played sport — everyone except those on detention, the sick and the 'special ed kids'. Although our academic needs were thoroughly catered for, sport was an area of the curriculum that was denied to us. Instead of being active with our peers, we sat in the unit and we worked with our teacher on a timetabled subject. I strongly objected to this. Leisure sports such as swimming and aerobics weren't available to the junior members of the school. We were supposed to compete in an inter-school team. None of these sports was suitable for students with sight deficiencies.

Ironically we were never compelled to do sport so that we could fit into the school. Everyone else *had* to do sport. While this was done so that we could easily be accepted in the school, it set up an imbalance between us and the other kids. This is something that should have been corrected for the sake of both integration and our physical needs. Whose brain doesn't need a rest now and then? Through my mother's insistent petitions to the school and my own lobbying, I was allowed to do aerobics with the senior students. Other visually impaired students followed my lead, and sports were made available to us — a small victory for equality!

As the years progressed, another hurdle arose. It concerned the number of subjects and the subject areas I chose to study. I loved the Japanese language. When the time came to choose my subjects, it was naturally on my list. However, as we were students with special needs, not only were our choices reviewed by the subject teachers, form teachers and school administrators, but they also had to be approved by the teachers in the unit. I was taken aside and quietly 'encouraged' *not* to do Japanese. It was felt that I might not be able to cope with character writing, and there was not a teacher in the unit with training in Japanese. They believed that my dependence on them was such that I might fail if they couldn't help me. I did have faith in myself and in my Japanese teacher. Despite her lack of training in special education and the disapproval of others, I studied Japanese and loved it. I, and my family, thought Japanese would be a valuable language to learn as it would enhance future employment prospects. When you have 'been handicapped', it's best to keep your options open.

I mentioned that the number of subjects I chose was also a problem. We, the 'special ed kids', had to do one less subject than was provided for in the school curriculum to make time for one tutorial session at the unit each day. Whether we needed six lessons of tutoring with a specialized teacher in our subject areas or not was never questioned by teaching staff or the administrators, it seems. While some students saw those subjects as a blessing, we still had no choice in the matter. It is vital that *all* people be allowed to make decisions.

My mother challenged what others were deciding for me. She was strongly 'advised' that if I took all six subjects, they wouldn't be able to help me, and did we think it right that we jeopardize my chances at success? What a way to narrow our chances for entry into higher education and the workforce!

The content of our lessons in the unit was determined by our exam results. Teachers' perceptions of what kind of assistance we wanted were examination driven. This bureaucratic reasoning was loosened as we progressed into the senior school where flexibility was apparent despite the rigidity of our unit timetable (maths on Monday, English on Tuesday . . .).

I also remember that I was chosen because of my good grades to participate in an extracurricular subject program. I was not allowed to continue in the program. The teacher in charge of the unit believed that if I fell behind in other subject areas because of the time devoted to the extracurricular program, they might not be able to help me to return to my former high standards! My mother protested, arguing for my inclusion in the extracurricular program. She fought a losing battle against those who 'knew what was best for me'.

Experiences such as this made me feel so useless and frustrated. I was made to feel like I was turning into a teacher's *project* or *case*, or be fed only predetermined information so that they could see what type of a successful item they could produce at the end of it all.

This account of how I made it through the obstacles in the school system, and left some dents in the system along the way, may seem trivial to some. However, there were many tears shed, many long discussions and telephone calls, a mountain of letters, some small victories and heartfelt losses. All of these things came from a little girl who *used* to be shy and certainly not outspoken. My family, whom most would consider an 'average' and easy going bunch, like me have had to adapt part of ourselves as we have attempted to change a system to meet our needs.

I've never regretted being part of the integration system, despite its imperfections, because anything is better than being segregated in a separate institution. This is one of the greatest injustices done to people with special needs. I didn't have the option of going to a school of my choice. Nowadays, technological support and advisers assist students with visual impairments to go to any school of their choice. The degree of assistance that they receive is based upon: the degree of visual impairment; their school results; and their practical classroom ability as documented by a trained observer/adviser.

Frequently I had to travel along the road those in superior, not necessarily more knowledgeable, positions thought most suitable for me. My choices became limited due to my lack of influence, and sometimes a lack of motivation or willingness to push for what I thought was right. The system was not initially designed to heed what the students, or their parents, felt they needed, but there has been change. I saw it.

Chapter 16

A Parent's Perspective on Integration

Amanda Lyons

As a parent, I believe implicitly that both my children and, in fact, all children have the right of access to the best education. Education is the foundation upon which we base many aspects of our lives, and school is our first involvement in a community outside our circle of family and friends. I see no reason for this scenario to be different for different children, and yet it is for those labelled 'disabled'.

Michael and I have decided to educate our sons in the Catholic education system. This started out as a personal preference; but as we set about attaining an appropriate education for our son, Joseph, it also proved to be the most accommodating.

I offer the following quotation, 'People just don't think logically about disability' (Laurie Alsop, quoted in Lawrence, 1988). As parents, we have faced illogical thinking, negative attitudes, incorrect assumptions, emphasis on our children's disabilities not their abilities, and generalizations. As an example, the statement, 'the children at the Centre are mostly non-verbal', was presented to us as sufficient reason to assess our son's school readiness with a test that relies on non-verbal responses — a child who, though physically disabled, has language and reading skills advanced beyond his age level. I wonder, then, at the accuracy of the information that would have been provided in the subsequent report.

This, to me, exemplifies one of the problems of education in segregated settings: individual abilities are lost among the labels and generalizations: 'the only label we need is the child's name' (Marsha Forest, quoted in Till, 1990).

In looking at achieving integration (inclusive education), there are a number of key issues involved, e.g., school of choice or local school, provision of adequate supports and resources, a flexible curriculum. 'The opportunity of a child to attend his or her local public school should not depend on ability, perceived ability, or administrative discretion. It has long been demonstrated that all students can benefit from integration in typical schools and classrooms' (Doug Biklen, quoted in Till, 1990).

Typically, children attend their local state or parochial school, or the school their parents choose for them. They walk, ride bicycles, take public transport, or their parents drive them. They typically do not take taxis. Of particular importance is the fact that they most often attend school with their siblings. I personally know of one family where siblings are attending separate schools because access was seen as too big an issue to be dealt with — at whose expense? The children's, of course.

It is also usual for parents to assist at school in activities such as reading, swimming, excursions, tuckshop; they may meet informally with the teacher after school; they may choose to attend P and C meetings at night. How do you do this when your child's school is many kilometres away from your home, and you have other children and family to consider? We have chosen to continue with our option to educate Joe in the Catholic school system, as we were informed that our options within the state school system were to send Joe either to a school in the far north or to one in the far south of the metropolitan area. As we live in the inner city, neither school could be considered to be within our local community — far from it!

We haven't been welcomed with open arms by every Catholic school we approached, but generally we have found a philosophy of inclusive education more akin to our own. We have now enrolled Joe in a small Catholic school that demonstrates a belief in inclusive education as well as a strong sense of community. However, we have had to move to a different part of town in order to be closer to school. The local state school, a few blocks away, would probably have been a lot easier, but this school to date is physically inaccessible for anybody using a wheelchair.

Learning at school is not just 'the three Rs'. It is also a place where one learns to be a friend, a valued member of a community, to be sensitive to and aware of other people's feelings, needs and abilities. 'Education is meant to teach active citizens' (Rainee Courtrage, quoted in Till, 1990). School is the basis for the rest of our lives — how restrictive the learning is in a segregated setting; children are learning to be different and they are devalued by being denied what every other kid on the block and their parents take for granted. 'The environments in which students with disabilities receive instructional services have critical effects on where and how they spend their post-school lives. Segregation begets segregation' (Lou Brown, quoted in Till, 1990).

We must realize that an education service that encourages segregated schools and segregated classrooms within regular schools is 'élitist with a separatist philosophy' (Marsha Forest, quoted in Till, 1990). Marsha Forest also states that we have to bring 'the ABC's into education — *A = acceptance, B = belonging, C = community.*' As a parent, I believe in my child's value to the community at large. I know any school will benefit from his inclusion: the 'problems' — access, toileting, difficulties with writing — can all be overcome if the people involved will just think positively instead of thinking, 'Oh no, we'll never cope.' Over and over, this has been the reaction when I chose to mention (foolishly) that Joe uses a wheelchair — I don't any longer when I'm making enquiries. Joe is Joe, a 6-year-old boy with so much to offer, like all his peers. He is a boy, first; someone with a different method of mobility, second.

All these beliefs were more than proven during six months in the USA in 1990. Joe attended one semester of school at a regular neighbourhood elementary school. He was enrolled in kindergarten class (the equivalent of our pre-school year) — a class of twenty children, three with special needs, one classroom teacher and three support teachers. Joe travelled to school each way on a school district bus equipped with a wheelchair lift; both able-bodied students and disabled students used the bus. The school, despite being built before the age of inclusive education, had been modified to enable access to a number of students who used wheelchairs. Joe's class was not 'astounded' to have a child in a wheelchair enter their class; because we lived locally, he was invited home to play after school; he could move independently around the school.

In this regular, integrated setting, Mike and I watched Joe mature, learn, develop friendships and establish himself as a valued member of the school community. There was never a day when he did not want to go to school, and there were many, many tears when it came time to farewell his 'American' school. This is what we want for Joe for all his school life; and this is what we believe is the right of each and every child. Essentially, we want to see children with disabilities educated with children who are not disabled. I would like to end with the following two quotations:

> Me and my friends feel happy having a special kid named Benny in our school because kids look different on the outside, but they look much, much the same on the inside.

> There is someone in our school who is developmentally delayed, and you should see him — he's great. (Michelle Kovac and Santina Gatto, quoted in Till, 1990)

References

LAWRENCE, A. (Ed.) (1988) *I Always Wanted to Be a Tap Dancer: Women with Disabilities*, Sydney, NSW Women's Advisory Council.

TILL, L. (1990) *Becky Belongs: Voices Raised in Support of Integration*, Sharon, Ontario.

Chapter 17

Integration: Another Form of Specialism

Mary Rice

The decision to write this chapter represents a departure from my usual practice in that, by and large, I have avoided making a case study of my experience as a parent of a child with an intellectual disability. The idea of treating my daughter as a special case runs counter to my belief that her life chances are best served by providing her with the same opportunities and experiences received by her older brothers. However, my concern at the way in which the process of integration is evolving compels me to share my experiences and voice my reservations in an effort to redirect what is happening. Perhaps the most fundamental problem associated with integration is that people have well entrenched views about what special education is and have imposed these views onto integration, rather than viewing integration as an opportunity to reconceptualize the issue of education for people with disabilities, indeed for *all* people.

What Do We Mean by Integration?

To me, integration is a societal issue. It cuts across all aspects of community life — employment, recreation, religion, club membership, education and so on. In fact, it is not unreasonable to suggest that the objective of most parents is to ensure that their children are integrated into and accepted in many facets of the society in which they live. Parents of children with disabilities are no exception in this regard. However, they have always had to struggle to have their children accepted in society, because of the prevalence of a 'separatist' view of disability. Integration in the education context is particularly significant because education has a powerful influence on the socialization of all children. To be excluded from the mainstream of education is to be excluded from this socialization process.

I believe integration to be the antithesis of special education. It occurs in an inclusive educational setting where all children, irrespective of differences, have the opportunity to learn with and from each other. In such a setting the modelling provided by peers reduces the amount of input required by the class teacher. Differences are accepted and valued, but the focus is on similarities which are common to all children. Integration is not an attempt to normalize children with disabilities, nor is it the re-creation of segregated practices within the mainstream school, with the attendant emphasis on labelling for ascertainment purposes. I

253

would suggest that these general principles are accepted by most people who support integration, rhetorically at least. Yet in the evolution of the integration process it has become what it was not supposed to be, that is, another form of specialism. As Lewis (1989) asserts, integration has resulted in the growth of new categories of people, integration teachers and integration aides who specialize in dealing with the group of clients labelled as 'integration children', a new class of disability. The integration of my daughter, Jane, illustrates this trend.

My experiences have led me to believe that society has much to gain by integrating children with disabilities into regular schools, for the benefits far outweigh any disadvantages that might be perceived. I believe, as Tomlinson (1982) does, that special education, by its very nature, emphasizes differences and socializes people out of mainstream society. In my experience, children in special settings learn how to be different and learn to expect special treatment and/or attention. I haven't always had these convictions, so let me backtrack and outline the circumstances which led me to this point.

The Early Years

When Jane was born eighteen years ago, little did I realize the extent to which my ideas about education, disability and life chances would change. Following her birth, the sanest and most enduring piece of advice I received came, ironically, from the paediatrician who attended her. This was, 'treat her as you would treat any other baby', a piece of advice which subsequently shaped many of the decisions made on her behalf. Jane became just another member of our family: she received the same attention, the same love, the same opportunities for learning and socializing that her brothers experienced (commensurate with position in the family). It soon became apparent, however, that even though we might treat her like any other baby, society didn't. Jane was definitely seen as a special case by those in authority, for she gained access to a number of 'services' which had not been provided for my sons. We found ourselves drawn into the world of disability with all its medical, paramedical and psychological trappings. We were expected to be grateful that society had seen fit to provide all these services for us. No doubt, there were positive outcomes of such a plethora of services, but in many respects I felt that they constituted an invasion of privacy, an imposition on our lives. For our family, the most fortunate aspect of these early years was that Jane had no serious health problems, so we were less subject to the medical 'merry-go-round' and specialist treatment that other families were caught up in.

When Jane was 3, she attended a Day Training Centre for the Intellectually Handicapped, as it was known then. Her easily recognizable label ensured that she automatically 'qualified' for a place in such a setting. Although I certainly had misgivings about this placement because it segregated Jane from the world of her brothers, I accepted it because it was the only educational opportunity open to her at that time. In fact, the sessions seemed to be appropriate as she was involved in the usual kindergarten activities such as painting, music, solving jigsaws and so on. However, two years later she was still doing the same things, albeit at a slightly more complex level. Although she was being well trained in such things as toilet habits and table manners, I began to realize that she was not being educated to the extent that I would have liked. Opportunities for academic learning were extremely limited because expectations were low and so much time was spent on aspects of training that are generally accepted as being the responsibility of parents. In short, I believed that Jane was capable of learning a great deal more than she was expected to learn at the centre.

Another aspect of Jane's attendance at the centre which disturbed me was that she began to mimic some of the idiosyncratic behaviours she observed in other children. In the absence of more acceptable role models, I believe that this behaviour feeds off itself and tends to become a tolerated norm for children in special settings. Added to this was the fact that children were transported to and from the centre in a bus which was clearly labelled 'for the intellectually handicapped'. I failed to understand why this patronizing discriminatory practice was necessary. Despite these misgivings, it was not an easy matter to change settings, though I was beginning to realize that it was imperative to try. I was encouraged in this regard by a family friend whose work in a special setting had led her to believe that all the people she taught should be in non-segregated settings.

Into the Mainstream

My first move towards integration came when I approached the directress of the centre about the possibility of sending Jane to our neighbourhood kindergarten. She was adamant that it would be a foolish move and added, 'we have tried that sort of thing before but it has never succeeded.' I refrained from pointing out that it had not been tried with my daughter before and that I would like to pursue the opportunity. There seemed little point in engaging in a 'battle' with her because she was inflexible in her thinking, so I decided to go directly to the local kindergarten. I took Jane along to meet the teachers and to nip any stereotypical expectations in the bud. After spending some time with her, they were happy to accept her for two sessions a week. This was not as much as I would have liked, but better than nothing. At that time parents' and children's rights were not recognized, so there was a very real chance that if I became too strident in my demands, it would be counterproductive. My approach had to be one of gentle persuasion. In any event I was pleased that Jane would have the opportunity of socializing with and learning from children with a range of abilities and hoped that the dual enrolment situation would be short-lived.

During and after Jane's experience at kindergarten she continued attending the centre. However, I was becoming increasingly dissatisfied with the limited educational opportunities being provided there. I knew that she was quite ready to learn how to read, but she was only being given one reading lesson a week at the centre. Lack of time and staff did not allow for any more than that, I was informed. More to the point was the way the program was structured with a strong emphasis on living skills. In any event, to supplement the reading lesson, I began teaching her at home and was delighted to find that she learnt with relative ease. In spite of this, she was still expected to attend a day training centre!

It was during this time that the integration debate began in a small way. It certainly reinforced my conviction that Jane should have the right to attend a regular school along with her brothers and neighbourhood peers. The fact that her educational needs were not being met in the special setting was added incentive to keep moving towards integration. I decided to approach the principal of our local primary school with a view to enrolling Jane in the school. I was really most heartened by his immediate, positive response. He could see no reason why she should not attend the school, providing one of the classroom teachers was prepared to teach her. Fortunately, this was not a problem: the fact that she was beginning to read no doubt helped in this regard.

Thus it was that my daughter became integrated, and I mean integrated in the true sense of the word. She was enrolled and admitted along with all the other school beginners and had her needs met in the same way that other children's needs were met, as a matter of course. There were no special procedures to follow, no ascertainment processes, no enrolment and support groups, no involvement in submissions for funding: in short, no discriminatory practices and no necessity to label. This is what integration meant, and still means, to me.

The Bureaucratization of the Integration Process

During Jane's early school years the debate on integration continued, and I was a member of a group which offered support to parents who were experiencing difficulties in their efforts to have their children integrated. We also acted as a lobby group to obtain assistance from the government and contributed significantly to advisory panels set up to inform the ministerial review policy on integration. In fact, I was one of many parents who argued that integration is philosophically, morally and educationally right. The report of the Victorian Ministerial Review Committee (1984) subsequently endorsed this stance through the framing of five guiding principles. In particular, the focus on the right of all children to attend mainstream schools without being subject to categorization procedures was an important milestone. However, the rhetoric of the policy was not easily translated into practice. Fulcher (1989) has emphasized the problematical nature of policy implementation and has recognized that the implementation of integration policy is a gradual process requiring significant shifts in attitudes. It soon became clear that the people charged with the responsibility of implementing ministerial policy — administrators, regional consultants and teachers — were ill-prepared for integration because they had little understanding of the nature of integration as expressed in the policy. As Fulcher (1989) points out, policy is made and remade at many levels. To many educators, integration is synonymous with special education, so special education practices have continually been applied to the integration process.

As integration became part of the educational bureaucracy, particular practices were set up which were specific to children with disabilities. In fact, the more bureaucratized it became, the more specialist and discriminatory the practices became. For example, the annual resource hunt and the establishment of Integration Support Groups, as they were called then, became important aspects of the process for schools. Though I realized that extra financial assistance was necessary to enhance the educational chances of many of the children, I was concerned that the granting of funding was largely dependent on the labelling of children, and that funding was not always sought on the basis of educational needs.

In an integrated setting all children should be provided with the appropriate support as and when it is needed. I felt that we were being drawn into yet another specialist system, the bureaucratized integration 'umbrella', something which we had not bargained for. Whereas previously Jane's schooling had followed the normal procedure, under the new system we were subject to forms of control that we neither wanted nor needed such as Integration Support Group meetings, parent advocacy, submissions for resources on the basis of a label. These practices appeared discriminatory to me because they were outside the regular school practices. For mainstream students, educational needs have always been determined after a child begins school, yet for students with disabilities, placement is now conditional upon allocation of resources, which in turn is conditional upon the deliberations of the Integration Support Group.

Indeed, from my observations it seems that the establishment of Integration Support Groups, far from strengthening parents' hands, actually increased the level of control exercised by schools. Consensus, which frequently relies on compromise, has to be reached before integration can proceed, and despite the use of parent advocates, parents are often overwhelmed by the opinions of professionals and were expected to support them. It was always perceived that the experts knew best! As far as Jane was concerned, there were no situations of conflict, so the Integration Support Group was virtually inoperative. Yet it irked me that this procedure had to be seen to be followed in order to safeguard Jane's placement.

Another aspect of the process which has skewed the meaning of integration is resource allocation. To obtain any sort of assistance, submissions had to be put for individual children and were much more likely to be successful if there was clear evidence of a well recognized label, irrespective of the particular needs of all children in the school. In our case funding was received by the school for a part-time integration aide, yet it seemed to me at the time that there were other children who were equally in need of such assistance but were unable to obtain it because their disabilities did not fit an acceptable medical category.

In the early years of integration there was an absence of clear guidelines about the role of integration teachers and integration aides. The integration aide assigned to my daughter perceived her role to be that of a quasi-teacher. Her practice was to withdraw children from the classroom for individualized learning sessions, thereby relieving the classroom teacher of the responsibility. The teachers quite genuinely believed that this was a desirable practice in the sense that the end justified the means. How could they think otherwise? They equated integration with special education and received no professional development which could have enabled them to redefine education for children with disabilities. So much for integration: treating the child became the norm just as it had always been.

During these primary school years Jane was experiencing integration quite differently in other aspects of her life. She joined the local Brownies' group, then proceeded in the usual way to becoming a Guide. In addition, she was a member of a church group for children. I always found it interesting to see how well she was accepted in these groups and how competently the leaders were able to include her in all activities without treating her as special in any way. There was a 'naturalness' about integration in these contexts which educators would do well to emulate.

Secondary School Years

When the time came to consider secondary school options for Jane, one of the considerations uppermost in my mind was to find a school which would be prepared to accept her as 'just another pupil'. I wanted her to be able to throw off the 'integration label' which had been attached to her in the latter stages of her primary school years. To this end I sought and gained admission for Jane in a small, Catholic girls' technical college which had the reputation of being able to cater well for individual differences. Some of the features of this school which attracted me included mixed ability groupings, no withdrawal of students from the classroom, individualized, goal-based learning and no emphasis on particular labels. An added bonus was that integration as a controlled, bureaucratic process had not become part of the Catholic school system, so there was no requirement to form an enrolment and support group. When Jane was accepted at this school, she was included in the regular school program just as other students were. Although there was some individualized assistance through the services of a teacher's aide, she was not assigned to particular children and was not employed specifically for integration. Furthermore, she remained in the classroom at all times working alongside the classroom teacher. I could not see any reason why this approach could not be used in primary schools. It retains the benefits of providing assistance for classroom teachers without the need to use the 'integration' label.

Three years after Jane began secondary school, funding was made available through the Catholic school system for the purposes of integration. Although the school was eager to obtain extra funding, the decision to apply was left entirely to me. In spite of the fact that there was no pressure to formalize Jane's position as an 'integration case', I felt obliged to give something back to the school which had accepted and integrated my daughter so well. All it required of me was to obtain a doctor's certificate confirming Jane's disability. After some deliberation and discussions with teachers, I supplied the certificate on the understanding that the money was to be used in ways which would benefit the education of *all* children in the school.

Now that Jane is nearing the end of her school years she faces the ultimate test, integration into the workforce. Despite its imperfections, the fact that she has been integrated into the mainstream of education leaves no doubt in my mind that she is better prepared for integration into the world of work than she would otherwise have been. She has not been socialized out of this opportunity.

Conclusion

In this chapter I have argued that the bureaucratization of integration has actually been counterproductive in facilitating inclusiveness of all children, the basic premise of integration. This has come about because of the application of special education principles to the implementation process. In a recent journal article Pickering (1992) referred to integration as 'a vision flawed', a view which is consistent with a special education perspective. I would argue that it is not the vision which is flawed; rather, the flaw can be found in the interpretation and implementation of the vision. An implementation process which leaves intact the disabling structures endemic to most schools will be extremely problematical. Furthermore, a process which is modelled on special education practices will, of course, be flawed because it is inconsistent with the real notion of integration. 'Real' integration should be invisible, a natural process which does not set apart any one group of people but which emphasizes practices inclusive of all children. The vision, therefore, is one which sees the classroom as an inclusive, accepting community within a flexible school structure. This is not unattainable, as Stainback and Stainback (1990) have demonstrated in their discussion on inclusive schooling. As a parent, I cannot help but agree with the words of Strully and Strully (1990), two other parents, who argue that we continue to ask the wrong questions in regard to integration. According to them:

> The only question that we should be asking is: 'What would it take to have this child in a regular classroom with his or her same-age peers?' This question allows us to focus our attention and efforts on what is most important — how to support *all* students in a fully inclusive classroom. . . . *It is right and it is time* to make inclusive education a reality.

If we do not strive for this, not only are people with disabilities socialized out of the mainstream community, but those in the mainstream are deprived of the worthwhile contributions of a significant number of fellow human beings.

References

FULCHER, G. (1989) *Disabling Policies: A Comparative Approach to Educational Policy and Disability*, Lewes, Falmer Press.

LEWIS, J. (1989) 'A Reflection on Five Years of Victorian Integration Policy', in MARKS, G. (Ed.), *Each an Individual: Integration of Children into Regular Schools*, Geelong, Deakin University, pp. 31–38.

MINISTRY OF EDUCATION-VICTORIA (1984) *Integration in Victorian Education: Report of the Ministerial Review of Educational Services for the Disabled*, Melbourne, Victorian Government Printer.

PICKERING, D. (1992) 'Integration: A Vision Flawed' (forthcoming).

STAINBACK, S. and STAINBACK, W. (1990) 'Support Networking for Inclusive Schooling', in STAINBACK, S. and STAINBACK, W. (Eds), *Support Networks for Inclusive Schooling: Interdependent Integrated Education*, Baltimore, Md, Paul H. Brookes, pp. 3–37.

STRULLY, J.L. and STRULLY, C.F. (1990) 'Foreword', in STAINBACK and STAINBACK (Eds), *Support Networks for Inclusive Schooling: Interdependent Integrated Education*, Baltimore, Md, Paul H. Brookes, pp. ix–xi.

TOMLINSON, S. (1982) *A Sociology of Special Education*, London, Routledge and Kegan Paul.

Notes on Contributors

Mel Ainscow is a Tutor in Special Educational Needs at the Cambridge Institute of Education and Director of a Unesco project which is producing teacher resource packs of educational materials for use in a number of countries. Mel's publications are numerous and include *Effective Schools for All*.

Stephen Ball is Professor of Education at King's College, University of London. Stephen's writing is extremely significant in the field of education policy analysis; his books include *The Micro-politics of the School* and *Politics and Policy Making in Education*.

Len Barton is Professor and Head of the Division of Education at the University of Sheffield. Len is the founder and editor of the international journal, *Disability, Handicap and Society*. The editor and author of numerous books and articles, his latest publication is co-authored with Jenny Corbett (1992) *A Struggle for Choice: Students with Special Needs in Transition to Adulthood*.

Richard Bowe is a Research Fellow at King's College, University of London. Richard has pursued extensive research into the impact of legislative reform in education in the United Kingdom.

Jenny Corbett is Senior Lecturer in the Department of Education Studies at the University of East London. Her major research interest is post-compulsory education and students with disabilities or learning difficulties. Jenny is the editor of *Uneasy Transitions: Disaffection in Post-compulsory Education and Training*.

Gillian Fulcher is a consultant researcher in policy and disability fields. Gillian was the principal author of the 1984, 'Integration Report' in Victoria which provided the basis for ensuing policy development. Since that time she has written *Disability Policies* and numerous academic papers and project reports.

Anne Gold is Lecturer in the Management Development Unit of the Institute of Education, University of London. Together with Stephen Ball and Richard Bowe, Anne is co-author of *Reforming Education and Changing Schools*.

Robert Henderson is a former elementary school principal and Chairman of Department of Special Education at the Universiuty of Illinois at Urbana, Champaign. He is the founding president of the Council for Exceptional Children's Division on International Special Education and Services (DISES).

Tony Knight is Senior Lecturer in the Centre for Curriculum Studies at La Trobe University. Tony has published widely and worked with schools in the area of developing inclusive school organization, curriculum and practice. Presently he is the co-chairman of Teacher Education Courses at La Trobe University.

Maeve Landman is Principal Lecturer in Education at Bristol Polytechnic. Director of the Policy and Provision in Education Section, she has a particular research interest in education policy and special educational needs.

John Lewis lectures in social policy and public administration at Royal Melbourne Institute of Technology, Coburg. Having taught in various special education settings, John was appointed by the Victorian Ministry of Education to the Integration Program Section. He is currently a member of the Disability Advisory Council of Australia.

Amanda Lyons writes from her experience as a parent advocating her child's place in the regular school. Amanda has travelled widely and is able to evaluate integration policy and practice on a comparative basis.

Genée Marks is Lecturer in Education at Deakin University. Genée is the editor of *Each an Individual* and has established an integration network in Victoria.

Daphne Meadmore is Lecturer in the School of Cultural and Policy Studies at the Queensland University of Technology. Her research interests include the formation and impact of education policy and the sociology of psychological measurement.

Arlene Ramasut lectures in education at the University of Wales, Cardiff College. She is the author of *Whole School Approaches to Special Needs* and continues to conduct research in the area of inclusive educational provision.

David Reynolds is Senior Lecturer in Education at the University of Wales, Cardiff College. David is a prolific writer and researcher in the field of effective schooling. He is editor of the international journal, *School Effectiveness and School Improvement*, and a co-director of the International School Effectiveness Project (ISERP).

Mary Rice writes with the authority of first-hand experience as a parent, a teacher and parent advocate. A Lecturer in Education at Deakin University, she has taught in the area of inclusive education. As a parent advocate in Integration Support Groups, Mary has been involved in advocacy, submission preparation and policy development.

Bob Semmens is a Senior Lecturer in Education in the Department of Social and Educational Studies at the University of Melbourne. Bob has a long and central involvement in the development of integration policy in the Victorian Ministry of Education. He is the founding coordinator of the International Forum on Education in Penal Systems (IFEPS).

Roger Slee is Director of the Leadership Research Concentration in the Faculty of Education at the Queensland University of Technology. Roger was seconded to the Victorian Ministry of Education to coordinate a review of integration policy implementation. He is the editor of *Australian Disability Review*.

Bruce Uditsky is Executive Director of the Alberta Association for Community Living, an international consultant in inclusive education and communities and a doctoral student in severe disabilities/special education at the University of Alberta, Canada. He is a co-founder of Integration Action Alberta and On Campus, an integrated post-secondary education program.

Becky Walsh is a student in the Teacher Education Program in the Faculty of Education at the Queensland University of Technology. Becky's experience of integration policy and practice is extensive and first-hand.

Index